Faroe-Islander Saga

Faroe-Islander Saga
A New English Translation

ROBERT K. PAINTER

McFarland & Company, Inc., Publishers
Jefferson, North Carolina

LIBRARY OF CONGRESS CATALOGUING-IN-PUBLICATION DATA

Names: Painter, Robert K., 1978– translator.
Title: Faroe-Islander saga : a new English translation / (translated by) Robert K. Painter.
Other titles: Færeyinga saga. English.
Description: Jefferson, North Carolina : McFarland & Company, Inc., Publishers, 2016 | Includes bibliographical references and index.
Identifiers: LCCN 2015043126 | ISBN 9781476663661 (softcover : acid free paper) ∞
Subjects: LCSH: Faroe Islands—History. | Sigmundr Brestisson, –1002. | Þrándr Þorbjarnarson, active 10th century. | Sagas—Translations into English.
Classification: LCC PT7281.F3 E57 2016 | DDC 839/.63—dc23
LC record available at http://lccn.loc.gov/2015043126

BRITISH LIBRARY CATALOGUING DATA ARE AVAILABLE

ISBN (print) 978-1-4766-6366-1
ISBN (ebook) 978-1-4766-2326-9

© 2016 Robert K. Painter. All rights reserved

No part of this book may be reproduced or transmitted in any form or by any means, electronic or mechanical, including photocopying or recording, or by any information storage and retrieval system, without permission in writing from the publisher.

Front cover image of the Faroe Islands © 2016 Jason Row/iStock/Thinkstock

Printed in the United States of America

McFarland & Company, Inc., Publishers
Box 611, Jefferson, North Carolina 28640
www.mcfarlandpub.com

For Lucy,
Queen of Argyll, Ross,
and the Western Reaches

Table of Contents

Preface   1

Introduction   5

Note on the Translation   27

1. The First Settlers in the Faroe Islands   31
2. Thrandur of Göta   32
3. Thrandur Earns a Fortune   34
4. Brestir and Beinir of Skufey   36
5. The Incident on South Island   37
6. Hafgrimur Seeks Allies   39
7. Standoff at Little Dimun   41
8. Hrafn Holmgard-Traveler   43
9. The Boys Are Set Free   44
10. Shelter from the Storm   45
11. Ulfur the Farmer   47
12. Sigmundur Comes of Age   48
13. Departure from the Farm   50
14. Ulfur's Story   51
15. Thorkell and Ragnhild   52
16. Thorkell in Exile   53

17.	Earl Hakon's Court	55
18.	Sigmundur in Denmark	56
19.	Sigmundur in Sweden	59
20.	Sigmundur's Reputation Grows	61
21.	Haraldur Iron-Skull	62
22.	Össur Hafgrimsson	65
23.	Departure from Norway	67
24.	Return to the Faroe Islands	68
25.	Earl Hakon's Settlement	72
26.	Sigmundur and Thurid	73
27.	The Jomsvikings	76
28.	King Olaf Tryggvason	77
29.	Sigmundur Converts to Christianity	78
30.	Christianity Comes to the Faroe Islands	80
31.	Thrandur Forced to Accept Christianity	82
32.	King Olaf Turns on Thrandur	84
33.	Sigmundur and King Olaf	85
34.	Earl Eirikur and Earl Svein	86
35.	The Earls Welcome Sigmundur	87
36.	A Growing Feud	87
37.	Hostilities Escalate	88
38.	A Narrow Escape	90
39.	A Partnership Comes to an End	93
40.	Thora Sigmundursdottir	94
41.	The Truth Comes Out	96
42.	The End of the Feud	98

Table of Contents

43. King Olafur Haraldursson — 99
44. A Bad Omen — 100
45. Trouble Brews Abroad — 100
46. The King Broods — 104
47. Karl-Maerskur — 104
48. Thrandur's Foster Sons Take Action — 105
49. A Cunning Trap — 109
50. Thorhallur the Wealthy — 112
51. Unwelcome Guests Arrive — 113
52. Gautur the Red on Sandey — 115
53. Leifur Thorirsson — 116
54. Death and an Omen — 117
55. Another Narrow Escape — 118
56. An Opportunity Arises — 120
57. Flight from Austurey — 121
58. The Vengeance of the Skuf-Islanders — 123
59. The Saga Ends — 126

Appendices
- A: Excerpt of *Jómsvíkinga saga*, Chapters 31–33 — 129
- B: Earl Hakon and *Þorgerðr Horðabrúðr* — 135
- C: Social Background and Technical Terms — 137
- D: Chronology — 141
- E: Genealogical Tables — 143

References and Further Reading — 145

Index of Proper Names — 149

General Index — 157

Preface

This book presents a new English translation of *Faereyinga saga,* or *Faroe-Islander Saga,* one of the lesser known Icelandic sagas, written by an anonymous author in Iceland sometime in the early 13th century. The central plot of the saga presents the history of the first settlers in the Faroe Islands in the early 9th century during the Viking Age, focusing on the feud between two rival chieftains, Sigmundur Brestirsson and Thrandur of Göta. This new literary translation aims to make *Faroe-Islander Saga* accessible to a wider readership in English, as this little read medieval work is just as engaging and profound as more commonly known Icelandic sagas such as *Njal's Saga, Laxdaela Saga,* or *Grettir's Saga.* The translation is faithful enough to the original saga text to be used as a reference for students learning to read Old Icelandic, but fluid enough to be accessible for any reader with a general interest in the Norse world and the Icelandic sagas. The English text is accompanied by a brief introduction which provides an overview on the saga and saga-writing, the Faroe Islands during the Viking Age, and some literary themes in the work. Also provided are brief explanatory notes highlighting cultural and historical aspects of the text; chronological tables; genealogies of families; as well as maps illustrating the Faroe Islands, the geography of the North Sea in the Norse World, and an overview of medieval Scandinavia.

The impetus for this new translation of an obscure Icelandic saga came almost ten years ago when I was a graduate student in linguistics at the State University of New York at Buffalo. I was taking a seminar in sociolinguistic research methods from the venerable Professor Wolfgang Wölck, one of the Grand Old Men in the field of sociolinguistics, who proposed that I research the linguistic profile of these islands between Shetland and Iceland, where unstable bilingualism exists between the colonial Danish, the globally threatening English, and the local Scandinavian dialect, Faroese. Having just completed a yearlong training in linguistic fieldwork, I found my head filling excitedly with grandiose ideas of completing a dissertation under Professor Wölck, punctuated by self-important research trips to the remote Faroe Islands to collect data, myself jammering heroically to the locals in a fluent, educated Danish or Faroese (languages which I did not and do not speak). But somewhere during that heady spring of 2007, two important things happened. First, scouring for books on Scandinavian languages among the dusty shelves of the university library, I found a battered copy of George Johnston's translation of *Faereyinga saga* from 1994, misleadingly titled *Thrand of Gotu*. The language was stilted, and the sentences were short, declarative, and dry; but the story gnawed at my imagination. It wasn't long afterward that I tracked down the original text from the formidable Íslenzk Fornrit series and began to translate. Then, the second thing happened: our daughter Lucy joined us in the world in September 2008. Notions of a doctoral dissertation based on sociolinguistic field data from the Faroe Islands were transmuted into a very different kind of library based study on the historical phonology of Germanic and Italic languages. The Icelandic sagas remained on my mind, however, and a highlight of a trip to Iceland in 2013 including visiting the wonderful Saga Museum in Borgarnes.

Reading the various Icelandic sagas, first through English translations and eventually in the Old Icelandic, I was hooked. Many arguments can be made for the intrinsic value of studying the sagas as Iceland's great contribution to world literature, or as important historical sources, but I follow the sentiment of two early 20th century University College London scholars, William Ker and Peter Foote, who explain their choice of Icelandic subjects as "merely a love of stories" (see Foote 1965, 9). The stories in the sagas are wonderful in their sober, matter-of-fact portrayal of their events, where the heroes are characterized by what they do, not what they say. Take two specific examples from *Faroe-Islander Saga*. In an early scene, two servants, Einar and Eldjarn, are sitting around a campfire idly discussing which of their kinsmen are the better men; a difference of opinion prompts Eldjarn to grab a brand from the fire and bash Einar on the shoulder with it; the following text states matter-of-factly, "and Einar took it badly; he grabbed an axe and struck Eldjarn in the head" (Chapter 5). The text does not say that Einar whined or considered his wounds or became angry or swore foully; rather the reader is simply invited to put himself in Einar's position and to consider the logical thing to do after being hit by a flaming stick. The action of seizing one's axe in rage seems wonderfully natural and almost inevitable in this context. In a later scene from the saga (Chapter 38), a band of Sigmundur's enemies makes a surprise attack against his farm when, unbeknownst to them, he is not at home; at the moment when the men are kicking down the door, the saga reads, "the lady of the house, Thurid, snatched hold of a sword and fought along with the household men." Again, it is not explicitly stated that Thurid fights as befits the wife of a great hero like Sigmundur, or that it might be in some way unusual for a woman to join the fight. Rather, all that is said about when her foes broke down the door is that Thurid went for her sword. The characterization of her bravery is read in Thurid's actions, never expressed directly. In the Icelandic sagas, this device of letting the facts speak for themselves and leaving out the commentary makes for rich storytelling, where the plot is driven relentlessly by a concatenation of one event, followed by the next.

With this new literary translation of the *Faroe-Islander Saga*, I tried to capture this sense of intrinsic energy and dramatic storytelling from the Old Icelandic original, something I felt was diluted or lacking from those rare, previous translations of this saga into English (see A Note on the Translation following the Introduction). This translation is fully original and dependent on none of the previous English translations. By attempting a novel start, I hoped to provide a fresh take on this lesser-known classic of the canon of sagas, something that was stylish and readable to a modern audience while still very faithful to the letter and spirit of what the saga-writer intended.

I would like to thank several people who contributed to the success of this project. Colleagues in the Linguistics Program at Northeastern University were constantly supportive and smilingly upbeat at all the right times, particularly Adam Cooper, Heather Littlefield, and Neal Pearlmutter. A special note of appreciation is also given to professors Thalia Pandiri and Craig Davis of Smith College, who were both supportive of my translation project.

Words of thanks are due to my undergraduate research students, linguistics majors Ana Piccirillo and Hannah Powers, who selflessly gave their time during the spring and fall semesters of 2014 to check the draft of the manuscript, and suggested numerous improvements to the translation and clarifications to the notes.

My father, James Russell Painter, nobly tested his draftsman skills to help produce the maps which accompany the text. My thanks to him for the maps and, of course, many, many other more important things.

Medievalist, colleague, and friend, Dr. Margaret McGeachy, a professor of English at D'Youville College, read the entire draft translation at several stages of completion, and her sharp eye for detail and careful editorial comments saved me from many historical or literary solecisms and plain old bad writing. The translation is much stronger than it was for her expertise.

Lastly, to Anna, Lucy and Henry, there are not thanks enough for being the family I can come home to after being lost for hours in an Old Icelandic dictionary, with my thoughts somewhere between Boston and the Faroe Islands.

The blame for any mistakes, errors, misinterpretations, or badly cast sentences in this book remains with me.

Introduction

The Faroe-Islander Saga

Written by an anonymous Icelandic author in the early 13th century, *Faroe-Islander Saga* (*Faereyinga Saga*) is the national saga of the Faroe Islands, taught in schools and widely beloved. Part history and part myth, the saga tells the story of the first generations of settlers from Norway to these North Atlantic islands at the edge of the known world, the haunt of grazing sheep and cliff-dwelling puffins. At the center of the saga is the enduring animosity and competition for power between the families of Sigmundur Brestirsson and Thrandur of Göta, rival chieftains whose bitter disagreements on the introduction of Christianity to the Islands and the interference of the Norwegian crown in Faroese affairs set the stage for a violent feud which unfolds over three generations of their descendants.

Much as *Orkney-Islander Saga* (*Orkneyinga Saga*) gives literary form to an oral tradition about the history and great figures of the Orkney Islands, *Faroe-Islander Saga* preserves the history of early chieftains and leading families on the Faroe Islands. The prevailing theme of the saga is the forceful introduction of Christianity into a pagan Norse society which is not ready or willing to abandon its heathen ways. The highwater mark of the saga—Sigmundur Brestirsson's mission from the proselytizing King Olaf Tryggvason of Norway to bring Christianity to the Faroes—is an episode which parallels the story of conversion in other sagas, such as Thangbrand's evangelic trip to Iceland in *Laxdaela Saga* and Leif Erikson's assignment to convert Greenland to the new faith in *Eirik's Saga*. As one scholar has suggested, the entire *raison d'être* of the *Faroe-Islander Saga* may be to give a literary backdrop to Olaf Tryggvason's role in conversion of the Islands (Foote 1965, 11). The Icelandic saga-writer portrays richly what must have been the historical tension between opposing forces: the hero Sigmundur's naive zeal to spread Christianity to the Faroe Islands is readily matched by the antihero Thrandur of Göta's recalcitrant refusal to "abandon his old friends" (i.e., the Norse gods). Their conflicting views on faith in the Faroes devolve into violence in a fashion which is all too familiar in the annals of history and which resonates with realism. The Icelandic saga-writer, who may well have been a monk in holy orders, is careful to show the ambiguity of the times. The saga does not present the adoption of Christianity and the shunning of pagan beliefs in the Faroes as a *fait accompli*. No less a character than the great christianizing monarch, Olaf Tryggvason, has a falling out with Sigmundur Brestirsson over a magic ring which imbues the wearer with everlasting luck; pagan black magic allows Thrandur to resolve the saga's great mystery; and the grand battle of the final chapters begins in the shadow of the wooden church built by Sigmundur, showing that early converts in the Faroe Islands placed the pagan value of dutifully avenging ones' kin over Christian forgiveness. Through the mosaic of these episodes, the saga-writer shows an evolving Norse world where the tenets of Christianity commingle readily with the superstitions and values of a heathen Germanic past.

For all its rich themes, hard fought battles, compelling characters, and wily intrigue, *Faroe-Islander Saga* is one of the lesser known Icelandic sagas for an English-speaking readership. Where masterful classics such as *Njal's Saga, Egil's Saga,* and *Laxdaela Saga* occasionally find their way onto the reading lists of comparative literature courses (aided in no small part by excellent translations by Magnus Magnusson, Hermann Pálsson, and Paul Edwards), this evocative medieval work is essentially unknown outside of the Scandinavian countries. The present literary translation seeks to make the vivid drama and artful storytelling of the original Old Icelandic saga accessible to a wider English readership.

The Faroe Islands in the Viking Age

Only slightly better known than *Faereyinga saga* itself, the Faroe Islands or "Sheep Islands" (Old Icelandic: *fær-* [sheep] + *-eyjar* [islands]) are a small cluster of seventeen rocky islands situated in the North Sea halfway between Scotland and Iceland, and a four-day sail from the west coast of Norway. The Islands have always had an allure of the unknown and unknowable. In the introduction to one of the few English language books on the history of the Faroe Islands, Jonathan Wylie refers to them as a *terra incognita*, adding: "The Faroes are an obscure corner of Scandinavia and, apart from Lapland, Scandinavia is perhaps the most obscure corner of the world" (Wylie 1987, 1). This mythologizing view was repeated

Introduction

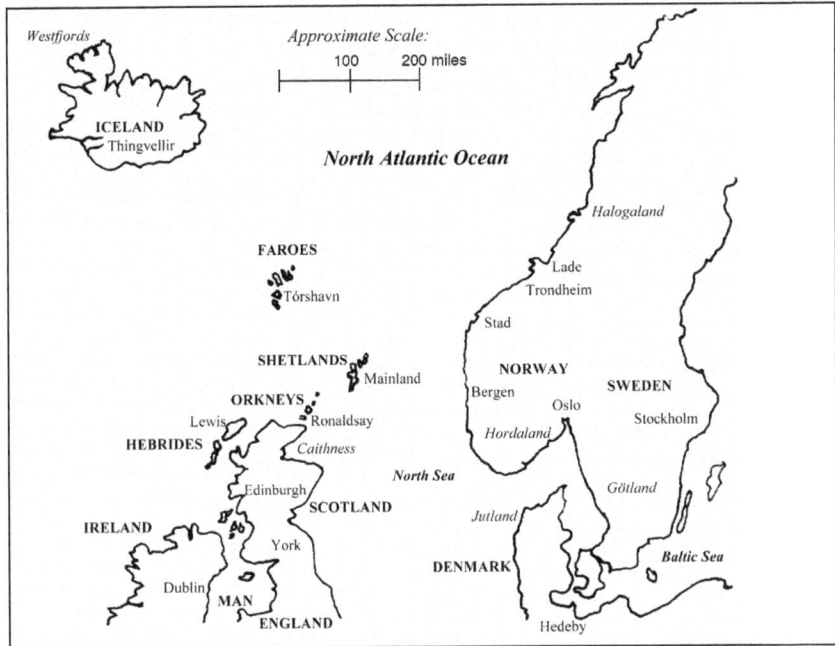

The Faroe Islands and the North Atlantic in the Viking Age

as recently as the November-December 2007 issue of the magazine *National Geographic Traveler*, where a feature on the Faroe Islands described them as "mysterious" and "authentic, unspoiled, and likely to remain so." Often enveloped in mist or shrouded by rain, the Faroes present a formidable profile of sheer cliffs, shores of broken rock, and emerald green meadows far above crashing waves. First approached from the sea, they are a place which might easily inspire legends.

The first serious reference to the Faroe Islands is found in a geographic treatise *Liber de mensura orbis terrae* (Book of the Measurement of the Earth) written at Aachen in the court of Charlemagne by the Irish monk Dicuil in 825:

> There are many other islands in the ocean north of Britain which can be reached from the northern islands of Britain [i.e. the Orkneys and the Hebrides] in a direct voyage of two days and nights with sails filled in a continuously favorable wind. A devout priest told me that in two summer days and the intervening night he sailed in a two-benched boat and entered one of them.
>
> There is another set of small islands, nearly all separated by narrow stretches of water; in these for nearly a hundred years hermits sailing from our own country, Ireland, have lived. But just as they were always

deserted from the beginning of the world, so now because of the Northman pirates they are emptied of anchorites, and filled with countless sheep and very many diverse kinds of sea-birds. I have never found these islands mentioned in the authorities [Dicuil, cited and translated in Wylie 1987, 7].

Modern scholars generally agree that Dicuil's archipelago is the Faroe Islands, and the monk's testimony corroborates a general picture we know from other historical sources and archaeology. During the 6th century, Irish missionaries of the Celtic Church of Ireland had established monastic bases in the Hebrides off the west coast of Scotland, and probing northward, they had reached the North Sea islands of the Orkneys, Shetlands, and lastly the Faroes Islands by around 700. Braving open sea in fragile leather boats known as *currachs*, these pious men lived as hermits on remote, windswept isles, seeking the solitude of the fringes of the explored world to commune with God. It is known that these stalwart Irish monks pushed much farther than the Faroes into frigid northern waters, because when the first Norwegians arrived in Iceland in 860, they found the Irish already there. Evidence for this is found in the first chapter of *Landnámabók* (Book of Settlement), the 13th-century source for the settlement of Iceland, which relates:

> Before Iceland was settled from Norway there were other people there, called *Papar* by the Norwegians. They were Christians and were thought to have come overseas from the west, because people found Irish books, bells, croziers, and lots of other things, so it was clear they must have been Irish. Besides, English sources tell us that sailings were made between these countries at the time [translated in Pálsson and Edwards 1972, 15].

Etymologically, the Old Icelandic word *papar* (sg. *papi*, pl. *papar*) is an Irish word, itself originally borrowed into Irish from Latin *papa* "father, bishop," and seems to mean an Irish hermit in this specific sense. There are various place names such as *Papey* and *Papli* (essentially, "Monk Island" and "Monk Land") found scattered across the North Sea zone on the Isle of Man and among the Hebrides, Shetlands, Orkneys, the Faroe Islands, and Iceland—linguistic traces which may attest to an early and lasting Irish presence (see Pálsson and Edwards 1972, 15).

Irish monks may have been the first inhabitants of the isolated Faroes, c. 700, but as they were chaste, unmarried men, their role in the peopling of the Islands is a minor, early chapter. Dicuil's account from 825 explains that these Irish settlers were driven off (or absorbed) when the Faroes Islands were settled en mass in the early 9th century as part of a larger movement westward by Norwegians seeking land and reprieve from the increasingly oppressive royal overlordship in Norway. The historical reality of the early settlement of the Faroes, however, might be more complex than Scandinavians simply ousting the odd Irish hermit. Julian Richards points out that no archaeological evidence for Irish anchorites has been found on the Faroe Islands; rather, the archaeology suggests that the first settlers of the Faroe Islands were "first- or second-generation Norse from the Northern Islands or Ireland" (Richards 2005, 98). The settlement of the Islands by individuals who were of mixed Norse/Celtic ancestry seems plausible as it explains the small share of Gaelic loanwords in the Faroese language and the common elements of Faroese and Irish culture (Richards 2005, 98; for an account of the distinctive Faroese culture, see Wylie 1981). Something of this mixed-population view may be corroborated by the first line of the *Faroe-Islander Saga* which names Grimur Kamban as the first settler. The given name "Grimur" is undoubtably Norse, while the family name "Kamban" is possibly Celtic. The traditional date given for Grimur Kamban's settlement on the Islands is 825 (Foote 1965, 9); modern archaeological evidence dates the period of more widespread Norwegian settlement to c. 875–900 (Richards 2005, 98).

The settlement of the Faroe Islands fits within the larger historical mosaic of the Norse expansion into the North Atlantic during the so-called Viking Age of the 9th to 11th centuries. For scholars, this age generally begins with the famous viking raid on the Lindisfarne monastery in northeastern England in 793, and tends to end with Haraldur Hardradi of Norway's defeat at Stamford Bridge by King Harold of England in 1066, three weeks before Harold was himself defeated by William the Conquerer at the Battle of Hastings (for a concise historical overview, see Robinson 1992, 69–73; for the Viking Age in general, Richards 2005). During this era, the Norwegians would raid, trade with, and help prop up petty Celtic kingdoms throughout northern Scotland and the Orkneys, the Hebrides, the Isle of Man, Wales, and Ireland. It is well-established that Irish cities such as Dublin, Cork, and Limerick had their start as Norwegian trading posts and bases of operations. Meanwhile, Viking bands from Denmark raided widely on the continental coasts of what are today France, Belgium, Holland, and northern Germany in the 8th and 9th centuries. A large Danish cohort—the so-called Great Army—landed in England in 865, ravaging for ten years. Eventually conquering the early English kingdoms of Mercia and (part of) Northumbria, the Danes formed the zone of control known famously as the Danelaw in England. Elsewhere in Scandinavia, the Swedes were actively establishing extensive operations eastward from Sweden into the Baltic region and Russia, navigating the Dnieper and Volga rivers, and trading as far south as the Black Sea and Constantinople. Famously, Swedish mercenaries, the Varangian Guard, even served as bodyguards for the Byzantine emperors throughout the 11th century.

Reflecting on the Viking Age, it is easy to fix on the stereotype of "viking as marauder," i.e., the northern scourge suddenly appearing from the sea in longships to loot and pillage civilized Europe to the south. Yet the Norwegians' expansion into the North Sea, including the settlement of the Faroes and Iceland, has a different character. "The significant factor about the westerward movement across the North Atlantic, as opposed to the Viking voyages further south, is that the prime motivation appears to have been settlement—land-taking and exploration—rather than raiding and looting" (Graham-Campbell et al. 1994, 164). The Icelandic sagas, including *Faroe-Islander Saga*, relate that around c. 874 the various petty kingdoms of Norway were unified under the overbearing King Haraldur Fine-Hair, who then ruled for fifty more years to c. 928, and whose consolidation of authority rankled many Norwegians. In particular, Haraldur imposed a tax on all freeborn landowners, exiled high-born men who refused to swear allegiance to him, and quashed all opposition to his rule—acts that according to Snorri Sturluson's cycle of sagas, the *Heimskringla*, led to widescale emigration. For instance, in a famous scene in the second chapter of *Laxdaela Saga*, Ketil Flat-Nose, a highborn Norwegian, proudly decides to lead his kinsmen from Norway to Scotland (his daughter, Aud the Deep-Minded, would be one of the first settlers and matriarch of a great family in Iceland):

> In the latter years of Ketil's life, King Haraldur Fine-Hair rose to such power that neither provincial kings nor other men of stature could prosper in Norway or retain their rank and title without his sanction. When Ketil learned that King Haraldur was intending to subject him to the same treatment as other chieftains, who had been forced to become the king's vassals and had been denied compensation for fallen kinsmen, he summoned his own kinsmen to a meeting and addressed them [*Laxdaela Saga*, Chapter 2, translated by Magnusson and Pálsson 1969, 48].

The sagas report that Norwegians took to the North Atlantic during the days of Haraldur Fine-Hair, stubbornly getting out of Dodge while the getting was good, but this is probably only half the story. The sagas are equally clear that daring exploits to unknown lands was a goal unto itself; this view is confirmed numerous times in the sagas, for example, in Chapter 3 of *Graenlendinga saga* (Greenlanders' Saga) the legendary Leif Eriksson decides to sail west from Greenland as "there was now great talk of discovering new countries" (Magnusson and Pálsson 1965, 54). Simply put, as part of their culture, the Norwegians were clearly predisposed to explore and settle new lands.

Regardless of the motivation, within a few short generations, there were Norse settlements in Ireland, Wales, the Hebrides, the Orkneys, the Shetlands, the Faroes, Iceland, Greenland, and even North America, as the archaeological evidence for a small Norse settlement in L'Anse aux Meadows on the northernmost tip of Newfoundland confirms (see Richards 2005, 108–116). In this context, it is worth repeating that the Norsemen were remarkable sailors and shipbuilders (see Richards 2005, Chapter 5), for whom the ocean was more of a superhighway than a barrier. Their ships were (generally) dependable and fast; as Magnusson and Pálsson (1965, 12) put it:

> [In this era] the northern seas were now swarming with sturdy ocean-going boats.... They were not the lean predatory longships built only for coastal waters, but high-stemmed and broad-breasted cargo boats propelled by one large rectangular sail and steered by a long rudder pinned to the starboard quarter.... Their ships, in good weather, were perhaps the fastest craft in the world at that time (it has been estimated that they could make about ten knots).

Despite the technological gains in seafaring and masterful seamanship, the journeys across open ocean still required a distinct courage. All trips were accomplished in open ships, exposing the crew, cargo, and livestock to salt-spray and the elements, though some ships may have had small cabins or berths (Gordon 1956, 26).

While the modern conception of the Faroes is that they are remote or isolated, in the Viking Age, the Islands (along with the Shetlands and Orkneys) were a frequent and common stopover point for ships sailing between Norway and Iceland, and could serve as a strategic base of operations for trading journeys or raids for plunder in the various Scottish, Irish, and English kingdoms to the south. According to one of the early chapters of *Landnámabók*, voyages to the Faroes from Norway were common well before Iceland was settled (the first settlement in Iceland dates to 874), and one manuscript version cites that the journey from Norway to Iceland took seven days, with the proposed route being four days to the Faroes, and three days further to Iceland (see Foote 1964, 10, n. 1). In fact, an errant trip to the Faroes resulted in one of the first recorded landfalls in Iceland:

> The story goes that some people wanted to sail from Norway to the Faroes—a viking called Naddodd, to name one of them. They were driven out to sea westwards, and came to a vast country. They went ashore in the Eastfjords, climbed a high mountain, and scanned the country in all directions looking for smoke or any other sign that the land was inhabited, but they saw nothing. In the summer they went back to the Faroes, and as they were sailing away from the coast a lot

of snow fell on the mountains, so they called the country *Snowland* [*Landámabók*, Chapter 3, translated in Pálsson and Edwards 1972].

During and after the Settlement of Iceland, sea traffic to and fro must have included island-hopping, though most sources are clear that runs across open-sea were also common. *Faroe-Islander Saga* (Chapter 1) probably reflects certain navigational truths when it relates that Aud the Deep-Minded reached Iceland from Caithness in Scotland by stopping first among the Orkney Islands and next among the Faroes.

That anyone could have settled on the Faroes is remarkable. The Islands are topographically defined by sheer, weathered cliff faces, high grassy meadows on the headlands, and few natural harbors. At 62 degrees north latitude, Tórshavn, the capital of the Faroe Islands, is situated farther north than such frigid locales as Helsinki, Finland; St. Petersburg, Russia; White-horse (Yukon, Canada); and Juneau, Alaska. The first Norwegian settlers needed to be a tough, self-reliant stock. Wylie outlines the nature of daily Faroese life around 1540, which was likely not radically different from life in the medieval period (Wylie 1987, 26):

> Men fowled, went whaling, cut peat for fuel, raised some barley (which, because of the short growing season, had to be reaped green and dried over peat fires), and kept sheep and cattle. But perhaps their most important pursuit was fishing: more than the keeping of sheep or cows, fishing seems to have determined whether the times were good or bad.

Farmsteads were established at natural harbors by the sea, though outbuildings, known as *aergi* or "shielings," would be built up in the hills for grazing sheep and cattle in the higher pastures in summer (see Wylie 1987, 9ff). Archaeology gives a sense of a typical Faroese farm in the Viking Age: a well-preserved farmstead of the period was excavated at Kvívík on the central island of Streymoy (see Graham-Campbell et al. 1994, 167). The main building was rectangular with stone and turf walls standing a meter high, with a large central firepit; a side entrance let out directly to a stream, a source for water. Next to the house, the remains of a barn was excavated which could hold up to twelve cattle in stone stalls. Traces of roof-beams of birch and turf sods were found; roofs were presumably turf, built at a 45 degree angle, as are sometimes still found in the capital at Tórshavn. Prime farming sites with access to the sea are few, and archaeologists suspect that most settlements have been continuously occupied since the Viking Age. For instance, there is very little reason to think that the footprint of the modern village of Hov on South Island does not correspond closely to the farm of Hof owned by Hafgrimur, the 10th-century chieftain introduced in Chapter 3 of the saga.

The *Faroe-Islander Saga* is clear that some farmers—such as the chieftains Thrandur and Hafgrimur—were freeholders, wealthy farmers whose family owned the land and raised cattle, goats, and sheep; other farmers were tenant farmers, paying annual rents to the landowner. Something of this system from the Saga Age lasts into historical times. Wylie reports that much of the land in the Faroes became owned by the Church before the Reformation and eventually by the king; tenant farms became known as "king's farmers" (*kongsbøndur*); "since the king's land is impartible, tenant farmers were traditionally rich men in the Faroes" (Wylie 1981, 7).

With extremely limited natural resources, the Faroes could not afford to be isolated. Much like Iceland in the medieval period, the Faroe Islands would export commodities such as wool, sheepskins, tallow, oil, butter and cheese in exchange for absolute necessities like metal, flour, and timber. As the Islands are virtually treeless, the Faroese-Norwegian settlers were at the mercy of ships from abroad to bring wood in order to build houses and ships (see Graham-Campbell et al. 1994, 167). Driftwood—mentioned as so vital a resource in Iceland during the Age of Settlement—was probably an important supplementary source of wood in the Faroes as well.[1] While most farmers would have had small skiffs to fish with, it is a sign of Thrandur of Göta's wealth in *Faroe-Islander Saga* that he has an ocean-going merchant ship bought in Norway. But given the right concatenation of ship-related calamities, the settlers on the Faroe Islands would have become imprisoned on their own islands. Looking ahead toward the end of the medieval period, Wylie notes that the lack of ships in the Faroes historically would constitute a tremendous problem: "By the end of the 13th century, and perhaps well over a century before, the Faroese were unable to carry on their own the trade upon which their survival depended" (Wylie 1987, 17).

The early Faroese were largely dependent on Norway for trade, and there was probably opportunistic bartering between the Faroes and the Scottish islands to the south (in a late episode in the *Faroe-Islander Saga*, a Hebridean trader makes a brief appearance). The extent to which the Faroe-Islanders traded and communicated with Icelanders in the medieval period is more of an open question. Foote notes that, "references to the Islands in the prolific literature of medieval Iceland are in fact remarkably

---

1. In early Icelandic society, the importance of driftage rights, which included the right to driftwood, flotsam, and beached whales, was worth fighting over; e.g., during a time of famine, a beached finback whale sparks a heated dispute between rival farmers in Iceland in *Grettir's Saga*, Chapter 12. Such rights likely played a role in early Faroese life, as well. The Faroe Islands are sometimes known, notoriously, for the controversial practice of whale-driving, the *grindadráp*, wherin Faroese men in skiffs herd a pod of whales to shore, where the whales are ritually slaughtered for their meat (see Wylie 1981, Ch. 5).

few, and almost all of them arise out of the dangers and difficulties of Faroese weather and Faroese waters" (Foote 1965, 10). The scholar also argues that with similar commercial products (wool, linen, etc.), based on almost identical rural economies, there was likely little reason for trade between the two countries (Foote 1965, 11). In 1262, Norway's King Magnús promised to send six trading ships a year between Iceland and Norway, and offered to send two supply ships between the Faroes and Norway; as Wylie concludes, "This suggests that trade with Iceland and the Faroes needed some artificial encouragement" (Wylie 1987, 17).

The local population on the Islands could never have been very large—a fact which makes the feuding between Sigmundur's family and Thrandur's seemingly reduce to so much mock-epic Hatfield-McCoy quibbling. In modern times, the population reported for the entire Faroes in 1801 was just 5,265, with 554 living in the capital at Tórshavn; by 1901, the population swelled to a modest 15,230 with 1,656 living in Tórshavn; and today, 2015, the current population of the Islands hovers just under fifty thousand inhabitants, with nearly half living in the capital city (for population data and analysis, see Wylie 1987, 114). During the era when the events of the saga take place, the population was probably less than three thousand, living in a few farms and hamlets scattered across the islands. Communication between these outposts was not overly frequent, and linguistically, many villages have distinctive dialects of the Faroese language (Wylie 1981, 13). One gets the sense that life in the Faroes was tenuous, between hard winters and poor fishing years. According to Wylie (1987, 14), the Black Death visited the Faroe Islands in 1350, wiping out a number approaching 70 percent of the estimated four thousand inhabitants.

Politically, according to the *Faroe-Islander Saga*, the early Faroe-Islanders adopted the Norwegian custom of parliamentary assembly, or *thing*, presided over by the *lógsógumaður*, the Lawspeaker, whose job it was to recite and interpret the full canon of law (on these terms, see Appendix C). As the saga-writer relates to the reader several times, the Faroese *thing*, known formally as the *Løgthing*, probably met annually in summer on a outcrop of land known as Thinganes in Tórshavn on the large, central island Streymoy. The Icelander who wrote the saga seems to equate (inaccurately?) the Faroese *thing* with the famous *Althing* of Iceland, established in 930, which served as both parliament and court. Robinson wryly notes: "The *althingi* had the authority to make the law but no way of enforcing it, leaving that up to the offended individual—a situation that led to the writing of many a saga of bloody self-help" (Robinson 1992, 72). The Faroese assembly presumably served not only as a legislative body and high court where cases could be heard, but also as a social gathering for visiting distant family and arranging marriages between eligible sons and daughters from different islands *à la* the Icelandic model.

The Faroe-Islanders' *thing* seemed to govern the internal affairs of the Islanders, and it is uncertain what status the Faroe Islands had in relationship to Norway in the saga era of the 10th, 11th, and 12th centuries (the events of the saga essentially run the fifty year period of 980 to 1030). At the beginning of *Faroe-Islander Saga*, the Faroes are divided into two fiefdoms, one controlled by Hafgrimur as a *len* or "fief" of Haraldur Grey-Cloak, the other by the brothers, Brestir and Beinir, as a fief of Earl Hakon of Trondheim. Foote and Wilson (1970, 132) envision the political arrangement as follows: "It is likely that … the king left the superintendence of his interests to some individual leader from one of the traditionally important families in the islands, a man who would doubtless be a member of his hird ['court'] and under vows of personal loyalty to him." In short, the Islands were largely left to administer themselves, save for a nominal presence of a king's bailiff who would send tribute home to the crown in Norway.

The ties of control between Norway and the Faroes would become more formalized in the 13th century. Wylie summarizes (1987, 11):

> [The king's official] was first called the sheriff, and in 1273 King Magnús Hákonarson decreed that "the sheriff shall have no more officers than two." Later on, the number of officials and the names by which they were called changed. The king's chief representative in the islands came to be called the bailiff (*fúti*). Six sheriffs (*sýslumenn*) stood under him, one for each of the Faroes' six districts (*sýslur*). The sheriffs were Faroese and as a rule lived in the districts they administered. Their duties included collecting taxes locally and bringing transgressions of the law to court. The bailiff was a foreigner.… As the system developed, the bailiff would come out to the Faroes with the first trading vessel in the spring. In the fall he returned to the continent. During the winter he was represented by a "winter bailiff" (*vetrarfúti*), who was a local man. The bailiff's principle duties included collecting taxes and prosecuting cases before the Løgthing. Then at some point (probably around the Reformation) he also began appointing the representatives (*løgrættumenn*) to the Løgthing.

This was later on, a century or so after the events described in the *Faroe-Islander Saga*. The saga itself is remarkable for portraying the historical shift between the early days when the Faroese settlers seem essentially to govern themselves to the latter days when the Norwegian crown is taking an ever firmer stance toward them. A running theme of the saga is that a power across the sea should not intervene in Faroese affairs. This view is embodied in Thrandur of Göta, who insists in several episodes the Islanders' right to take charge of their own affairs; for example, he denies Sigmundur the opportunity to impose Christianity at the Tórshavn *thing* in Chapter 30, and foils the king's bailiff, Karl-Maerskur, in his attempts to collect tribute in his territory, in Chapter 48. On the other hand, the saga-writer balances Thrandur with historical personage of King Olafur Haraldursson, who takes three Faroese men (Gilli Lawspeaker, Leifur Ossursson, and Sigurthur Thorlaksson) as his retainers on the condition that they collect royal tribute (Chapter 43)—this would be reflective of the relationship with Norway during the saga-writer's day. When two royal ships are lost at sea (Chapters 43 and 44), the king deputizes Karl-Maerskur to reestablish the crown's presence in the Faroe Islands. In this way, the saga-writer captures the developing political scene from the Age of Settlement into the modernity of his own 13th-century age.

Culturally and linguistically, the modern Faroese are a Nordic people, and the main language, Faroese (*Föroysk*), is closely related to Icelandic, and somewhat less so to western dialects of Norwegian; in Einar Haugen's introduction to Jonathan Wylie's 1981 book, *Ring of Dancers: Images of Faroese Culture*, he says of Faroese: "What I heard was surprisingly familiar. With a little good will on each side, I could make out most of what I heard, and my Norwegian functioned as a viable instrument.... This language of the Faroes ... the intonation, flexible diphthongs, the burred *r*, the sharp consonant clusters—I had heard them before, from speakers of Sogn and Voss, Hardanger and Rogaland [in Norway]" (Wylie 1981, xiv). Additionally, practically all Faroe Islanders are bilingual in Danish for historical reasons. In 1380 the Faroe Islands became a province of the newly unified Dano-Norwegian Kingdom, and political ties to Denmark only weakened in semi-recent times with limited Faroese independence coming from the Home Rule Act of 1948. This Act arose from the de facto aftermath of the Second World War, when communications between the Islands and Denmark were effectively cut off by German operations in the North Sea. Fuller autonomy in international affairs for the Faroe Islands was earned with the Foreign Powers Policy Act of 2005, an agreement between the Faroese and Danish government which took four years of careful negotiation (for a full account of Faroese development of a national culture and growing independence from Denmark, see Wylie 1987). With their own North Germanic language, distinct culture, and heritage, the Faroese are rightly proud of their past, and their saga—with its very different heroes, the shrewd Thrandur of Göta and quintessential champion Sigmundur

Brestirsson—is an embodiment of the fierce nationalistic feeling in the country. To the nature of the saga, we now return.

The Icelandic Sagas and Faroe-Islander Saga

The Icelandic noun *saga* means "something said or told, a story, a history," and it is related etymologically to the Icelandic verb *segja* "to tell," a cognate of the German verb *sagen*, and the English *to say*. Though elements of many of the sagas must have been passed down originally as oral stories, the Icelandic sagas as we have them are carefully composed works of literature (see, e.g., Gordon 1956, 45; Robinson 1992, 76). While saga-writing in various forms took place over nearly three centuries from c. 1120–1400, most of the thirty or so major sagas date from the century between roughly 1200–1300, with some sagas (*Egils saga* and *Fóstbrœðra saga* [*Sworn-Brothers' Saga*]) composed slightly earlier and others (*Grettis saga*) slightly later in the broader range (see Gordon 1956, 44ff). As this is not the place to review the full development of Icelandic saga literature, the broad pattern is that earlier sagas covered more religious and historical themes, where later sagas tended to shift focus to the more secular, historical feats of specific individuals and families. Two of the first sagas, for instance, composed around 1180, detailed the lives of two pious Norwegian kings, Olaf Tryggvason and Saint Olaf Haraldursson; these sagas were soon followed by lives of two Icelandic saints, Saint Jón of Hólar and Saint Thorlak of Skálholt (see Gordon 1956, 44). These religiously themed sagas gave way to more purely historical sagas in Snorri Sturluson's *Heimskringla* (c. 1230), an ambitious work which documents the lives of the kings of Norway from the time of legend up to Snorri's own day. After the so-called King's Sagas recorded in *Heimskringla*, there appear a large number of sagas of the Icelanders, or Family Sagas, which tell of the exploits of the first families of settlers of Iceland, sometimes focusing specifically on a heroic individual. To these collected sagas belong some of the greatest works of Old Icelandic literature, such as *Njal's Saga, Erybyggja Saga, Laxdaela Saga,* and *Grettir's Saga*, among many others. In addition to these well-known classic sagas, there were numerous 13th-century works written in Iceland based on or translated from ballads and stories popular in continental Europe, for example, *Ivens saga, Parcevals saga,* and *Tristrams saga*.

With few exceptions, the authors of the great sagas of the Icelanders are unknown. Snorri Sturluson may have composed *Egil's Saga* in addition to *Heimskringla*, but generally the writers seem to have been anonymous

Icelanders, perhaps monks or priests associated with the monasteric centers of learning at Hólar and Skálholt, but also possibly well-educated laymen (on the authorship question, see Gordon 1956, 53–54). Gordon notes that the Icelandic sagas often "reflect a family pride and incipient national pride" (1956, 53), which points to a lay author who was interested in promoting their own family's rich history and genealogy. However, this line of thinking can go too far; it is clear from textual evidence of the sagas themselves that the authors of several sagas were often not natives of the places where the saga's events unfold. In some cases, the saga-writer was composing someone else's story. Peter Foote, for example, takes the author of *Faroe-Islander Saga* to task for this: "How much the Icelandic author of *Faereyinga saga* actually knew about Faroese conditions is a puzzling question: He introduced some Faroese place-names, but not many, in his story, and he got [the islands of] Skúvoy and Stóra Dímun mixed up" (Foote 1970, 159).

In a sense, factual and historical inaccuracies were less important to the anonymous saga-writers than being able to tell a good story. The impetus behind a work like the *Faroe-Islander Saga* or *Orkney-Islander Saga*, detailing people and exploits of exotic lands, was the inherent fascination that Icelanders brought to the recording and telling of stories. Indeed, the Icelandic saga-writers were considered peerless in this respect. Consider the words of the contemporary, medieval Danish historian, Saxo Grammaticus, in his Latin opus *Gesta Danorum* (History of the Danes, c. 1200):

> The Icelanders ... take great pleasure in learning and recording the history of all peoples, and they consider it just as meritorious to describe the exploits of others as to perform it themselves [cited and translated in the introduction to *King Harald's Saga*, Magnusson and Pálsson 1966, 20].

The existence of a saga describing the petty skirmishes and feuding between families who are essentially first cousins in the Faroe Islands attests to the importance the Icelandic author placed on "recording the history of all peoples." The *Faroe-Islander Saga* is thus written partly as a quasi-historical document—an amalgamation of oral or written tales of powerful chieftains in the Faroes. In part, the saga is designed merely to entertain. As mentioned earlier, the saga-writer may also have had a specific interest in describing the spread of Christianity throughout the Norse world. As Peter Foote theorizes about the saga-writer (Foote 1965, 11):

> [...] Icelanders were not much interested in the Faroe Islanders in general and did not know much about them in particular. The first historical interest of any significance may well have come when Icelandic authors, in the years before and around 1200, began to consider the Christian history of Norway and its colonies and especially their conversion to the

faith in the reign of Olaf Tryggvason. Their accounts of the career of this missionary king seem to provide the immediate literary background of the *Saga of the Faroe-Islanders*.

Nothing further about the saga-writer is known. The date of composition of the saga is taken to be before roughly 1220 and 1230, as Snorri Sturluson seems to make reference to certain passages in *Faroe-Islander Saga* in his *Saga of St. Olaf* which is more securely dated to that ten year period (see discussion in Foote 1965, 11).

Synopsis of the Saga

The Faroe-Islander saga has the literary hallmarks of 13th century saga writing: a focus on drawing out characters' motives through their actions, a compression of time and events to drive the dramatic narrative, and a plot where one event is the stimulus for the next, so that the entire story arc unfolds as a natural progression of a jagged fault line stemming from a single epicenter. The structure of the present saga can be described as episodic with blocks of chapters focusing rather neatly around each generation of several families.

Spoiler alert: For those readers who wish to read the saga for themselves on its own terms, safely skip to the beginning of the translation.

Prelude (Chapters 1–7). The saga opens in the late 9th century with men fleeing the tyranny of King Haraldur Fine-Hair of Norway whose overbearing rule forces many to seek land elsewhere. Grimur Kamban is named among the first settlers of the Faroes; the name is Celtic, pointing to early Irish influence in the prehistory of the Islands. Aud (Unn) the Deep-Minded, traveling from disastrous events in Scotland and the Orkneys to Iceland stops on the Faroes, and marries off her grand-daughter Alofa, daughter of Thorstein the Red, who is the matriarch of the Götuskeggjar family of Austurey (Chapter 1). The reader is introduced to the wily Thrandur, who inherits his father's farm at Göta, before sailing abroad to earn a secret fortune through a clever and opportunistic strategem in Denmark (Chapters 2–3). An accidental killing of a servant of the local chieftain Hafgrimur of South Island creates simmering hostilities between Hafgrimur and the rival chieftains, brothers Brestir and Beinir Sigmundursson of Skuf Island (Chapters 4–5). Outflanked legally in seeking compensation for his servant, Hafgrimur recruits Thrandur of Austurey and Bjarni of Swine-Island to move against Brestir and Beinir, leading to the deadly standoff at the island of Little Dimun (Chapter 6). In the aftermath, the Sigmundurssons' orphaned young boys, Sigmundur Brestirsson and Thorir Beinirsson, are threatened with death by Thrandur, only to be spared by Swine-Island Bjarni (Chapter 7).

Sojurn in Norway (Chapters 8–17). The course of saga then follows the next generation and Sigmundur Brestirsson's exploits as a young chieftain of growing reputation. Sold into slavery by Thrandur, Sigmundur and Thorir are transported to Norway from the Faroes by Hrafn Holmgard-Traveler (Chapter 8–9). Freed from slavery and left to their own devices, the young boys become lost in the mountains during a snowstorm on their way to Earl Hakon's court in Trondheim. Stumbling upon an isolated farm, Sigmundur and Thorir are given lodging for the winter by Ulfur/Thorkell, the matchless hunter and outlaw, who fosters the boys to manhood. Romance grows between Sigmundur and Ulfur's daughter Thurid (Chapter 10–13). Coming of age, the boys travel to Trondheim to appeal to the friendship and generosity of Earl Hakon. On the journey, Ulfur/Thorkell tells the story of his youthful love for Ragnhild and the unlucky events which led to his own outlawry (Chapters 14–16).

Sigmundur in the service of Earl Hakon (Chapters 18–23). At court, Sigmundur and Thorir earn the patronage of Earl Hakon and his sons, Earl Eirikur and Earl Svein (Chapter 17). Sigmundur gains growing fame and a following by leading Viking raids first in Denmark, then in Sweden over subsequent summers (Chapters 18–19); in his third summer, Earl Hakon tasks Sigmundur to hunt down the outlaw chieftain Haraldur Iron-Skull in the Orkney Islands. Tracking Haraldur to Wales, Sigmundur fights with but then befriends Haraldur, and promises to reconcile Haraldur with Earl Hakon (Chapter 20–21). Planning to return to the Faroe Islands to avenge his father's death, Earl Hakon gives Sigmundur Brestirsson a magic ring from the pagan goddess Thorgerd Horda's-Bride, which imbues the wearer with good luck (Chapter 23). In the meantime, word of Sigmundur's growing reputation abroad reaches the Faroe Islands, and Hafgrimur's son, Össur Hafgrimursson, who has seized the farms which are Sigmundur's inheritance, begins to make defensive preparations for the boys' return (Chapter 22).

Sigmundur's Return to the Faroe Islands (Chapters 24–27). Sigmundur and Thorir make their long-awaited return to the Faroe Islands accompanied by Haraldur Iron-Skull, though a storm at sea separates the kinsmen from each other. Sigmundur captures one of his father's killers, Swine-Island Bjarni, and persuades him to help their attack on Össur Hafgrimursson and Thrandur. In a daring raid on Össur's defensive works on Skuf Island, Sigmundur kills Össur, and takes up possession of his paternal farm. Reuniting with Thorir, the boys press Thrandur of Göta for compensation for the deaths of Brestir and Beinir. At the Torshavn assembly, no settlement is reached between the two parties, and Sigmundur resolves that the dispute should be settled by Earl Hakon in Norway; Sigmundur arrives at court in Trondheim, only to find that Thrandur has not made the trip from the Faroes as promised (Chapter 24). Earl Hakon settles the case unilaterally for Sigmundur, making Sigmundur chieftain over all the Faroe Islands, and assessing Thrandur multiple counts of compensation for his actions against his kinsmen, Brestir and Beinir (Chapter 25). Though Thrandur contrives to avoid payment for several years, arguing that Sigmundur should pay compensation to Leifur Össursson, orphaned child of Össur Hafgrimursson. Eventually, full blood-money is paid by Thrandur to Sigmundur and Thorir for the death of their fathers and for Thrandur's attempt on the boys' lives years ago at Little Dimun (Chapter 26). Sigmundur's reputation as chieftain over the Faroe Islands grows, and Sigmundur and Thorir rush to the aid Earl Hakon and his sons when Norway is invaded by the mysterious Jomsvikings (Chapter 27).

Christianity Comes to the Faroe Islands (Chapters 28–33). At the center of the saga, the evangelizing King Olaf Tryggvason brings Christianity to the northern countries, circa 1000, and the king gives Sigmundur Brestirsson the task of bringing Christianity to the Faroe Islands (Chapter 28–29). Arriving at Tórshavn for the Faroese Assembly, Sigmundur begins to preach the new faith, but meets stiff public opposition led by Thrandur, who exacts a promise from Sigmundur on threat of death that he will not teach Christianity among the Faroes (Chapter 30). Turning the tables in a daring raid on Göta, Sigmundur captures Thrandur, forces his conversion, and compels him to convert the Islands to Christianity (Chapter 31). Sigmundur returns to Norway alone, unable to force Thrandur to accompany him to deliver Faroese tribute to King Olaf (Chapter 32). Sigmundur competes with King Olaf at some sporting games, but Sigmundur earns his ire by refusing to give Olaf the luck-ring which Earl Hakon had given him, and Sigmundur returns to the Faroes (Chapter 33).

A Growing Feud in the Faroes (Chapters 34–42). With Earl Hakon's sons, Eirikur and Svein, ruling in Norway, Sigmundur's status as chieftain of all the Faroe Islands is reaffirmed (Chapters 34–35). Back at home, old tensions between the families of Sigmundur Brestirsson and Thrandur of Göta are flammed by the conversion of the Faroe Islands to Christianity. Hostilities escalate when Thrandur and his foster sons (Sigurthur, Thorthur, Gautur, and Leifur Össursson) attempt two unsuccessful ambushes on Sigmundur and Thorir (Chapters 36–37). At the saga's climax, Thrandur and his foster sons move against Sigmundur's farm on Skuf Island and set it ablaze. Sigmundur's wife Thurid leads the household in defense, while Sigmundur, Thorir, and servant Einar escape out a secret tunnel (Chapter 38). Thrandur's posse pursues Sigmundur into the night, and corners them on cliffs high above the ocean. With a daring leap, Sigmundur and his fellows escape by swimming to South Island, but only Sigmundur survives the seas, weak and defenseless, only to be killed by a tenant-farmer of Thrandur's who sees Sigmundur's luck-ring and determines to steal it. The farmer, Thorgrimur, buries Sigmundur and Thorir and covers up Sigmundur's murder (Chapter 39).

Reconciliation between the two rival families begins when Leifur Össursson seeks to marry Thora, daughter of Sigmundur and Thurid. Before consenting to marriage, Thora demands that Leifur discover the identity of her father's killers (Chapter 40). Thrandur and Leifur visit Thorgrimur, discover the luck-ring, and Thrandur uses the old pagan faith to summon the ghosts of Einar, Thorir, and Sigmundur to learn how they died (Chapter 41). Thorgrimur is found guilty of Sigmundur's murder, and the way is open for Leifur to marry Thora Sigmundursdottir. Leifur Össursson takes up his grandfather's farm and becomes a respected chieftain (Chapter 42).

Feuding in the Next Generation (Chapter 43–59). The king of Norway, Olafur Haraldursson, summons several leading Faroe Islanders to court to arrange tribute from the Faroes to the crown (Chapter 43). After two royal messenger ships are lost in the North Sea crossing, Thoralfur Sigmundursson travels to Norway to reestablish relationships, followed by a ship crewed by Thrandur's good-for-nothing foster sons, Sigurthur, Thorthur, and Gautur. When Thoralfur is killed abroad under mysterious circumstances, the king points the blame on the foster sons, who promptly slip out of the country under the cover of darkness (Chapter 44–45). Anxious to receive the overdue tribute from the Faroes, King Olafur deputizes the mercenary Karl Maerskur to reassert royal influence among the Islanders (Chapter 46–47). Befriending the king's retainers, Leifur Össursson and the Faroese Lawspeaker Gilli, Karl Maerskur attempts to collect tribute at the annual assembly, but encounters treachery by Thrandur and his foster sons, who murder the king's servant in cold blood (Chapter 48). Exiled from the Faroes, Sigurthur, Thorthur, and Gautur make for Iceland, only to be shipwrecked on their home island, where they steal money and food around Austurey. Through yet another deception, Thrandur turns the tables on the weaponless Leifur and Gilli at the next assembly, arranging for his foster sons' triumphant return from outlawry. Rule of the Faroe Islands is divided between Thrandur, Leifur Össursson, and the sons of Sigmundur Brestirsson. As part of the settlement, Thrandur takes Leifur's and Thora's son, Sigmundur, as a foster son back to Göta (Chapter 49).

Finally tiring of their desolate ways, Thrandur turns his foster sons out of his house. Sigurthur worms his way into an influential position by having an affair with Birna, wife of a wealthy farmer, Thorhallur (Chapter 50). When some unscrupulous merchants shipwreck nearby, Sigurthur takes them into Thorhallur's house, where an altercation between Thorhallur and one of the merchants leads to the cuckolded farmer being murdered (Chapter 51). Another foster son, Gautur the Red, similarly insinuates himself into the home of Thorvaldur, another wealthy farmer, and has an affair with his wife Thorbera; and it is only a matter of time before Thorvaldur ends up dead too (Chapter 52). With the reputation of Thrandur's foster sons thoroughly blackened, a deadly series of events is set in motion when Leifur Thorirsson, son of Thorir Beinirsson, is accidentally killed in a dispute between Sigurthur and one of his tenant farmers (Chapter 53). Leifur Thorirsson's death reawakens the old hatreds between Thrandur's family and Sigmundur's family, as both Thurid and Thora, Sigmundur's wife and daughter, demand that Leifur Össursson take action against this killing of their kinsmen (Chapter 54). General sentiment of the Faroe Islanders turns against Thrandur's foster sons (Chapter 55).

When the third foster son Thorthur seeks to marry Sigmundur's widow, Thurid, Leifur and Thora devise a plot to bring about Thrandur's and his foster sons' downfall (Chapter 56). Visiting Thrandur nominally to arrange the marriage but in actuality to kidnap the young Sigmundur Leifursson back home, Leifur and Thora sabotage all the boats on Austurey, making them unseaworthy, before slipping off in the morning from a groggy Thrandur, one of the most poignant yet humorous incidents in the entire saga (Chapter 57). With premonitions of the danger, Sigurthur and Thorthur journey to Skuf Island to finalize the wedding between Thorthur and Thurid. Sigurthur meets with Thurid at the family farm on Skuf Island, when the trap is closed. At Thurid's signal, her sons attack Sigurthur who manages to fight his way away from them, killing Thurid's and Leifur's son Heri in his escape, becoming fatally wounded by a vengeful Leifur. Pursued back to Austurey by the Skuf Islanders, Sigurthur, Thorthur, and Gautur are brought down in an epic final battle, where several of Sigmundur Brestirsson's sons are also wounded or killed (Chapter 58). The feud ends with the death of Thrandur and his foster sons, and Sigmundur's descendents rule over the Faroe Islands justly and uncontested, and Christianity takes a strong foothold in the islands (Chapter 59).

Some Remarks on Character in the Faroe-Islander Saga

The *Faroe-Islander Saga* presents a seductive picture of the Islands as a place where myth and reality blend. The question is often raised, how historically accurate is a saga like this one? From a certain perspective, it is a non-question. Magnusson and Pálsson argue, "The great Family Sagas of Iceland, like *Njal's Saga* or *Egil's Saga* or *Laxdaela Saga*, were more concerned with the character and fate of individuals than with strict historical accuracy.... The 'success' of a saga does not depend on its historical accuracy so much as on the skill with which its individual characters are portrayed" (1966, 14).

Faroe-Islander Saga is successful as a whole through its vivid portrayal of its two main characters. Consider the character of Thrandur. As a hero-villain of the saga, Thrandur is magnificent in ability to stay in power; in the timeframe of the saga, six kings hold sway in Norway, but there is only one Thrandur. His character is one of the best drawn in the saga—he is shrewd and stingy with money; he is an expert in the law; he is relentless in manipulating events in his favor; and he can summon shaman magic and influence the weather when he needs to. Moreover, Thrandur's ability to dissemble is boundless; Peter Foote devotes over half his monograph, *On the Saga of the Faroe-Islanders*, to analyzing what he calls Thrandur's "genius for fraud" (Foote 1965, 20); and a medievalist colleague of the present translator suggested that all Thrandur's remarks be rendered into English in indirect or passive constructions to reflect his craftiness. And yet, Thrandur is not a monolithic villain. In subtle ways, the character of Thrandur ages in the saga. The freckled, haughty young man in his prime who fleeces a fortune from King Haraldur Gormsson (Chapter 3) and proposes to kill his young cousins in cold blood at Little Dimun (Chapter 7) is not the same Thrandur whose eyesight starts to fail before the Torshavn *thing* the year Karl-Maerskur arrives (Chapter 48), or dotes on the toddler Sigmundur Leifursson (Chapter 57), or dies of grief when he learns his foster sons have been killed (Chapter 59). His cunning remains, but there is a sense that humanity comes with age to Thrandur.

If nothing else, the saga-writer makes sure that we know that Thrandur, as a great chieftain, always seems to have the best interests of the Islanders at heart, denying the right of the Norwegian crown to meddle in Faroese affairs (Chapter 24) or to impose Christianity without the Islanders' consent (Chapter 30). Much of Thrandur's more treacherous actions, such as being complicit in the murder of the Karl-Maerskur (Chapter 48), are softened when viewed from the perspective of Thrandur's belief that the Faroe Islands should govern themselves.

Moreover, the motives of a character like Thrandur are often in sharper relief to the original readers of the saga than to modern ones. For instance, it may seem ironic that Thrandur is the prime agent in the failed raid against Sigmundur's farm which leads directly to his rival's demise at the hands of Thorgrimur (Chapters 38–39) and yet it is Thrandur himself who doggedly (and fantastically) tracks down Sigmundur's murderers (Chapter 40). The linguist E.V. Gordon gives some insight into explaining Thrandur's motives (1956, 34):

> In Icelandic society revenge for manslaughter was a sacred duty ... most men in the sagas did not feel vengeful in their vengeance, but were merely dutiful [...]. As the duty of revenge supplied one of the strongest motives of that society, the heroic authors frequently used it as a choice of a tragic alternative, in which duty and honour are weighed against one of the more natural ties, such as kinship.

Put simply, Thrandur would have felt it his duty to avenge his kinsman (he and Sigmundur were first cousins, once removed) even though he was equally guilt of seeking to kill Sigmundur himself—there is no irony here. His duty to clear the way for his foster son Leifur's marriage with Thora by finding her father's killer is almost secondary (see Chapter 40).

If Thrandur is the quintessential antihero of the saga, Sigmundur Brestirsson is the hero, the golden boy who is tragically orphaned at the age of nine at Little Dimun and forced to be raised by one of his father's killers (Chapter 7). A cut above his older cousin, Thorir, in all respects, he grows into a powerful warrior in a sequence of greater accomplishments which play like the "training montage" of a modern Hollywood blockbuster, coping with ever tougher foes: he defeats a ravaging bear (Chapter 12); the pirate Randver in Denmark (Chapter 18), the knight protectors, Vandill and Athill of Sweden (Chapter 19); and matches swords with a battle-tested Haraldur Iron-Skull (Chapter 21), before fighting against the indomitable and legendary force of the Jomsvikings, and killing no less than their leader, Bui (Chapter 27). The various battles in the *Faroe-Islander Saga* are intended to be entertaining, and scenes such as Sigmundur heroically climbing up the handle of his ax onto the defensive works to fight Össur on his return to Skufey (Chapter 24) can have readers on the edge of their seats. But the battles can become monotonous, if not disturbing in their bloodlust; the modern reader's evaluation of Sigmundur character suffers when we see him killing every living soul on board the enemy ships after the encounters with the Vikings in Chapters 18 and 19. Here again, some perspective is needed:

> The chief evil in life which men had to face in those violent days was death by the sword. That is why Norse authors usually have feuds or battles as the setting of heroic story. Their motives in doing so are often misunderstood, for many critics have attributed to them a delight in battle and killing for its own sake; but, on the contrary, *they saw in it the greatest evil, the one that required the most heroic power to turn into good. The authors' delight was only in the man who had this power* [Gordon 1956, 31; emphasis added].

While the saga-writer's portrayal of Sigmundur's character may not have the depth of Thrandur's, Sigmundur should be read as more than a bloodthirsty Viking warrior. Rather the saga-writer is at pains to present his actions as heroic in the face of ever-greater danger; and how a character behaves in the face of stiff adversity is the true measure of a hero. Sigmundur exemplifies what a Norse champion should in the epic battle against the Jomsvikings (Chapter 27), loyal to his chieftain and unflinching against harm: "Sigmundur called back [to Earl Hakon], 'To reward those many honors you have bestowed me, your grace, and because I want you to rely on me in your hour of the greatest danger, I will move against Bui.'"

This is not to say that Sigmundur is not without his faults; but his character is more realistic for the flaws. As a teen in Norway, he dishonorably decides to leave Thorkell's farm essentially because he is embarrassed that he got his daughter Thurid pregnant (Chapter 14); he is quick to temper, ranting at Earl Hakon over the settlement with Haraldur Iron-Skull (Chapter 21), and threatening to plunge an axe into an unarmed Thrandur over wergild (Chapter 26); and he sulks moodily in his farm all winter when the Faroe-Islanders reject his attempts to teach them Christianity (Chapter 30). But it is clear that he and Thurid are happy together on his father's farm with their kids (Chapter 36) and his family, particularly Thorir, loves him deeply (Chapter 39).

For those about to read the saga for the first time, there are a host of other well drawn characters: the farmer-outlaw Thorkell, covered in reindeer skins, and sniffing at the boys' arrival on his farm (Chapter 10); Bui, the piratical leader of the Jomsvikings (Chapter 27); the long-winded and pompous Olaf Trygvasson (Chapter 28); Sigmundur's wife, the strong-willed Thurid Strong-Widow, fighting among the household men to ward of Thrandur (Chapter 38); the loveable brigand, Karl Maerskur (Chapter 47); and the beautiful and fiendishly devious Thora Sigmundursdottir, a lethal maiden who succeeds in outfoxing Thrandur where her male relatives have failed (Chapter 40).

The present translator's express hope is that the life and energy of these characters has made the translation from Old Icelandic into English.

A Note on the Translation

This new translation is based on the standard text of *Faereyinga saga* from the Íslenzk Fornrit edition, volume 25, edited by Ólafur Halldórsson.[1] This text is based mostly on the manuscript of the saga which appears in *Flateyjarbók*, with supplemental readings from the version in *Ólafs saga Tryggvasonar* (*Olaf Tryggvasson's saga*).

The translation of excerpts of *Jómsvíkinga saga* in Appendix A is based on the edited Old Icelandic text in Blake (1962) which reproduces the Codex Holmianus 7, 40, manuscript containing the passage mentioning Sigmundur Brestirsson in Chapter 33 that does not appear in manuscripts from *Flateyjarbók*.

Following the practice of the saga translations produced by Magnus Magnusson, Hermann Pálsson, and Paul Edwards for the Penguin Classics, I have added chapter titles to the saga and appendix excerpts, both for ease of reference and to provide a sense of the contents of each chapter for the reader. No such titles occur in the saga manuscripts.

Faereyinga Saga has not found its way to as wide an English speaking readership as classics such as *Njal's Saga* or *Laxdaela Saga*, but the saga has been translated into English at least five times before. Two early translations are either archaic or rather out-of-date: *The Tale of Thrond of Gate Commonly Called Faereyinga saga—Englished by F. York Powell* (London 1896) and *The Saga of the Faroe Islanders*, translated by A.C. Muriel (London 1934). Hard to find, but more modern is *The Faroe Islander Saga, freely translated ... by G.V.C. Young and Cynthia Clewer* (Belfast 1973). The two most widely available translations are George Johnston's 1994 popular but very stilted version of the saga, which appeared under the misleading title *Thrand of Gotu*; and Icelander Volundur Lars Agnarsson's 2012 serviceable translation into English with facing Old Icelandic text,

---

1. Ólafur Halldórsson, ed., *Faereyinga saga/Ólafs saga Tryggvasonar eptir Odd Munk Snorrason, Íslenzk Fornrit*, 25 (Reykjavik: Hið Íslenzka Fornritafélag, 2006).

Faereyinga Saga, designed primarily for students of the language wishing to read the saga in the original. Translations exist in other languages, notably Faroese, Danish, Norwegian, Swedish, German, and French; for these references, see pages lxxix–lxxx in the Íslenzk Fornrit introduction to volume 25.

The current translation was made independently of all these other works, and the translator's goal was not simply to render the content into English, but rather to attempt an exciting literary translation in fresh, readable prose.

For the translation of chapters 31–33 of *Jómsvíkinga Saga* in Appendix A, I have consulted and benefited from studying the excellent and still very readable translation of N.F. Blake (Blake 1962). For these passages, the translation is new and original, though I am indebted to Blake's work for the occasional word choice or suitable phrase.

In terms of orthography, Old Icelandic diacritical marks for short and long vowels were omitted; that is, <á, é í, ó, ú, ý> are written simply as <a, e, i, o, u, y>. Such marks crop up in edited texts but only appear sporadically to mark long vowels in the saga manuscripts; any serious reader working linguistically with Old Icelandic will quickly be able to trace them. The Old Icelandic vowel written as <ö> (IPA [ø]) is a front, rounded mid-vowel, phonetically different from the vowel <o> (IPA [o]), a back, rounded mid-vowel; in this case, it was considered better to retain the umlaut over the vowel in the spelling to keep <o> and <ö> distinct.

Much consideration was given to the translation of Icelandic proper names. The practice was adopted where proper names were given in their original Old Icelandic forms with only minor transliteration of the Icelandic letters "thorn" <Þ> and "eth" <ð> for the digraph <th>, e.g., *Þrándr* becomes *Thrandur*.[1] The masculine singular morphological element /-r/ was also retained as <-ur> for masculine names, e.g., *Sigmundur* and *Olafur*, rather than anglicizing these to, e.g., *Sigmund* and *Olaf*. I feel that anglicization can impart a false sense of a continental Germanic epic such as the Middle High German *Nibelungenlied*; and earlier translations of the saga which refer to *Thrándr* from *Göta* as "Thrond of Gate" seem to have gone too far from the original North Germanic character of the sagas. For female names, where final /-r/ occurs, it was omitted and a final <-ð> was written as <-d>; for example, *Þorgerðr* becomes *Thorgerd*.

---

1. Some translators render Icelandic "thorn" <Þ> and "eth" <ð> as English <th> and <d>, respectively, e.g., Magnusson and Pálsson, in their translation of *Njal's Saga* (Magnusson and Pálsson 1960, 33).

Place names are given as simple transliterations from the orthographic values supplied by the text, except where a particular location is historically significant, e.g., the Earl's home at *Lade* (not *Hlað*). Thus the names of the Faroe Islands generally appear in their archaic form, e.g., Old Icelandic *Austurey* versus Faroese *Eysturoy*. In the notes, place names are usually given once in their Old Icelandic form and once in their modern form, e.g., Thorshaven (*Tórshavn*). In the translation, some island names appear in both transliterated and translated forms, e.g., *Skufey* and *Skuf Island*, *Sviney* and *Swine-Island*. The variation is generally functional, e.g., allowing for the farmer *Bjarni* to be referred to as *Swine-Island-Bjarni*.

As with reading all saga literature, outlandish names of people and places take some acclimatization, and I hope these conventions for rendering Old Icelandic into English are accessible and straightforward for the general reader.

1. The First Settlers in the Faroe Islands

There was a man named Grimur Kamban who was the first to settle in the Faroe Islands. In those days, a great number of men were seeking refuge from the tyranny of King Haraldur Fine-Hair; some men settled themselves in the Faroe Islands and farmed there, while other men sought land on other islands.[1]

When Aud the Deep-Minded was traveling to Iceland, she came first to the Faroe Islands.[2] There she married off Alofa, daughter of Thorstein the Red, from whom descends the entire family line of Faroe-Islanders called the Götuskeggjar who live on Austurey.[3]

---

1. Haraldur Fine-Hair (c. 850–c. 932) became king of Norway in c. 872, after uniting several petty kingdoms under his overlordship; his story is told in Snorri Sturluson's *Heimskringla*. The nickname comes from the fact that Haraldur refused to cut or comb his hair until all Norway was under his power, a period from roughly 864 to 872. Many high-born men fled Norway under Haraldur's rule as the king claimed all the country's land for himself and required freeborn landowners to pay tax to the crown. The first settlers of Iceland arrived in 874, and there was much land-taking among the North Sea islands of the Hebrides, Orkneys, Shetlands, and Faroes. The contribution of Haraldur's overbearing rule to the settlement of Iceland is referred to in Chapter 2 of *Laxdaela Saga*, and some backstory to the political situation and Haraldur's conquest of North Sea Islands appears in *Orkneyinga Saga*, Chapters 4–6.

2. Aud the Deep-Minded, daughter of the Norwegian Ketil Flat-Nose and mother of Thorstein the Red, was a matriarchal figure in the Settlement of Iceland. This account of Aud's trip to the Faroes is nearly identical to that in *Landnámabók*, Chapter 97. In Chapter 95 of the same source, Aud sails from Caithness (Scotland) to the Orkney Islands, where she arranged the marriage of her granddaughter Groa, from whom descends the family line of the Earls of Orkney whose history is told in *Orkneyinga Saga* (*Orkney-Islander Saga*). The fact that the Götuskeggjar family of the Faroe Islands descends from Aud situates the settlement of Faroe Islands within the same grand mythology of the settlement of Iceland.

3. Austurey "East Island" (Faroese: *Eysturoy*), the second largest of the eighteen Faroe Islands, is located in the northeast of the archipelago, between five northern islands (Kalsoy, Viðoy, Fugloy, Svínoy, and Borðoy) and the big island of Streymoy.

2. Thrandur of Göta

There was a man called Thorbjörn the Götuskeggur who had a farm on Austurey in the Faroe Islands. His wife was named Guthrun, and they had two sons together: the older was named Thorlakur, and the younger, Thrandur. Both were promising young men. Thorlakur was big and strong, and Thrandur would come to have the same build when he was fully grown, as there was a large difference in age between the brothers. Thrandur was red-haired with freckles, and he was rather handsome.[1] His father Thorbjörn was a rich man and already old when this saga takes place.

Thorlakur married there on the island, and yet he still lived at home with his father at Göta.[2] Right after the wedding, Thorbjörn the Götuskeggur died, and he was buried in the old way because all the Faroe Islands were still heathen at that time.[3] His sons set to work dividing the inheritance among each other, but they both wanted the main farm on Göta as that was the most valuable share. They cast lots for it, and Thrandur won.[4]

After this outcome, Thorlakur begged his brother for the home farm if Thrandur could have more of the livestock in return, but Thrandur refused. Then, Thrandur went off and got himself another farm there in the Islands.

Thrandur rented out the land in Göta to some kinsmen, charging as much rent as possible for it. In the summer, he loaded his ship with some cargo and sailed for Norway, where he took lodging for the winter. He always seemed to be in a foul mood.

---

1. In the Icelandic sagas, the physical characteristics of being red-haired and freckled were stereotypically equated with being a rascal or troublemaker. Foote notes that there was an intriguing medieval association of red-hair color in humans with the rusty pelts of the fox, the quintessential wily animal (Foote 1965, 17).

2. Göta (*Gøta*) is a modest village on the east coast of Eysturoy, with a population today of about five hundred. In the area known as *Norðragøta*, the remains of Thrandur's (*Tróndur*) large farm can still be found and it is a popular tourist site in the Islands.

3. "*Buried in the old way*" could refer to the pagan practice of cremation, which was discouraged by the Church, and archaeological excavations of grave sites throughout Scandinavia show that cremation gave way to the practice of inhumation during the 10th century. However, as one scholar points out: "There was no single pre–Christian burial rite and there was tremendous regional variation throughout Scandinavia" (Richards 2005, 22). The phrase may refer to a practice whereby individuals were buried fully clothed with various grave-goods, such as jewelry, drinking horns, and other fineries, regardless of whether the body was cremated or inhumed. After the introduction of Christianity, grave sites throughout Scandinavia show a decrease in grave-goods (see Richards 2005, 19–28).

4. Casting lots for dividing property and settling other disputes was common in mainland Scandinavian law, but not a usual procedure in Icelandic law at the time; this episode seems to show that the early generations of Faroese followed Norwegian laws (see Foote 1970, 165).

2. Thrandur of Göta

Haraldur Grey-Cloak ruled over Norway at that time.[1]

The following summer, Thrandur traveled with some merchants south to Denmark and arrived at Haleyri before the season was out.[2] There was a large crowd assembled there, and it is reported that many people had come to the northern lands to conduct business at the market. At this time, King Haraldur Gormsson, known as Haraldur Bluetooth, ruled over Denmark.[3] King Haraldur himself was at Haleyri that summer with a great band of his men.

Two of the king's retainers were with him that summer, named Sigurthur and Harekur. These brothers went about the market place, looking to buy the largest, most precious gold ring they could find. They went into one booth which was exceptionally well-appointed. Inside sat a man who welcomed them and inquired what they wanted to buy. When they replied that they wanted to buy a large gold ring of the highest quality, the man told them that he had a good selection. The brothers asked the merchant's name, and he was called Holmgeir the Rich. Holmgeir brought out his treasures and showed the brothers an enormous gold ring which happened to be the most precious of his wares; in fact, it was so expensive that they didn't think they could produce the silver which he was asking for it then and there, so they asked him to hold off from selling the ring until the next day, and Holmgeir agreed. They left the booth with the matter settled, and the night passed.

In the morning, Sigurthur went out of their tent, while Harekur stayed behind. A short time later, Sigurthur came back to the tent-flap and whispered sharply, "Harekur! Quick! Give me the purse with the silver set aside for buying the ring, since the payment is now due. You wait here in the meantime and guard the tent."

Harekur handed Sigurthur the silver-purse through the tent-flap.[4]

---

1. Haraldur Gunnhildarson "Grey-Cloak" was King of Norway from 961 to 975; he was grandsson of Haraldur Fine-Hair and son of Eirikur Bloodaxe. He rose to power through the support of his uncle, King Haraldur Bluetooth of Denmark. Note that the action of the saga has jumped nearly 75 years from the Settlement Period of the Faroes.

2. Haleyri is identified as a seasonal market-town on the coast of Skaane, the southernmost region of Sweden which was part of the Denmark until 1658. There were several such market centers in Skaane, which was among the most important trade regions in the 12th and 13th centuries. See Graham-Campbell et al., 1994, 84ff.

3. Haraldur Gormsson "Bluetooth" was King of Denmark from c. 958 to his death, c. 987. He is usually credited for conquering Norway in the early 960s, bringing that kingdom under the sphere of sovereignty of Denmark. The piratical-sounding nickname may refer to a dark complexion; the word for blue (*blá-r*) in Old Icelandic refers to a wider range of colors than the English word, encompassing all shades of blue into black, e.g., the blueish-black of a raven.

4. This is a difficult scene to interpret because the saga-writer is deliberately vague for dramatic effect. Foote's interpretation (1965, 14–15) is probably correct, namely, that the individual who comes to the tent and asks Harekur for the money through the tent-flap is not actually Sigurthur, but someone impersonating Sigurthur. Foote believes the saga-writer leaves open the possibility that the thief might even be Thrandur, but this is perhaps infering too much.

3. Thrandur Earns a Fortune

Sometime later, Sigurthur returned to the tent to his brother and said, "Hey, hand over the silver; the payment is due."

Confused, Harekur replied, "But I just gave it to you."

"That's not right," said Sigurthur, "I didn't ask for it."

They argued over this for a while, and then they informed the king and the rumor spread. When the king learned that his attendants had been robbed, he placed a travel embargo so that no ship could sail abroad until the situation was resolved. In the eyes of many men, it was a serious misuse of the king's power to keep them detained at Haleyri.

In the meantime, the Norwegians held a meeting about their plans. Thrandur was at the meeting, and muttered, "Here's a sorry group of dithering men!"

They asked him, "Do you know what to do?"

"So it seems," replied Thrandur.

"Let's hear your plan then," called the merchants.

"It won't be without its price," said Thrandur.

The group wanted to know how much he was asking for, and he answered, "Each of you must give me an ounce of silver."[1]

They argued that an ounce apiece was quite a lot, but they agreed that each man would give him half an ounce beforehand, and another half-ounce if his plan was carried out to their benefit.[2]

On the following day, the king convened a *thing* and decreed that those gathered would never be free from the embargo until the matter was resolved.[3] Then, a young man, whose red hair flowed from his head and who was freckly and looking rather stern, stood up to speak. He called out, "Here I see a sorry group of dithering men!"

The king's advisors asked what he proposed to be done, to which the young man answered, "I think that each man here lay out whatever amount of silver the king demands, and that all the money be pooled together. Then let him make compensation to the men who have suffered losses.

---

1. Not a modern ounce; the unit *eyrir* "ounce" was an eighth of a mark of silver, approximately weighing 25 grams.
2. Accurate conversions of the value of an ounce of silver into modern terms are impossible, but eight ounces of refined silver by weight was known as a mark, and a mark of silver was equivalent to the value of four milch cows. Thrandur's bargain for an ounce apiece is therefore akin to half the value of a cow; a fortune indeed.
3. A *thing* was a public assembly, usually held on a broad field where lawsuits and other communal business would be heard and resolved (see Appendix C).

The king would gain for himself the honor which comes from these actions.[1] I know that he will make the right choice as to whom he should listen to, since people remain here, not bound by adverse weather, but rather detained here through such a great injustice."

This proposal quickly gained the support of the entire assembly, for men said that they would present the money willingly to the king out of respect owed to him rather than sit there in their dishonor. So the plan was adopted and the money in the king's pool grew; it was something of a fortune.

After this, the travel ban was lifted and a great number of ships sailed abroad. The king held a *thing*, bringing the treasure in a sack to compensate his retainers for their loss. Then, the king discussed with his men what should be done with this huge fortune. It was then that a man rose to speak, saying, "My lord, what worth do you place on that man who came up with the plan?"

Everyone now saw that the speaker who stood before the king was the same young man that had made the proposal earlier.

King Haraldur declared, "This entire fortune is to be divided into two equal shares; my men get one share, and the other share will be further divided into half-shares. This young man will receive one of these, and I will keep the other half-share myself."

Thrandur thanked the king handsomely for this and offered his pledge of friendship. The fortune Thrandur now possessed was so great that he could scarcely transport it back to the market. At last, King Haraldur sailed away, soon followed by all the commoners and merchants.

Thrandur sailed to Norway with the same Norwegian merchants with whom he had traveled to Denmark, and they paid him the amount which he had stipulated. Thrandur bought himself a large sea-worthy cargo ship in Norway, loaded it with the enormous fortune acquired on this trip, and finally, he set course for the Faroe Islands. He had good luck on his journey with all his treasure intact and settled down on the farm at Göta in the spring.[2] He was never lacking money from then on.

---

1. Both English and Scandinavian monarchs at this time were essentially chieftains of men in the ancient Germanic tradition whose authority stemmed from the awarding of friendship and gifts to their followers.

2. The belief in "luck" played an important role in pre–Christian Norse culture. Good luck or bad luck (compare German: *Glück* "good luck" versus *Pech*, "extreme bad luck"), were viewed as inherent qualities possessed by an individual, and a person's luck could be passed down across generations; for example, Leif Eirikursson, the discoverer of Vinland in North America, was felt to have inherited his luck from his father Eirikur the Red; Leif earned the nickname Leif the Lucky for having successfully rescued fifteen men stranded on a reef off the coast of Greenland (in *Eiriks saga*, Chapter 4). Here, Thrandur is portrayed as possessing good luck, a fact which would not have been lost on the 13th century audience of the saga.

4. Brestir and Beinir of Skufey

There was a man named Hafgrimur, who farmed on South Island in the Faroe Islands.[1] He was a tough, powerful man, wealthy in land and livestock. His wife was called Guthrid, and she was the daughter of Snaeulfur.[2] Hafgrimur was the local chieftain over half of the Islands and watched over the district as a fief of King Haraldur Grey-Cloak, who was then ruling over Norway.[3] Hafgrimur was very impetuous in character and was not known for being a wise man. He had a servant named Einar, who was called the South-Islander[4]; there was another man in Hafgrimur's household called Eldjarn Comb-Hood. This man was a rumor-monger and abusive, stupid and malicious, cowardly, sniveling, and altogether a liar and a slanderer.

Important in this saga are two brothers who lived on Skufey, one was named Brestir Sigmundursson, and the other, Beinir Sigmundursson.[5] Their father, Sigmundur, and Thorbjörn the Götuskeggur, the father of Thrandur, were brothers.[6]

Brestir and Beinir were excellent men, and they were chieftains over the other half of the Islands. They ruled their half as a fief of Earl Hakon Sigurtharson,[7] who at that time wielded some power in Trondheim.[8]

---

1. South Island (*Suðuroy*) is the southernmost of the Faroe Islands; it is particularly known for being surrounded by a number of smaller islets and skerries.
2. Lit. "Snow-Wolf."
3. The term *höfðingi* "chief, leader" in this context seems to mean the same as *goði* "chieftain" which meant various things in the Norse world. Generally, chieftains were wealthy and thus influential farmers who possessed certain duties and powers either through inheritance or specific appointment by the king (of Norway or Denmark). Fox and Pálsson explain that chieftains once had a partly religious role but "by the 11th century the chieftains had only legal and administrative functions" (Fox and Pálsson 1972, 194). The authors continue: "It is important to emphasize that these chieftains did not form any sort of feudal ruling class: 11th century Iceland is best described as a confederation of free farmers" (Fox and Pálsson 1972, 194). This remark would apply to the Faroe Islands as well; the chieftains were wealthy farmers influential among their fellow farmers, a leader among equals.
4. The nickname South-Islander is ambiguous between referring to *Suðurey* "South Island" in the Faroe Islands and southern islands off the coast of Scotland, i.e. the Orkneys or Shetlands.
5. Skufey (*Skúvoy*) is a small island in the Faroes, comprising just four square kilometers, located south of Sandoy and north of Suðuroy. Archaeologists unearthed a number of stones engraved with crosses on Skufey, indicating early settlement by Irish *papar*.
6. Brestir and Beinir Sigmundursson are thus first cousins of Thrandur Thorbjornsson; all the kinsmen are of the Götuskeggjur family line, see Chapter 1.
7. The powerful Hakon Sigurtharson (c. 937–995) was King of Norway after Haraldur Grey-Cloak from 975 to 995, but was first the Earl of Trondheim after the death of his father in 961. His successor was King Olaf Tryggvason (995–1000).
8. Trondheim was the medieval capital of Norway during the Viking Age under King Olaf Tryggvason until 1217. Today it is the country's third largest city with about 170,000 inhabitants.

Brestir's men were retainers of Earl Hakon and both brothers were his most beloved friends. Brestir was the greatest and strongest of all men and a better warrior than any other man who lived in the Faroe Islands at that time. He was a handsome man and excelled at all sports. Beinir was much like his brother in many ways, yet he was not quite his equal.

In contrast to the brothers, few people liked Thrandur, despite close ties of kinship among the Islanders.

The brothers were not married; they had mistresses. Brestir's mistress was called Cecilia, and Beinir's was named Thora. Brestir's son was named Sigmundur, and he was a promising young man from an early age. Beinir's son was named Thorir, who was two years older than Sigmundur. The brothers had a farm on Dimun, which was smaller than their farm on Skuf Island.[1] The boys were much younger at the time when the following story takes place.

Snaeulfur, Hafgrimur's father-in-law, farmed on Sand Island.[2] He was from the Hebrides originally but had fled from those islands because of a killing and because he was such a confrontational man, and so he had come to settle in the Faroe Islands. He had been on viking raids in the earlier part of his life, and even then he had been overbearing and hard to deal with.

5. The Incident on South Island

There was a man named Bjarni who lived on Sviney, and who was known as Swine-Island Bjarni.[3] He was a prosperous farmer and had many cattle; he was also a very shrewd man. He was the brother of Thrandur of Göta's mother.[4]

---

1. Dimun (*Stóra Dímun* "Big Dimun") is a small island between South Island and Skufey of just one square mile, neighbored by Little Dimun (*Lítla Dímun*). The islands are approachable only in calm seas due to the steep cliffs surrounding both.
2. Sand Island (*Sandoy*) is the fifth largest of the Faroe Islands, just north of Skufey. Graham-Campbell et al. (1994, 168): "The recent discovery of a group of pagan graves at Sandur on Sandoy has provided fresh evidence of an early Viking presence. Excavations close to the church here have revealed extensive settlement remains, including an important series of early timber churches, the earliest of which is associated with an 11th century hoard of coins. [This site] clearly has had a history of settlement as long as any in the Faroes."
3. Sviney "Swine Island" (*Svinoy*) is a smaller island located in the northeast of the Faroes, with a population today of just 50 inhabitants; there is a church in the one town in which stands a memorial stone thought to mark the burial place of Swine-Island Bjarni.
4. Thrandur's mother was Guthrun. Her brother, Bjarni, is thus Thrandur's maternal uncle.

5. The Incident on South Island

The assembly place of the Faroe Islands is on Straumey,[1] where there is a harbor called Thorshaven.[2]

Hafgrimur, who farmed on South Island in that bay called Hof,[3] was very much a heathen, inasmuch as all the Faroe Islands were heathen at that time. There was one autumn at Hafgrimur's farm on South Island when Einar the South-Islander and Eldjarn Comb-Hood were sitting together at the fire roasting sheep heads. They were making a comparison of the best men in the Islands: Einar championed his kinsmen, Brestir and Beinir, while Eldjarn favored Hafgrimur and claimed him as the superior man. It came about that Eldjarn leapt up and made a swing at Einar with a tree-branch which he had been stirring the fire with. The blow struck Einar's shoulder, and he took it badly. Einar grabbed an axe and struck Eldjarn Comb-Hood in the head; he fell over unconscious and soon died.

Since Hafgrimur would need to be compensated for the killing, he sent Einar off the island and told him to go directly to his Skuf-Island kinsmen, seeing as how Einar sided with them.[4] Halfgrimur added, "I'll come, too, sooner or later, so that we can dine sumptuously at the Skuf-Islanders' expense."

Einar sailed off and made his way to the brothers, and told them why he had come. They welcomed him warmly, and he was cared for well on their farm that winter.

Einar asked his kinsman, Brestir, to handle his case, and he agreed to this. Brestir was a clever man and skilled in the law.

That same winter Hafgrimur sailed in his ship to Skuf Island. He met with the brothers and asked how they intended to compensate the crime Einar had committed against Eldjarn Comb-Hood. Brestir answered that

---

1. Straumey "Stream Island" (*Streymoy*) is the largest and most populous of the Faroes, sitting in the center of the archipelago. *Streym-* is a cognate of English "stream," and the Old Icelandic form *straumr* means "stream" or "current." Wylie suggests that the early Norse settlers found the name Stream Island appropriate for the coursing water and tidal action which flowed through the narrow inlets and channels of this island (Wylie 1981, 18).
2. Thorshaven "Thor's Harbor" (*Tórshavn*), then as now, the capital of the Faroe Islands, situated on the southeast peninsula of Streymoy. It is the largest city and the hub of economic and cultural activity in the Faroe Islands, with a population around 12,000.
3. Hov, to this day, is a small village on the east coast of Suðuroy.
4. In Norse society, a murder was not the black crime it is today, provided that the killer make his deed known publically. The relatives of the victim could either seek revenge against the murderer or demand compensation in the form of wergild, a kind of blood money (see Appendix C). The awarding of compensation was a formal legal matter and followed an established scale of payment for such killings with the amount of wergild owed being determined by the rank of the victim and other mitigating factors of the incident. Hafgrimur, rather callously, is more concerned in recouping some money from Eldjarn's death than over the loss of his servant.

they should settle the case at the *thing*, judged by the best men in the Islands, so that there might be a settlement on equal terms. Hafgrimur replied, "There won't be any settlement other than what I decide alone."[1]

"Then there won't be a settlement at all, and nothing will come of it," countered Brestir coldly.

Then Hafgrimur summoned Einar to appear before the *thing* on Straumey, and they parted company with matters standing as they were. Immediately after the incident had taken place, Brestir had circulated an account of the assault which Comb-Hood had made on Einar.[2]

Now both sides came to the *thing*, each with a band of men. But when Hafgrimur went before the assembly and sought to present his case against Einar, the brothers Brestir and Beinir took up places on the other side of the field with a large gathering. Brestir prevented Hafgrimur from bringing the case on Comb-Hood's behalf, since under the established laws, it was felt that the victim had started the fight against an innocent man. Then Brestir's men broke up the court by force right in front of Hafgrimur; the result being that they sentenced Eldjarn to outlawry and bearing the full guilt for the incident.[3] Hafgrimur said that this outrageous insult would be avenged. Brestir declared that they would be ready and said nothing further in response to his threats.

Both sides parted ways with matters standing as they were.

6. Hafgrimur Seeks Allies

Shortly after this, Hafgrimur set out from home and went down to his ship, along with six men and his wife Guthrid. They sailed to Sand Island, where his father-in-law, Snaeulfur, farmed.

As they approached the island, they saw nobody out fishing in the

---

1. In special cases, the plaintiff in a legal suit could be granted the right of "self judgment" (*sjálf-dæmi*) by the defendant wherein he would decide unlaterally what compensation he thought appropriate. Hafgrmur is trying to claim the right self-judgment without cause.

2. Brestir, being a clever legal mind, had circulated a version of the incident at South Island which highlights that Eldjarn Comb-Hood had struck Einar first; when the case came to trial, Einar's subsequent killing of Eldjarn could be judged as an act of self-defense. The term *frumhlaup* "assault" used here is a legal term for the offence (see Foote 1970, 166).

3. An interesting episode, according to Peter Foote in *On Legal Terms in Faereyinga Saga* (Foote 1970, 167–8): "The breaking-up of a court by force was doubtless possible under many circumstances... It is found elsewhere in Icelandic stories. Here it seems to be a dramatic extra, since the legality of the defence and the counter-charge [assault] seem unquestionable."

bay or up on the island.[1] They hiked up to Snaeulfur's farm and into the farmhouse, but no one was there. They went into the sitting room, to find that the table was set with food and drink, but nobody seemed to be home. This seemed strange to them, and they stayed there that night.

The next morning, they prepared to set off and they made their way along the coast. They rowed the ship in a different direction from which they had approached the island, and came across a group of people. They recognized them as Snaeulfur the farmer and his entire household. Hafgrimur rowed toward them and called out to his father-in-law, but Snaeulfur did not return the greeting. Then Hafgrimur asked what advice Snaeulfur had for him concerning the dispute with Brestir and Beinir, so that he might have his revenge. Snaeulfur replied, "It went badly for you, considering that better men attacked you without cause, but just accept the worst of it."

"You were wrong if you thought I wanted a scolding from you," said Hafgrimur, "and I won't listen to you."

Snaeulfur grabbed a spear and threw it at him. Hafgrimur raised his shield in defense and the spear pierced it deeply, but he was not wounded. The two men parted company as matters stood, and Hafgrimur sailed home to South Island, very dissatisfied with the meeting.

Hafgrimur and his wife Guthrid had a son named Össur; he was only nine years old when these events took place, but he was already a very promising young man.

Now some time passed. Hafgrimur left home and sailed to Austurey to visit Thrandur. Thrandur welcomed him warmly, and Hafgrimur sought counsel as to what he would advise him concerning the dispute with the Skuf-Islanders, Brestir and Beinir. Hafgrimur added that Thrandur was the wisest man in the Islands and that he earnestly wanted to do something to get the better of them. Thrandur said that it was a strange thing to ask, since Hafgrimur wanted him to take part in a plot against his own cousins.

"Indeed, you cannot be serious," continued Thrandur. "Should I take part in your scheme, just because you want other men to fall in league with you? You will stop at nothing to get the better of them just for vengeance."

---

1. The towering cliffs and rock ledges of many of the Faroe Islands are dramatic. The Icelandic saga-writer seems to have an awareness of the topography of the islands as illustrated by phrases such as "up on the island." In general, scholarly opinion holds that the saga-writer did not know much about Faroese conditions (see Foote 1970, 159).

"You've got that right," growled Hafgrimur; "I want to get the better of them. You must be on my side, if I am to take the brothers' lives."

Thrandur replied, "I will come on the raid against the brothers; however, in return for my help, you will repay me with the value of two cows every spring and two hundred ounces of silver every autumn,[1] and this debt will be binding forever from this day forward. But I am still not prepared to act, unless more men ally themselves with you. I want you to meet with my mother's brother, Bjarni, on Swine Island, and get him to join you."

Hafgrimur agreed to this and sailed out to Swine Island and met Bjarni, seeking him as an ally just as Thrandur required. Bjarni responded by saying that he would not go along with this plan, unless he got some profit out of it in return. Hafgrimur told him to name his price. Bjarni said, "You must give me the value of three cows every spring and three hundred ounces of silver, payable in slaughtered meat, every autumn."

Hafgrimur agreed to this and went home as matters stood.

7. Standoff at Little Dimun

Now the saga returns to the brothers, Brestir and Beinir. They had two farms, one on Skuf Island, the other on Dimun. Brestir had a wife by that time, who was called Cecilia and was Norwegian by birth.[2] They had a son named Sigmundur, who was nine years old when this part of the saga takes place, and he was both strong and manly in his appearance. Beinir had a mistress named Thora, and a son by her, named Thorir. He was eleven years old at the time and a promising young man.

There was one time when the brothers, Brestir and Beinir, were at

---

1. In Old Icelandic, "hundred" in monetary terms usually refers to a "strong hundred," a base unit of exchange of 120. Here, "ounce" seems to refer to weight. The figures two and two hundred (and three and three hundred, below) appear in the original, but these amounts are dizzyingly high, used to heighten the drama. Hafgrimur's farm at Hof has little arable land, and today the area is better known for its off-shore salmon fishing; even if Hafgrimur collected extensive rents from tenant farms, it is hard to imagine his producing 200 ounces of silver worth of cattle-meat per year to pay off Thrandur (equivalent in the system of reckoning to 64 milch cows), let alone 500 worth of meat (160 milch cows) to pay off both debts annually.

2. Compare Chapter 4, where Brestir is said to be unmarried (*eigi ... kvángaðir*) and Cecilia is described as his mistress (*friðla*). Note that Brestir's son, Sigmundur, is legitimate, while Beinir's son, Thorir, is not; this clumsy addition of a pedigree seems to be included as appropriate for the chieftain and champion Sigmundur is to become, and further serves dramatically to set Sigmundur apart in character from Thorir.

their farm on Dimun and they sailed over to the island of Little Dimun, which was uninhabited. There they let their sheep roam free and penned them only when it was time to slaughter them. Their boys, Sigmundur and Thorir, begged to go with them. The fathers gave in, and then they all set out for the islands. They all brought their weapons with them.

It is said that Brestir was powerful, strong, and better with a sword than any man; he was a wise man and beloved by all his friends. His brother Beinir was also accomplished in his own right, yet he did not quite come to equal his brother.

They were just sailing out to Little Dimun when they had cleared Big Dimun and saw three boats heading for them, each loaded with armed men; there were twelve men in each boat. The brothers recognized these men immediately: there was Hafgrimur of South Island in the lead, Thrandur of Göta on the second ship, and Bjarni of Swine Island on the third ship. These men put their ships between the brothers and the islands, keeping them from landing, and then drove their ship into a narrow inlet. There was a rocky crag above the brothers and they leapt up onto it with their weapons; they put the boys down near them on the rock. The rock was wide on top and a good place for a pitched fight.

Now Hafgrimur's posse closed in, and they too sprang at once from the ships in the inlet up onto the rock. Hafgrimur and Swine-Island Bjarni's men charged the brothers, but they defended themselves courageously. Thrandur and his crew walked along the beach and were not part of the attack. Brestir was defending the rock on the right-hand side of the attackers, the harder side to defend. The men skirmished for a while, but they could not dislodge the brothers.

Then Hafgrimur cried out, "I had a deal with you, Thrandur, that you would back me up with men if I gave you my cattle!"

Thrandur answered, "You are a bigger coward for every minute that you can't cut down two men with two dozen! It's just like you to always blame others for your faults, and how little nerve you have to get near any real danger! Let this be my advice: if there is any backbone in you, go be the first man to take down Brestir, and the others will follow your lead, or else I will know for certain that you are completely useless." Thus, Thrandur goaded him on as vehemently as possible.

After this, Hafgrimur leapt up onto the rock and thrust at Brestir with a spear, driving it into his stomach and clean through him. When Brestir saw this was a fatal wound, he lashed out at Hafgrimur and struck him with his sword. The blade cut into Hafgrimur's left shoulder, cleaving it and his side wide open, and lopping his hand off. Hafgrimur fell dead off the rock, and Brestir fell onto him. There each man died.

Now they attacked Beinir on two sides. He defended himself well, but it ended then and there, and Beinir was cut down.

It is said that Brestir was the death of three men before he killed Hafgrimur, and that Beinir had slain two men. After the battle, Thrandur proposed that they should kill the boys, Sigmundur and Thorir.

"I'm not going to kill them," replied Bjarni evenly.

Thrandur frowned, "If they go free, someday these boys will be the death of nearly every man here."

Bjarni answered, "I wouldn't kill them any more than I would kill myself."

"I wasn't being serious just now," said Thrandur lightly. "I just wanted to test you to see how you would react to it. Now I will make amends with the boys for all this, since I was forced to take a stand against them; I will offer to be a foster-father to them."

The boys sat on the rock and looked up at this news. Thorir burst into tears, but Sigmundur said, "Let's not cry, cousin, but just mark this day for a long time."

After this episode, they sailed from Little Dimun, and Thrandur had the boys come home with him to Göta. Hafgrimur's body was brought to South Island and buried there in the heathen way, while friends of Brestir and Beinir transported their corpses home to Skuf Island and dug graves for them, also in the old manner.

Afterwards, news of these events became known throughout the Faroe Islands and every man mourned the death of the brothers.

8. Hrafn Holmgard-Traveler

That same summer, a ship from Norway landed in the Faroe Islands. The captain's name was Hrafn,[1] a man from the Vik region of Norway, who owned a farm in Tønsberg.[2] He routinely sailed from Sweden to

---

1. Lit. "Raven."
2. Viken "The Vik" (Old Icelandic "inlet" or "creek") was a loosely defined district in southeastern Norway centered around Oslofjord, the strait separating Norway and Sweden (and often in saga times under the control of Denmark which lies across the sound). Tønsberg was a major trading outpost in the region.

Holmgard, and on account of this he was called the Holmgard-Traveler.[1] The ship was harbored in Thorshaven.

It is said that one morning, while the merchants were still unloading their cargo, Thrandur of Göta arrived in a skiff and asked to speak with the captain, Hrafn, in private. Thrandur told him that he had two persons to sell to him as slaves. Hrafn replied that he would not buy them before he had seen them. Then Thrandur led two boys forward; their heads were shaved and they wore white cloaks. Both were handsome, but their faces were swollen with grief.

When he saw the boys, Hrafn said, "Thrandur, these boys are the sons of Brestir and Beinir, whom you so shamefully murdered, aren't they?"

"I think you know they are," replied Thrandur.

"I am not taking them into my charge," Hrafn said, "if I have to pay money for them."

"I'll agree to that," answered Thrandur. "Here are two marks of silver, which I am giving you on the condition that you take these boys away with you and see to it that they never come back to the Faroe Islands."

Then he poured out some silver on the table in front of the captain, counted it, and presented it to him. It *was* very fine quality silver, or so it seemed to Hrafn, and so the deal was struck that he would take the boys with him. Thereafter, Hrafn set sail out of Thorshaven with a favorable wind at his back and made the voyage to Norway, then heading east to Tønsberg, as was his habit. He spent the winter there, and the boys were well looked after at his home.

9. The Boys Are Set Free

In the spring, Hrafn prepared his ship for the trip east and he asked the boys if they wanted to come with him. Sigmundur answered, "Yes! It beats what we got to do when we lived with Thrandur."

Hrafn asked, "Do you know about the arrangement between me and Thrandur?"

---

1. Holmgård is the Scandinavian name for the Russian city of Novgorod, situated on the Volkhov river. It was one of the most important trading centers in the Baltic in medieval times under the Kievan Rus', a confederation of Slavic tribes who held sway between the Baltic Sea and Black Sea from the late 9th century until the 13th century. Noteworthy for historians is the fact that the saga-writer portrays travel from such distant lands as the Faroes to the Baltic as resoundingly normal.

"Of course," said Sigmundur.

"I think it best for my sake," said Hrafn, "that you travel wherever you want to without me, and that silver which Thrandur gave me for you both, I think it would be better that you have it to live from. You have been brought unfairly to a foreign land."

After they concluded their talk, Sigmundur thanked him and bid him a safe journey.

Now the saga returns to Thrandur. He took all the Faroe Islands under his rule, including the livestock and property which had belonged to the brothers, his kinsmen, Beinir and Brestir. He also took Hafgrimur's boy, Össur, and raised him as a foster son.[1] Össur was ten years old when he went to live with Thrandur. After this, Thrandur ruled over the entire Faroe Islands, and nobody dared to oppose him.[2]

10. Shelter from the Storm

That same summer in which the brothers Brestir and Beinir were killed, there was a change of rulers in Norway: King Haraldur Grey-Cloak was slain, and Earl Hakon replaced him. He was the first vassal earl of King Haraldur Gormsson, and his authority stemmed from the king.[3] This was the end of the reign of the Gunnhildarsons; some were slain, and some fled from the country.

The saga now returns to Sigmundur and Thorir. They stayed two years in the Vik after Hrafn had set them free. When they had used up the silver which Hrafn had given them, Sigmundur was only twelve years old and Thorir was fourteen. When they heard about the rule of Earl Hakon, they decided to present themselves to him at court, if they could; it seemed to them the most likely plan for any success, since their fathers had also served him.

They travelled from Vik to Uppland, then headed west after Heidmark

---

1. Throughout the early Scandinavian world, it was a common practice for a man to send his child to be brought up by a foster father, often his social inferior (see Fox and Pálsson 1974, 11).

2. Recall from Chapter 4 that Hafgrimur ruled half the Faroes as a fief of King Haraldur Grey-Cloak and that the brothers had ruled half for Earl Hakon of Trondheim. As a chieftain Thrandur is now in control of both territories, with no authority from the crown in Norway sanctioning his rule.

3. This is to say that the Earl ruled over the united kingdom of Norway which itself was subject to the rule of the King of Denmark, King Haraldur Blue-Tooth. Earl Hakon Sigurtharson ruled Norway from 970 to 995.

and north to Dofrafjall.[1] They arrived just at the onset of winter; the snow began to pick up and a storm began to set in, yet they kept on trekking towards the mountain with little sense of direction, and became lost. Having run out of food, they camped in the open until morning. Thorir, who was giving up hope, asked Sigmundur to save himself and press on searching for the pass, but Sigmundur said that they would make it through together or neither of them would. He was the stronger of the two of them, so he lifted Thorir onto his back and carried him onward.[2] Both boys were now completely exhausted; towards evening they found a little dale in the pass and, making their way through it, they recognized the smell of woodsmoke. Not long afterwards, they came across a farmhouse; they went inside and found themselves in a sitting room. There sat two women, one older and the other, a younger girl. Both were extremely beautiful. They welcomed the boys, stripped off their wet clothes and gave them some dry ones as replacements. They then served them some food to eat. Afterwards, they prepared beds for them and led them off to sleep, warning that they wanted the boys to be gone by the time the master of the house came back; he was an ill-tempered man.

A short time later, Sigmundur woke up as a man of enormous stature stomped into the house. He was clad in reindeer skins and carried a dead reindeer on his back. He tilted up his nose and frowned, asking who else was in the house. The housewife told him that two boys had arrived, two frostbitten wretches who were so exhausted that they were almost dead.

The man replied, "It might kill us, your taking men into the house! I've told you that often enough!"

"I couldn't bear it that such noble-looking men would die right in front of our house," cried the housewife.

The farmer told her to let the matter rest. They sat down to dinner and afterwards went to bed.

The two boys were sleeping in one sleeping room; the farmer and his wife slept in another, and the farmer's daughter slept in the loft.[3] Beds were made up for the boys there in the bunk-house.

---

1. Uppland (*Uppland*) and Heidmark (*Heiðmark*) are regions south-central Norway; the boys are traveling from southeastern to northwestern Norway up to Trondheim. Dofrafjall (*Dofrafjall*) is a huge mountain range that divides the country essentially in two, separating eastern Norway from the Trøndelag, the western area of which includes the court at Trondheim. Even today, the mountain roads through the Dovrefjell region are often impassable for weeks in winter due to heavy snowstorms.

2. This scene foreshadows the dramatic events in Chapter 39.

3. Farms in medieval Scandinavia were composed of several single-purpose buildings surrounding an inner and outer courtyard, including stable, hay barns, kitchen or cook house,

In the morning, the farmer got up early and addressed the boys, "It seems to me as though the women want you to rest here today if you think you need to."

They admitted that they would like that.

11. Ulfur the Farmer

The farmer was gone during the day, but he came home in the evening and was in good spirits toward Sigmundur and Thorir. The next morning, the farmer came to the boys and said, "Fate would have it that you two happened upon my house. Now, it makes sense to me that you stay here for the winter, if it makes sense for you, too. The women think highly of you, and you've wandered considerably off the main road. It's a long way to get to another settlement in all directions."

Sigmundur and his cousin thanked the farmer for his offer, replying that they would gladly stay for the winter.

The farmer said that they should graciously accept the housewife's hospitality and help themselves to whatever they needed, and added, "I will be out each day to find us game, if there is any to catch."

So the boys stayed at the farm and it suited them. Moreover, the women were happy, and it seemed like a good arrangement having the boys around, as the farmer was gone every day.

The farmhouse was well-built, sturdy, and comfortable. The farmer was named Ulfur[1]; his wife was Ragnhild; and their daughter, Thurid. Thurid was the prettiest of girls with a commanding presence. A mutual affection grew between Sigmundur and Thurid; they would talk with each other for hours, and the farmer and his wife did nothing to discourage this.

The winter now passed and the first day of summer came.[2] Then, Ulfur came to talk with Sigmundur and said, "So, you spent the winter with us after all. Now, if you don't have anything better to do, you should

---
bake-house, guest-houses, bunk-houses for men and women, outhouses, and various other structures with a specific use.

1. The name means "Wolf" in Old Icelandic.
2. The Icelandic calendar divided the year into two equal seasons, summer (*sumar*) and winter (*vetr*), though "spring" and "fall" were discussed informally. "Summer" ran from the middle of April to the middle of October; the first day of summer was reckoned in Iceland as the last Saturday in the winter season, but in Norway, the date was April 14.

feel free to spend your teenage years here. It might be that a greater future is in store for you both. But I will warn you about one part of that future: do not wander into the forest that lies north of this farm."

They swore not to do this, and thanked Ulfur for his offer, which they accepted gladly.

12. Sigmundur Comes of Age

Not far from the farmhouse was a small lake where the farmer was in the habit of going for a swim. Afterwards he would lead the boys to a raised mound, his shooting bank, and they practiced their aim with throwing spears. Sigmundur quickly became an expert in all the woodsman and fighting skills Ulfur could teach him, such that he soon became a very skilled young man. Thorir got the same training, and yet he did not quite come to equal Sigmundur in ability.[1] Ulfur was a tall, powerful man, and the boys decided that he was the most skilled of any man alive.

They remained at the farm for three winters; Sigmundur was then fifteen years old and Thorir was seventeen. Sigmundur was big for his age, indeed both boys were, yet Sigmundur was more formidable in every respect, even though he was two years younger.

There was one time in the summer that Sigmundur asked Thorir, "What's to stop us from going into the forest just north of this farmyard?"

Thorir said, "It doesn't interest me."

"Well, I feel differently," said Sigmundur, "and I'm going there."

"You'll get an earful if we go back on our word to our foster-father," replied Thorir.

So they went off north and Sigmundur carried a wood axe along with him; they went into the forest and came to a pretty clearing. They had not been there for long when they heard a loud crack from the woods, and suddenly they saw an incredibly huge and savage-looking bear. It was a great bear, wolf-grey in color. The boys turned and ran back along the deer path by which they had come. The path was narrow, and Thorir was running in front with Sigmundur at his heels. The bear started chasing after them, and as the path became narrower, they fumbled through the

---

1. Astute readers will notice the parallel description of the brothers Brestir and Beinir in Chapter 4. Like fathers, like sons.

12. Sigmundur Comes of Age

branches as they ran. Then Sigmundur turned quickly on the path between some trees and waited there for the beast to come up to him. With two hands, he struck the beast right between the ears; the axe sank into its brain and the creature keeled over and died instantly without any death throes.

Thorir had now doubled back, and said, "This heroic feat was destined for you, brother, but not for me. It seems fated that I should always be following in your wake."[1]

Sigmundur said, "Let's see if we can't get this bear lifted up."

They set to work and managed to lift the bear up, propping it against a tree so that it could not fall over. They positioned sticks in its jaws, so the beast seemed to gape open at the mouth. Having accomplished this, they went home.

When they got back to the farm, their foster father, Ulfur, was standing in the home meadow, having just come back from an outing to search for them. He scowled and asked where they had gone.

Sigmundur answered, "It's bad news, foster father. We went against your advice and a bear chased after us."

Ulfur replied, "I expected as much that you would go off, but I don't want that bear to come after you any more. Despite the fact that he is a such beast, I'm not sure that you boys didn't rile him up. Nevertheless, we should now try to kill him."

Ulfur went inside, took out a spear, and then marched off to the forest with Sigmundur and Thorir. When Ulfur saw the bear, he charged at it, ran it through with his spear, and the bear fell to the ground. Then, he realized that the beast was already dead and laughed out, "You're having your fun with me! So, which one of you boys killed this creature?"

Thorir said, "No credit for this is mine, foster father. Sigmundur killed the brute."

"This is the most heroic feat I have ever seen," said Ulfur, "and many more will follow this great achievement, Sigmundur."

Then they went home, and Ulfur had a great deal more respect for Sigmundur after this episode.

---

1. Lit. "that I be your *eftirbátr*." The "after-boat" was a smaller boat towed behind a ship for shore landings; a distinctly Norse concept and phrase.

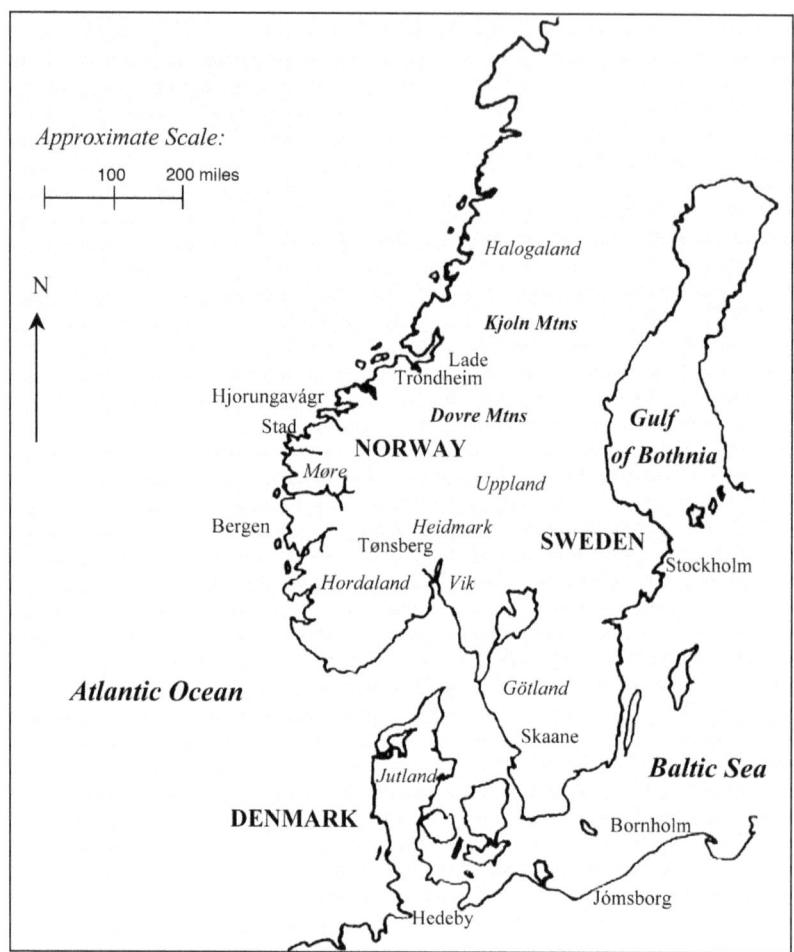

Norway in the 10th and 11th centuries.

13. Departure from the Farm

The boys stayed with Ulfur until Sigmundur was eighteen years old and Thorir was twenty. By then, Sigmundur was a man of exceptional stature, good looks, and experience; it was said about him that he was second only to Olaf Tryggvason[1] in terms of accomplishments.

---

1. Olaf Tryggvason was King of Norway from 995 to 1000. He is famed for converting Norway, Iceland, the Shetlands, Orkneys, and Faroe Islands to Christianity.

Finally, the day came when Sigmundur said to his foster father Ulfur that he wanted to go out into the world: "And it seems to me that Thorir's and my destiny will be less impressive if we do not make a name for ourselves among other men."

"Then you should do what you intend to," said Ulfur.

While they were at the farmhouse they had come to learn that Ulfur would be away on trading trips for seven nights or longer every fall and spring, and consequently, he had many provisions in store at home: linen, clothes, and other goods which the household might need.

Ulfur had new clothes made for the boys and made sure they were well-equipped to travel. The preparations delighted the women as it seemed a fitting gift for the boys' farewell, even though it was hard for the young girl, Thurid. When they left the farm, Ulfur went with them on the way, leading them through Dofrafjall up to a place where they could see north to Orkadale.[1] There, Ulfur sat down and said that he wanted to rest, and so everyone took a seat.

It was then that Ulfur said, "I am curious at long last to know who it is I have fostered, which family you both are from, and what your native land is."

The boys told him everything about their lives and what they had endured. Ulfur expressed great sorrow for them.

Then Sigmundur said, "And now, foster father, would you please tell us about your life and what you have gone through?"

"I will now tell you my story," Ulfur said.

14. Ulfur's Story

"To begin, there was once a farmer named Thoralfur who lived in Heidmark in Uppland. He was a powerful man who served as bailiff for the kings of Uppland. He was married to a woman named Idun, and they had a daughter named Ragnhild, who was among the most beautiful of all women.

The farmer on the neighboring land was named Steingrimur, a good man and extremely wealthy. Steingrimur's wife was called Thora, and

---

1. The Orka river flows from northern side of the Dovrafjall mountains into the Orka valley; the region today is part of Sør-Trøndelag county in Norway. The region was a wealthy petty kingdom before Haraldur Fine-Hair united the country.

together they had a son named Thorkell. Thorkell was a promising young man, well-built and strong.

One of the jobs that Thorkell performed on his father's farm was to place markers on the shore each fall when the frost set in and the lakes froze over. He and his friends would hunt game across the pack ice; he was an exceptional hunter. Because of this, he became known as Thorkell Hard-Frost.

There was one occasion when Thorkell came to talk to his father. Thorkell said that he wanted his father to arrange for his engagement and to ask for the hand of Ragnhild, Thoralfur's daughter. His father replied that Thorkell was aiming high, but in the end, they made their way to Thoralfur and brought up the matter of Thorkell's proposal to Ragnhild. Thoralfur answered reluctantly and said that he had higher hopes for her than marriage to Thorkell, and nothing could come of the proposal, though he had every wish to continue their friendship. They parted company as matters stood, and Steingrimur and Thorkell went home.

15. Thorkell and Ragnhild

Sometime after this, Thorkell set out from home with another man one night when he had been informed that Thoralfur was gone on some errand and not at his farm. Thorkell and his accomplice slipped into Thoralfur's house and found Ragnhild in her bed; he pulled her to him, carried her outside, and brought her back home with them. His father became furious when they arrived; he said that his son had taken on more than he could handle and ordered Thorkell to bring the girl back home immediately. Thorkell responded stiffly, "I won't do that."

His father, Steingrimur, told him to leave the farm and hide and that's what Thorkell did; he went off with Ragnhild and they hid in the forest. Eleven men went with them on the journey; they were Thorkell's companions and childhood friends.

Sometime later, Thoralfur the farmer came home and discovered what had happened. He gathered some men at once and soon had a posse of one hundred men; they rode to Steingrimur's farmstead and demanded that Steingrimur hand over Thorkell and return his daughter into his possession.

Steingrimur said that they weren't there.

Thoralfur's men ransacked the farm but didn't find what they were looking for. Afterwards, they went to the nearby forest and searched for Thorkell and Ragnhild, dividing themselves into search parties. Thirty men stayed with Thoralfur.

One day, Thoralfur spotted twelve men in the woods, trailed by a woman. Making out who they were, Thoralfur and his men started after them.

Some of Thorkell's companions raised the alarm that Thoralfur's men were approaching them, and asked Thorkell what they should do. He said, "There is a hill not far from us, and we should head there; it will make a good stronghold. We should take up positions among the rocks there and mount a defense."

They reached the hill and prepared themselves for battle.

Soon Thoralfur's men came to the hill and immediately made an attack against them, but Thorkell's men defended themselves bravely.

Finally, the battle ended with twelve of Thoralfur's men slain, along with seven of Throrkell's men. Five of Thoralfur's men were badly wounded and later died. Thoralfur himself had been dealt a life-threatening wound.

After the battle, Thorkell and his companions ran off into the woods and split up; Ragnhild got left behind and was brought home with her injured father. When Thoralfur made it back to his farmstead, he died from his wound. The rumor among his men was that it was Thorkell who had given him his death blow.

News of these events now spread. Thorkell came home to his father scarcely wounded, but most of his companions were wounded more seriously. By and by, they all recovered.

16. Thorkell in Exile

Soon afterwards, the Upplanders held their assembly and Thorkell Hard-Frost was declared an outlaw.[1]

---

1. Outlawry (*útlegð*) in the Icelandic tradition was divided into two types, "Lesser Outlawry" and "Full Outlawry." In "lesser outlawry," the outlawed individual had to leave Iceland for a period of three years; "full outlawry" meant that the convicted person must leave the society from which he'd been outlawed forever. The outlaw could be killed by anyone from that society, even abroad, and it was strongly forbidden to harbor or aid an outlaw in any way; in Iceland, a bounty of eight ounces of silver were placed on the outlaw. Ulfur is a full-outlaw, a man with a price on his head. For more detail on this sentence, see Appendix C.

16. Thorkell in Exile

When Thorkell and his father heard the news, Steingrimur said that Thorkell could not be caught at home while everyone was looking for him:

"My son, you will need to travel during these years of outlawry which have now so shamefully fallen on you. There are vast, craggy ravines up the river; among those steep cliffs is a cave. Nobody knows about that hiding spot except me. You should go there now and take some food with you."

Thorkell arranged to live in the cave while everyone was searching for him. He was not discovered, but he was lonely there, so when some time had passed, he left the cave and made his way to the farmstead where Thoralfur's kinsmen were. He absconded with Ragnhild a second time and set off for the mountains."

"...and I came to this land here," continued Ulfur, "where I have now built my farmstead. I have been here with Ragnhild ever since, for eighteen winters, the age of our daughter, Thurid. Now I have told you both my life story."

"It seems like an impressive story to me, foster father," said Sigmundur, "but now I need to tell you that I have not repaid your hospitality very well. When we left, your daughter told me that she is pregnant and there is no one to blame for it but me. I am going away mostly because I think you and I will have a falling out over this."

Ulfur replied, "I've known for a long time that you loved each other and I didn't want to stand between you."

Sigmundur said, "My foster-father, I would ask you not to marry off your daughter, Thurid, because I plan on marrying her and will court no other woman."

Ulfur answered, "I could not give my daughter away to anyone better, but I am going to make this one request, Sigmundur. If you ever come to be influential among men of rank, bring my case forward. Reunite me with the men of my district and restore my rank in society, as I am very unhappy in exile."

Sigmundur promised to do this if he could.

They then parted ways, and the cousins walked until they came to Earl Hakon's court in Lade.[1] They went before the Earl, and he received them kindly. He asked who they were, and Sigmundur replied that he was Sigmundur Brestirsson:

"My father was the same Brestir who was your bailiff for a time in

---

1. Lade (*Hlaðe*) was an estate on the eastern fringes of Trondheim where Earl Hakon and his sons were often in residence.

the Faroe Islands before he was killed. I seek your audience and good grace, my Earl, and I offer my hand to you in friendship."

Earl Hakon replied that he knew little of Sigmundur, "...but you are not unlike Brestir. When you yourself come of age to avenge your kinsman, I will not stand in your way." Then he offered them a seat among his retainers.

A young Svein Hakonsson was among his father's men at this time.[1]

17. Earl Hakon's Court

Sigmundur started talking with Svein Hakonsson and very skillfully ingratiated himself to him, and the Earl's son took a liking to Sigmundur.

Sigmundur told Svein his story and asked him to bring forth his case so he could win some favor with Svein's father. Svein asked what he wanted.

"I would very much like to go raiding," answered Sigmundur, "if your father will support me."

Svein replied, "Such things are thought of highly."

The winter season was now approaching Yule. At Yuletide, Earl Eirikur Hakonsson arrived from the east from Vik, where he had a residence.[2] Sigmundur arranged to speak with Earl Eirikur and told him about his difficulties. Earl Eirikur promised his backing and said that he and his brother would not overlook to arrange things between Sigmundur and Earl Hakon.

After Yule, Sigmundur brought up the matter again with Earl Hakon, asking whether he could support him in some way and if he might show him some favor on account of his father, Brestir, who had been the Earl's retainer.

Earl Hakon replied, "I certainly gained two loyal servants when Brestir was murdered. He was a bailiff for kings, one of the most courageous too. Those who killed him are the lowest scum in my estimation. So what are you asking for?"

---

1. Svein Hakonsson would be co-ruler over Norway with his brother Eirikur Hakonsson from c. 1000 to 1015, after the death of Olaf Tryggvason.

2. Eirikur Hakonsson, the elder son of Hakon Sigurthurson, was co-ruler of Norway with his brother Svein Hakonsson from c. 1000 to 1012, having been in exile under the reign of Olaf Tryggvason. He raided in England from 1014 onward with Canute the Great and eventually became Earl of Northumbria in northern England.

Sigmundur said he wanted to make viking raids and thereby gain some renown or die in the undertaking.[1]

The Earl said that the man had spoken well.

"And you will learn in the spring, when men are making preparations for such journeys, which ones I will allow to take place."

When the winter passed, Sigmundur tried again to redeem his promise from Earl Hakon. The Earl replied, "I will grant you a single longship, Sigmundur, along with forty men-at-arms. Assembling even that small band will be difficult since most of them will not want to follow you, an unproven foreigner."

Sigmundur thanked the Earl and told Eirikur about his father's offer.

Earl Eirikur spoke: "A minor help, but it still might be useful to you. I will get you another ship and forty more men." The ship which Eikur provided him was very well-built.

Next, Sigmundur told Svein about the assistance of his brother and father.

Svein answered, "I'm not in an equal position to equip you with my friends as my brother and father, but I will give you a third ship and another forty men. They will be my own companions, and I know that they will be the most loyal of all the men who are signing on to follow you."

18. Sigmundur in Denmark

Sigmundur now prepared to set off with his men and when he was ready, they sailed east to Vik and then on to Denmark, passing over the straits. They explored all around the islands that summer and plundered wherever they went. He encouraged each man to fight bravely and to drive against the defenders of opposing ships, though he always allowed the merchants themselves to go in peace. He continued sailing eastward for the duration of the summer, until he came to the Elfarsker, which has always been a good base for raiding.[2]

---

1. Viking raids had as their purpose pillage and conquest, but just as frequently they involved trading in far-off lands and voyages of exploration. Going "a-viking" could be a warlike or mercantile trip; it is not clear that the Norse or Danes of the period made much of a distinction between the activities (for fuller discussion on this point, see Richards 2005, 2–7).

2. Elfarsker "the River Skerries," presently known as the Southern Gothenburg islands, lay off the southern coast of Göteborg, Sweden. They were notorious during the Viking Age as the stage for *holmganga*, the early Scandinavian practice of dueling.

18. Sigmundur in Denmark

When they had lain anchor in a narrow inlet, Sigmundur scrambled up onto the rocks to scout the area. On the far side of the island, he saw there were five ships; the fifth one was a dragon-warship.[1] He went back down to his men and told them there were five Viking ships anchored on the far side under the cliffs:

"I want to say that I think fleeing this fight would be total cowardice. We could earn all kinds of fame if only we run the risk."

They asked him to decide what to do.

"Let's load stones onto the ship," said Sigmundur, "and make it look like we are a promising target. Then, we'll place our ships on the outer side of the inlet we just sailed through, as it's the narrowest spot. I noticed this evening, when we sailed in, that a ship could not get past us if we stationed three ships side-by-side. It will work to our advantage if they can't direct all their strength at us."

The crew put Sigmundur's plan into action.

In the morning, when they had positioned their ship on the far side of the inlet, the five Viking ships began rowing toward them almost immediately. In the bow of the dragon-ship stood a great bruiser of a man who asked at once who commanded these vessels. Sigmundur announced himself and asked who the man was. His name was Randver[2] and he was sailing east from Holmgard; he gave them a choice—either they surrender their ships and themselves as prisoners, or they defend themselves. Sigmundur replied that there was a third choice: the raiders could try to withstand their weapons. Randver ordered his men to bring up two ships, since all five could not engage Sigmundur's crews, and he wanted to see first how the battle progressed.

Sigmundur skippered the ship which Svein, the Earl's son, had given him, and Thorir commanded that which Earl Eirikur had provided.

They positioned themselves and the battle began. Sigmundur's crew started throwing rocks so fiercely that, at first, their enemies could not do anything but protect themselves. When they ran out of rocks, they kept up a steady barrage of arrows, which killed several of the vikings and

---

1. The saga-writer includes the detail of a dragon-headed warship as colorful romance. Surveying the archaeological evidence for Scandinavian ship-building, Richards (2005, 47–52): "Dragon-headed longships, shields down their sides, their red-and-white striped sails catching the wind, have become an important element of the Viking cliche. What is the reality?... [...]. Viking sails have not survived but we have striped designs from Bayeux. On the Gokstad and Skuldelev 5 ships there are battens for shields to be hung along the sides of vessels. Dragon-prowed ships exist as graffiti and as literary metaphors, but the best we can do archaeologically is a beast-headed bedpost from Oseberg!"

2. Lit. "Robber" or "Bandit," more-or-less a *nom-de-guerre*.

wounded many others. Then, Sigmundur's crew grabbed weapons for hand-to-hand fighting. The tide of battle was turning against Randver. When he saw the lack of courage among his men, he said they were fully worthless wretches if they didn't overcome boys who were not even men yet. Randver's men complained that he always liked to drive them forward, while he kept himself safely in the rear, and they told Randver to bring his ship into battle. He ordered his crew to do so. The dragon-warship now advanced, followed by the remaining two ships loaded with fresh fighters. They approached Sigmundur from the other side and attacked; the battle was more bitterly fought than before.

Sigmundur was in the forefront of the fighting on his ship; he struck his opponents hard and lightning-quick. His kinsman Thorir fought bravely too. They had been fighting so long in the thick of things that they could not tell who was winning.

Then Sigmundur called to his men, "We can't defeat them unless we test our courage. I'm going to charge up the gangplank of the dragon: if you're brave, follow me!"

Sigmundur boarded the dragon with twelve men and cut down one defender, and then another; his men followed his lead. Thorir also joined the attack on the dragon with five men. Now, all resistance gave way before them. When Randver saw this, he charged forward at Sigmundur and they clashed, fighting in single combat for a long time.

Here Sigmundur showed his skill; he tossed his sword with a flourish aloft and he caught it with his left hand, holding his shield in his right. He slashed at Randver with his sword and cut his right leg clear off below the knee. Randver pitched over, and Sigmundur gave him a blow to the neck which severed off his head. At this, Sigmundur's men gave a war-cry and it was over; the vikings fled in three of their ships. Afterwards, Sigmundur's party cleared out the dragon-warship, and killed every living soul on it.

At last, they counted their losses. Thirty men of Sigmundur's crew had been killed. They anchored their ships, took care of their wounds, and stayed there for several nights.

Sigmundur took charge of the dragon-warship and the other ship which had flanked him. They discovered a tremendous treasure hoard, including weapons and other valuables. Then, they sailed away for Denmark and north on to Vik, where they visited Earl Eirikur, who welcomed Sigmundur warmly and invited him to stay. Sigmundur thanked the Earl for the offer, but said that he first wanted to go north to see Earl Hakon. He left the two ships in Earl Eirikur's safekeeping, so he travelled north in his smallest ship.

Next, they went to Earl Hakon who welcomed Sigmundur and his crew. Sigmundur stayed with the Earl that winter and quickly became famous on account of his exploits.

At Yuletide that winter, Sigmundur was made a retainer of Earl Hakon along with Thorir, and they spent the winter season at court, enjoying the generous hospitality.

19. Sigmundur in Sweden

King Eirikur the Victorious ruled over Sweden at this time.[1] Eirikur was the son of Bjarn Eirikursson and his grandfather was Eirikur Eyvindsson. He was a very powerful king.

One winter, twelve Norwegian merchants had travelled east over the Kjölen mountains into Sweden. When they entered the kingdom of Sweden, they set up a market for the peasants in the countryside, but a dispute broke out at the marketplace and one of the Norwegians killed a Swede. When King Eirikur heard of this, he sent some of his liegemen out and had the twelve Norwegian merchants killed.

That spring, Earl Hakon asked Sigmundur where he intended to sail during the summer. Sigmundur said that he was at the Earl's service.

Earl Hakon replied, "I want you to sail somewhere in Sweden and give a reminder to those Swedish fools who killed twelve of my men last winter over a slight misunderstanding that they have not yet felt my vengeance."

Sigmundur answered that he would undertake the venture if that was what the Earl wanted.

So, Earl Hakon provided Sigmundur with men hand-picked from his court and arranged to levy ships. This time, everyone was eager to follow Sigmundur. They set course east to Vik and met with Earl Eirikur, who gave Sigmundur a fine company of warriors, so that Sigmundur now had well over three hundred men and five well-equipped ships. From there, they sailed south to Denmark and then east into Swedish territory. They landed their ships somewhere along the coast of Sweden.

---

1. Eirikur Bjarnsson the Victorious was King of Sweden from 970 to 995, and was perhaps the first king of Sweden, though the extent of his kingdom in relation to the borders of modern Sweden is unclear.

19. Sigmundur in Sweden

Before disembarking, Sigmundur addressed his men, "Here's where we'll start our foray inland. Let's make it a glorious raid."

They marched inland and came to a settled district of about three hundred men. They killed them all, ransacking and burning farmsteads. The people of the district fled to the forest, disappearing among the trees.

Not far from where Sigmundur's men were pursuing the stragglers, the district was protected by a sheriff of the king, named Björn. When he heard rumors of the invasion, the sheriff began assembling some men to fight and an army soon formed, with Björn in command.

One day, while out scouting, the sheriff's force spotted the invaders. At once, Sigmundur's men asked their leader what his plan was.

"We've faced large forces before," he said, "and often our opponents' size hasn't given them the advantage when their lines are packed with men quaking in their boots. Here's what we'll do: let's draw up our own battle-line as a triangular phalanx[1] with Thorir in the lead, two men behind him, three behind them, and so on. Everyone on both sides will lock shields. Then, we'll charge right into their formation and when the Swedes see us coming at them like that, they won't be able to keep their nerve."

They formed up as a phalanx and ran at the Swedish army, charging right into them. A huge melee ensued and many Swedes were felled at once. Sigmundur cut his way forward easily, fighting with a two-handed sword. When he came upon Björn's standard-bearer, he dispatched the man with a lethal blow. He called to his men to break their shield formation when he saw Björn himself directly ahead. A gap was made as Sigmundur flew at Björn, and there was a fierce exchange of blows, but Sigmundur quickly overpowered the sheriff and dealt him his death-blow. At this, the Vikings let out their war-cry, and the Swedes fled.

Sigmundur said that they shouldn't pursue them, as they didn't have the supplies or knowledge of the terrain to track them in this unknown land. After this, they acquired a huge share of plunder from the district and they took it back to their ships. They sailed east from Sweden to

---

1. The phalanx was a mainstay of ancient Greek warfare where men would stand in close formation with locked shields, and the long spears of each successive line of men would stick out beyond the row of shields, creating a near-impregnable screen of spear points. Sigmundur's plan, involving interlocking shields, seems to be non-typical tactics for the Norwegian warriors. It is not clear that the typical Viking shield would have been appropriate for the task. According to Graham-Campbell et al. (1994, 53), Norse shields were typically circular, no more than 1-meter in diameter, made of wood and leather, with an iron boss in the center to protect the carrying hand. As such, the shields would be too small to interlock in the fashion of the ancient Greek hoplites.

Holmgard and raided for the rest of the summer around the islands and coastlines.

The saga names two brothers in the service of the Swedish king, Vandill and Athill. They were knight-protectors for the king of Sweden, and they were never equipped with less than eight ships and two dragon-warships.

When the king learned that there was widespread raiding in his kingdom, he sent word to the brothers, bidding them to destroy Sigmundur and his companions. They readily agreed to do this.

That fall, Sigmundur's party was sailing back west when they came to an island which lay off the coast of Sweden. Sigmundur said to his men, "We won't meet any friends here among the Swedes. Be on guard. I'll go up on the island to look around."

He climbed up to the top of the island and saw that there were ten ships on the other side; two dragon-warships and eight others.

Sigmundur relayed the news to his men, telling them to get ready and to unload their plunder from the ships and load stones in its place. The crew spent the night making preparations.

20. Sigmundur's Reputation Grows

Early in the morning, they rowed swiftly toward the enemy ships. The captains of each vessel called out, demanding to know who was approaching. Sigmundur gave his name, and no sooner had the captains heard it than they realized there was no need to inquire about his intentions. Crewmen grabbed their weapons, as Sigmundur and his men would not have come in peace.

Vandill brought his dragon-warship alongside Sigmundur's and put up a hard defense against the raiders. After the fighting had been going on for a while, Sigmundur called to his men encouragingly, "Like before, we won't overtake them unless we push ourselves forward. I'm going to jump across to their ship; follow close behind me!"

Sigmundur jumped onto the dragon-warship, and a large group of men followed after him. Sigmundur quickly became the death of one defender, then another, and corpses soon littered the decks beneath them.

Vandill rushed at Sigmundur and they dueled for some time, but Sigmundur showed the same finesse as before: sword in one hand, shield in another, he struck at Vandill's left side and cut off his sword-hand. The sword itself rattled to the deck, and then Sigmundur lunged forward and killed him. At that, Sigmundur's men shouted their war-cry.

Athill then spoke to his crew: "The tide has turned; Vandill is dead. Anyone who wants to save themselves, let's make our escape."

Athill's men fled in five ships, but five of their ships were left behind, including the dragon-warship. Sigmundur's crew boarded them and killed everyone who was still on board. At last, Sigmundur sailed from the island and came to Denmark, which seemed like a suitable place to lay low and recover, so they stayed there for a while to let their wounds heal.

When they were well-rested, they sailed to Vik and met with Earl Eirikur, who gave them a kind welcome. They lingered there for a while, before making their way north to Trondheim to meet with Earl Hakon, who welcomed Sigmundur and his men warmly and thanked him for the great service they had performed for him that summer.

Sigmundur and Thorir stayed with the Earl that winter, along with a small band of men, but they needed to find lodgings for the rest of their followers elsewhere.[1] From then on, they were never short on money.

21. Haraldur Iron-Skull

In the springtime, Earl Hakon asked where Sigmundur planned to go raiding that summer, and Sigmundur replied that he would go wherever the Earl wished. The Earl spoke:

"I will not force you to go harass the Swedes again. Instead, I would prefer that you travel west across the open sea and sail in the vicinity of the Orkneys this summer.[2] There are rumors that a man named Haraldur Iron-Skull may be there; he is an outlaw and a blackguard who caused great unrest in Norway before I exiled him. By right, he is a great chieftain; nonetheless, I want you to kill him if you come across him."

---

1. The implication is that Sigmundur (with Thorir) has become such a great chieftain in his own right that he has too many followers to be lodged at the royal court.

2. The Orkney Islands played a great role in the North Sea traffic from Norway to Scottish kingdom of Caithness and were of central strategic importance; the history of the Earls of Orkney is found in *Orkneyinga Saga*.

21. Haraldur Iron-Skull

Sigmundur said that he would pursue Haraldur if that was what the Earl wanted.

That summer, Sigmundur set sail from Norway with eight ships; Thorir now commanded Vandill's dragon-ship, while Sigmundur captained Randver's. They sailed west out into the open ocean and stirred up trouble by raiding throughout the summer months. Toward the end of summer, they landed at Öngulsey,[1] which lies in the English Sea. There, in the harbor, they saw ten ships ahead of them; the largest one in their midsts was a great dragon-warship.

Sigmundur knew at once that these were Haraldur Iron-Skull's ships.

As night was approaching, Sigmundur's men discussed their plan of attack for the morning.

At the reddening of dawn, they broke out their weapons and attacked. The fighting lasted all day and into the evening; only the gathering darkness separated the two sides. That night, the crews debated how to best press their attack again in the morning.

The next day, Haraldur called over to Sigmundur's ship to ask if they wanted to fight again. Sigmundur answered that he had no reason to consider anything else.

Haraldur continued, "Well, consider this: I am now forced to say what I wasn't prepared to say before. I propose that we cease all fighting and enter into a partnership."

The crews of each side expressed their approval and added that there was good reason for these two chieftains to make peace and join forces, since there would be few who could stand against them together.

Sigmundur replied that he had one objection to this proposal.

"What's that?" asked Haraldur.

Sigmundur answered, "Earl Hakon sent me after your head."

"That was wishful thinking on his part," sneered Haraldur. "You and he are men of a different sort: you are obviously very brave, while Hakon is a sniveling coward."

"We will have to disagree on that point," said Sigmundur.

Yet, the crews had their way in making their chieftains come to terms, and so the two sides settled their differences. They pooled all their spoils of war, and together they raided far and wide for the remainder of the summer; and none could withstand them.

---

1. Öngulsey (*Anglesey*) is a large island immediately off the northwest coast of Wales across from the city of Bangor. It lies in the Irish Sea, east of Ireland and south of the Isle of Mann.

Then, in the fall, Sigmundur said that he wanted to set course for Norway.

Haraldur replied, "Then we will need to split up."

"No, we won't," said Sigmundur. "I think we should go to Norway together. I plan to ask Earl Hakon if I can bring you before his court."

"Why would I seek an audience with my greatest enemy?"

"Just let me worry about everything."

"I trust you completely," said Haraldur, "especially as this will be difficult for you, so have it your way."

After this, they sailed north to Norway and arrived at Hordaland.[1] They were told that Earl Hakon was away in the north at Bergen. They sailed there and harbored their ships at Steinvog. Sigmundur went into Bergen with twelve men in a row boat, as he wanted to meet with Earl Hakon alone first; in the meantime, Haraldur remained behind at Steinvog.

Sigmundur went to Earl Hakon's court and found him sitting at the drinking tables. He approached the Earl and greeted him warmly; the Earl welcomed him in a friendly manner, bidding Sigmundur to sit down on the opposite bench and regale him with the events of the summer. They spoke for a while as Sigmundur told the Earl about his travels, but he did not mention that he had found Haraldur Iron-Skull. However, when Hakon sensed that the story was coming to an end, he asked outright whether Sigmundur had found Haraldur.

"In a manner of speaking," said Sigmundur, and he told the Earl how he had come upon Haraldur and how they had made peace.

At this news, the Earl became silent. His face turned red, and he spoke only after a moment had passed: "You have carried out my errands better in the past than you have now, Sigmundur."

"Haraldur has come here into your power, my lord," replied Sigmundur. "And it was my intention to assure you that Haraldur wishes to reconcile with you so that he may regain his rights of safety of life and freedom to live in this country."

"That will never happen," rejoined the Earl. "When my men arrest him, I will have him killed."

---

1. Hordaland, then as now, is a county in western Norway, the locale of Bergen, Norway's second largest city. That Earl Hakon is at Bergen is perhaps anachronistic, as the events of the saga in this chapter are taking place in the early 980s (see Appendix D); and Bergen was not established as much more than a trading post until roughly the 1020s or 1030s. Wylie (1965, 15) writes: "Before King Ólaf Haraldursson [c. 1070], Bergen had evidently been a fishing village of no particular importance." The saga-writer must be projecting the importance of the city in the 13th century back to saga times.

Sigmundur said, "I am willing to make compensation on his behalf for as much money as you demand, my lord."

"There's no amount that would be enough to buy his freedom from me," snarled the Earl.

Sigmundur replied, "I have not served you long or well enough, if I cannot obtain a settlement for a single man's life in return?! I am leaving this country and I will serve you no longer! All I wanted was to reconcile you and Haraldur, rather than your killing him!"

Sigmundur sprang up and stormed out of the drinking room, while the Earl just sat there in silence, not having enough courage to call for Sigmundur to come back.

Finally, the Earl spoke, "Sigmundur was furious just now, and it would be a great loss to my kingdom if he leaves when he wasn't being serious."

"He seemed serious to us," said his men.

"Go after him, then," cried the Earl, "and we will settle this just as he wants."

The Earl's men went after Sigmundur and told him the news, and Sigmundur came back inside. The Earl greeted him just as warmly as before, agreeing that they should settle the matter as Sigmundur had proposed, adding, "I don't want you to leave me."

Sigmundur accepted the truce and arranged the settlement with Earl Hakon on Haraldur's behalf. Then he went to Haraldur and explained to him how matters stood, and that Haraldur should now come forward to settle and discuss things. Haraldur said it would be a bad thing to trust the Earl, but they went to the Earl's court and the former enemies were reconciled. Haraldur then traveled north to Halogaland,[1] while Sigmundur stayed with the Earl that winter on the friendliest of terms, along with Thorir and a large party of men.

Sigmundur lavished his men with both clothes and weapons.

22. Össur Hafgrimsson

The saga now returns to events in the Faroe Islands. Össur Hafgrimsson lived under the foster care of Thrandur of Göta until he was fully

---

1. Halogaland was the northernmost of the Norweigan provinces and a kingdom during the Viking Age before unification under Haraldur Fine-Hair.

grown into a handsome and noble-looking young man. Thrandur arranged for him to marry the daughter of one of the wealthiest farmers there on the Islands, and after the wedding, Thrandur said he would divide the authority and rulership over the Islands in two. Össur could rule over the half of the Islands which once belonged to his father Hafgrimur, while Thrandur would take the share formerly ruled by the brothers, Brestir and Beinir. As part of the arrangement, Thrandur thought it only fitting that Össur receive all the money, farmland, and livestock which had belonged to the brothers in addition to the inheritance from his father, Hafgrimur. Everything was thus arranged according to Thrandur's wishes. After the division, Össur owned two or three farms: the one at Hof, his inheritance from his father on South Island; the next on Skuf Island; and the third on Dimum, the latter two being the rightful inheritance of Sigmundur and Thorir.

The Faroe-Islanders received reports that Sigmundur had become a famous man, and they made great preparations for his homecoming. Össur had defensive positions built at the farm on Skuf Island and stayed there most of the time.

Skuf Island takes its name from the fact that its cliffs are so sheer that it makes a natural stronghold[1]; there is only one break in the rockface which leads up onto the island, and it is said that the island is so impregnable that just twenty or thirty men could defend it no matter how many attackers tried to storm it.

Össur travelled among his farms with twenty men, and he always had thirty men staying with him at home among the servants. There was no man as powerful as Össur in the Faroe Islands, except for Thrandur.

The Islanders never knew about the large sum of silver Thrandur had acquired at Haleyri, though he was an extremely wealthy man,[2] and he alone ruled over everyone in the Faroe Islands, since Össur and his followers weren't as sly and devious as he was.

---

1. This may be folk etymology as the saga-writer seems to associate the name of the island with the verb *skúfa* "push, ward off," i.e. Skufey = Guard Island; and several scholars have noted that the saga-writer seems to be confusing the topography of Skúvoy, which has gentle harbors, and Stóra Dimun, which has imposing fortress-like cliffs (see Foote 1970, 159). Some sources maintain that Skufey takes its name from the species of *skua* birds which nest by the multitudes in the cliffs on the island.

2. Thrandur's great fortune was acquired in Denmark in Chapter 3.

23. Departure from Norway

The saga now reverts to Sigmundur. He told Earl Hakon that he wanted to cease these viking expeditions and go home to the Faroe Islands. He was sick of hearing that he had not avenged his father, Brestir, and having people think less of him for it, so he asked the Earl to support him and give his advice about how to go about it.

Hakon replied, "It's difficult to approach the Islands undetected and there's rough surf at the landings, so one can't go in warships, but I will have two merchant ships built for you and provide you with men to crew them so that you will be well-equipped."

Sigmundur thanked the Earl for his generosity, and he prepared for his journey all winter. That spring, the ships were finished and the Earl's men were ready for action.

Haraldur met with him in the spring and asked to accompany him. When they were nearly ready to set off, Earl Hakon came to speak to them:

"So it has come to pass that the boy who left is coming home a man."

The Earl accompanied Sigmundur to the door, and asked, "Can you tell me someone in the Faroes you trust?"

Sigmundur answered, "I trust in my own strength and abilities."

The Earl replied, "That's not enough. You shall have a source of support on which to rely, someone I have complete faith in, Thorgerd Horda's-Bride.[1] We will start off your journey by meeting her and she'll bring you luck on your travels."

Sigmundur thanked him for this advice.

They walked alone out along the road through the forest and took a little side-path into the woods. They emerged into a clearing, and there stood a house with a yard enclosed by a wooden fence. The house was very well-appointed, trimmed with gold and silver decorations. Earl Hakon and Sigmundur and a few retainers went inside, where a good many people awaited them. There were several glass windows in the house, such that there were no shadows. A woman stood opposite them, magnificent in a robe. The Earl cast himself down at her feet and kneeled there for a

---

1. Sigmundur's and Earlk Hakon's visit to Thorgerd (Þogerður Hörðabrúður) recalls a scene from the Jomsviking Saga (*Jómsvíkinga saga*) where the heathen Earl Hakon leaves his men to visit Thorgerd, a pagan goddess, to solicit her magical aid against the marauding Jomsvikings (see Chapter 27 below, part of which is missing in *Faroe-Islander Saga*, and the excerpted scene in Appendix A). What little is known about this pagan goddess is discussed in Appendix B.

moment; then he stood up and whispered to Sigmundur that they ought to present her with some offering, and he produced some silver from his purse to give to her.

"We must give her something of value," continued Earl Hakon, "which she will accept in exchange for the fact that I want her to take off the ring she has on her hand. The wearer receives good luck from that ring, Sigmundur."

Then the Earl proceeded to try to take her ring, but Sigmundur noticed that the woman kept bunching her fingers into a fist, so that the Earl couldn't remove it. The Earl threw himself down before her feet again, and Sigmundur noticed that the Earl was weeping. At last, he stood up and grabbed the ring on her hand, took it off, and handed it to Sigmundur. Then he told Sigmundur never to lose or sell this ring, and Sigmundur promised he would keep it safe always.

They parted now with matters standing as they were. Sigmundur went to his ships and it is said that he had fifty men on each merchant-ship. They put out to sea with favorable winds for as long as they could still see the seagulls over the islands, the two ships sailing together.

Haraldur Iron-Skull was on Sigmundur's ship, while Thorir was at the helm of the other ship.

A storm swept over them and the ships lost sight of each other. The storm raged on, separating them for days.

24. Return to the Faroe Islands

At last, a gentle breeze filled Sigmundur's sails, and they sailed onward to the Faroe Islands. They caught sight of an island due west, and some of Sigmundur's men knew from the silhouette that it was Austurey. Sigmundur said he could not have chosen a better landfall, since his aim was to take Thrandur from power. But as they headed for the shore, the tide worked against them and a squall rose up, making it impossible to get near the island.[1] Although his men were skilled sailors, the ship was blown to Sviney. They landed at dawn and ran straight up to the farm, forty men in all, while ten stayed behind to guard the ship. They surrounded the

---

1. Here and elsewhere in the saga, Thrandur seems to be protected by pagan magic linked to the weather, which happens to be adverse whenever hostile forces are working against him.

farm, broke into the farmhouse, grabbed Swine-Island Bjarni from his own bed, and led him out.

"So who's the leader of you sorry lot," demanded Bjarni.

"I am," said Sigmundur, stepping forward.

"So, you're cracking down hard on those who seemed to wish you nothing but harm back then when your father was killed. I won't deny I was there, but you should remember something of what I said about you at the time. When it was proposed that you and your kinsman Thorir should be killed, I said that I would no sooner kill you than I would myself."

"That I remember very well," said Sigmundur.

"Doesn't that count in my favor?" asked Bjarni.

"Almost," answered Sigmundur. "You'll be spared, but I want some local intelligence from you in return."

"Certainly," said Bjarni with relief.

"You're going to come with us to Austurey," continued Sigmundur.

"With the wind blowing the direction it is, you'll end up in Heaven before you land there," replied Bjarni.[1]

"Then you'll go with us to Skufey, if Össur is at the farm there."

"If you say so," said Bjarni, "And I think that Össur *is* at home."

That night they sailed to Skufey and reached the island when it was still dawn. Luck was with Sigmundur because they encountered no one on the narrow path which gives access to the island. They made their way up the island, all fifty men along with some of Bjarni's, and reached the defensive outposts just as Össur and his men were arriving to work on them. Össur demanded to know who these strangers were; and Sigmundur informed him.

"Don't think we didn't get reports of your coming! I want to offer you terms for a settlement," began Össur, "the best men in the Faroe Islands will judge your case."

"I won't accept any terms, except ones I make," replied Sigmundur.

"I won't agree to give you self-judgement of your own case," said Össur. "I won't accept your decisions on men's characters and I won't allow a lawsuit brought against me."

Sigmundur answered that his men would attack the fortifications if no arrangement could be met, adding, "I'll keep my own counsel as to what I take for myself."

---

1. Bjarni's use of "heaven" (Old Icelandic: *himinn*) is linguistically anachronistic; the year is probably c. 983–984, and the Faroe Islands will not be converted to Christianity until c. 1000.

Haraldur Iron-Skull was opposed to all talk and dissuaded Sigmundur from any settlement.

Össur had thirty men in the fortifications; it was a difficult place to overcome by force. Össur had his son named Leifur with him who was still a young boy.

Then Sigmundur's men attacked the fortifications, and their opponents mounted a fierce defense.

Sigmundur rushed along the fortifications and sized them up. He was armed with a helmet and sword-belt, and carried his best weapon, a silver-ornamented double-axe with an iron-wrought shaft. He wore a red tunic beneath a lightweight chain-mail jacket, and there has never been anyone, friend or foe, in the Faroe Islands to rival him.[1]

He noticed a spot where the wall of the fortification had sagged, but there were no other weak points. Sigmundur took a step back from the defenses, and then, running at full speed, he leapt up against them, dug his axe into the walls, and pulled himself up the axe-shaft, and managed to climb up onto the fortification. Someone came at him immediately, slashing down at him with a sword. Sigmundur deflected the blow with his axe, then quickly thrust out, plunging the pointed axe-head into the man's chest, killing him instantly. When Össur saw what was happening, he ran at Sigmundur and swung at him, but Sigmundur parried the sword, and slashed at Össur with his axe, hewing off his right hand; the sword dropped to the ground. Sigmundur struck again, catching Össur in the torso, and Össur fell. Other defenders rushed at Sigmundur, but he leapt backward off the fortification and landed on his feet below.

The defenders on the wall crowded over Össur as he died.

Then Sigmundur called out to them that they had two choices: either he would keep them penned without food in the fortifications, then burn it down on top of them, or else they should agree to his original terms and he would let them go. The men conceded his right to judge his own case, then gave themselves up.

---

1. The details of Sigmundur's dress and armament point to his tremendous wealth and status as a chieftain. The axe, in particular, is noteworthy for its ornateness; consider Graham-Campbell (1994, 55): "[Axes] were made in a quite simple way: a sharp cutting-edge was welded onto a shaped block of iron, and the butt end was then slotted over a wooden handle and wedged tight. Most battle axes were undecorated and are indistinguishable from working axes; their attribution as battle axes results from the fact that they have been found at graves with other weapons. A few examples are much more splendid and must have been made for ceremony or display. The finest by far is the ax from the royal or aristocratic burial at Mammen, Jutland. This is inlaid with silver in the elaborate patterns that give their name to the Mammen art style, and it is difficult to imagine it ever being used in battle; it was probably a symbol of wealth, status, power."

24. Return to the Faroe Islands

The saga now returns to Thorir. He had set course for South Island where he met up with Sigmundur, after these events had taken place.

Now messages were exchanged between Sigmundur's faction and Thrandur about reaching a settlement. A truce was agreed to, and a meeting between the two sides was arranged to take place on Straumey at Thorshaven, the assembly place for the Faroe-Islanders. Sigmundur and Thorir arrived with a huge bodyguard; Thrandur was in an extremely cheerful mood. This is how the settlement went. Thrandur confessed, "I was dishonorable during the incident where your father was slain, kinsman. I would like to grant you whatever terms are most honorable for you and that you will be most content with—I merely wish that you and Thorir arrange all terms of the settlement just between ourselves among Faroe-Islanders."

"I won't agree to that," said Sigmundur. "I want Earl Hakon to set the terms of the settlement, or we won't be reconciled. That is only proper, I think. So we should both go to Earl Hakon's court if there is going to be any peaceful agreement between us."

"I am absolutely willing to do just what you decide, kinsman," said Thrandur, "but I want it stipulated by the Earl that I retain my land rights and powers-to-rule which I now have."

"There will be no conditions except the ones I set," responded Sigmundur coolly.

When Thrandur saw that Sigmundur was intractable, they made peace on these terms, agreeing to travel to Norway the following summer.

One ship sailed to Norway in the fall with a contingent of Sigmundur's followers, but Sigmundur and Thorir stayed on Skuf Island that winter, along with Haraldur Iron-Skull and many of their men. Sigmundur restored his father's farm to a magnificent state with good quantities of provisions.

The winter came and went, and Sigmundur readied his ship. Thrandur prepared the merchant-ship which he still owned. Each kept an eye on the other's progress. When he was ready, Sigmundur set off at once. On the voyage with him were Thorir and Haraldur Iron-Skull and nearly twenty other men. They came to Norway at Sunnmøre[1] and learned that Earl Hakon was not far away, so they went straight to find him.

Earl Hakon welcomed Sigmundur and his crew. Sigmundur told him about the settlement with Thrandur.

The Earl responded, "You haven't been as clever as Thrandur. I don't believe he would come readily to an audience with me."

---

1. Sunnmøre ("Southern Møre") is a coastal region in the southwest of Norway.

The summer passed. Thrandur didn't come. A ship arrived from the Faroe Islands, reporting that Thrandur had been driven back and his ship damaged so that he couldn't travel.

25. Earl Hakon's Settlement

At this news, Sigmundur demanded that Earl Hakon deliver a verdict regarding his case against Thrandur, even though he hadn't come.

The Earl replied, "So be it. I rule as follows. Thrandur must pay two counts of wergild,[1] one for each of the brothers, Brestir and Beinir; and a third count of wergild for the plot against your lives when Thrandur wanted to murder you after your fathers' deaths. Lastly, a fourth count must be paid on account of the fact that Thrandur sold you into slavery. Moreover, the quarter of the Faroe Islands, which you owned by right, should be expanded by taking those two shares from Thrandur and the inheritance from Össur, such that half the Islands shall now become your possessions. The other half will revert to me as compensation for Hafgrimur and Thrandur murdering my servants, Brestir and Beinir. No wergild will be paid for Hafgrimur's death in the battle with Brestir due to his conduct toward innocent men. Nor will money be paid for Össur, as it was wrong of him to take possession of your property, and he was slain for it. You should divide up the wergild with Thorir as you see fit. Thrandur can keep his right-to-reside[2] in the Faroes so long as he meets these conditions. The entire Faroe Islands you will hold for me as a fiefdom, and pay tribute to me for my half."

Sigmundur thanked the Earl for this great award. He stayed with the Earl for the winter.

In the springtime, he travelled to the Faroe Islands with Thorir, but Haraldur Iron-Skull remained in Norway.

They had a safe crossing to the Faroes; then they summoned Thrandur to the *thing* at Thorshaven on Straumey. Thrandur came with a large band of men.

---

1. Wergild is the money owed to the family of the victim in legal compensation for the slaying of a man after the killer has come forward publicly. The Earl's settlement, awarding four counts of wergild, is extremely favorable to Sigmundur and Thorir.

2. Earl Hakon grants Thrandur the right-to-reside in his country (*landsvist*) as opposed to full outlawry—perhaps the one favorable outcome of his arbitration of the matter.

Sigmundur made it known that Thrandur received little from the settlement, and then told him of the Earl's adjudications. Sigmundur asked if Thrandur would honor the settlement or whether he would break it.

Thrandur replied that Sigmundur could judge that for himself and that he was pleased that Sigmundur had become such a great man.

Sigmundur told Thrandur not to blow smoke about this. Once again he asked for a plain "yes" or "no" as to whether Thrandur would conduct himself appropriately. Sigmundur reminded him that he could still choose not to be reconciled and face the consequences.

Thrandur chose to accept the terms but asked to defer the payment of the wergild, even though the Earl had decreed that the blood-money should be paid in a single sum. In reply to his request, Sigmundur agreed to allow the wergild to be paid over three years.

Thrandur expressed how wonderful it was that his kinsman Sigmundur would now be taking up governance of the Islands, wishing him at least as long a reign as he had: "And now things are as fair as they could be."

Sigmundur told him to stop uttering such empty platitudes; they were growing tiresome.

At this, they parted ways, with the matter settled.

Thrandur offered to foster Leifur Össursson on his farm on Göta, and the boy grew up there.

Meanwhile, Sigmundur got his ship ready that summer for the trip to Norway and Thrandur paid the first third of the wergild, though he had been extremely reluctant to. Before he sailed from the Islands, Sigmundur collected the tribute for Earl Hakon.

Sigmundur's ship had an easy voyage to Norway, and he went directly to the Earl's court and delivered the tribute. The Earl gave a warm welcome to Sigmundur, Thorir, and all their companions, and they stayed with him that winter.

26. Sigmundur and Thurid

Before Yule that same year, Sigmundur travelled with the Earl to the Frosta *thing*,[1] where Sigmundur interceded on behalf of his foster-father,

---

1. Frosta is a small municipality just north of the Earl's seat in Trondheim in Norway, apparently with jurisdiction over Uppland, the region from which Thorkell was exiled.

Thorkell. He petitioned Earl Hakon to convene a session where cases might be presented, and asked the Earl to grant Thorkell his full right of return from exile. The Earl agreed to his retainer's request without hesitation, and he sent for Thorkell and his household. That winter, Thorkell, Ragnhild, and their daughter, Thurid, were the Earl's guests at his home. Thurid had given birth to a baby girl during the summer when Sigmundur and Thorir left the farm, and she was called Thora.

The following spring, Earl Hakon bestowed Thorkell Hard-Frost a stewardship out in Orkadale, and Thorkell settled on a farm with his family and he was there all the time. The saga now returns to the present.

Sigmundur travelled to Orkadale and met with Thorkell, who was very glad to see him. Sigmundur proposed marriage to Thurid and asked her father for his permission. Thorkell took this proposal well, and it seemed to everyone—father, daughter, and suitor—that much honor and worthiness could be found in this arrangement. Soon, Sigmundur celebrated his wedding at Lade with Earl Hakon, who held a wedding-feast for the couple for seven nights. At the wedding, Thorkell Hard-Frost was made a liegeman of the Earl and became one of his dearest friends. After the guests went home, Sigmundur and his wife stayed with the Earl until the fall; then Sigmundur and Thurid and their daughter Thora sailed to the Faroe Islands.

The winter was uneventful on the Islands.

In the springtime, people went to the *thing* on Straumey, and a crowd soon gathered. Sigmundur and a small body of his men were there. When Thrandur arrived, Sigmundur demanded the second third of the wergild, even though, he said, he had a right to ask for everything.

Thrandur replied, "It so happens, kinsman, that Össur had a son named Leifur, and I brought the boy into my household when you and I were reconciled. I would ask you to accord Leifur some honor on account of his father, whom you murdered, and I could grant him the money that you are owed by me."

"I won't do that," said Sigmundur. "You will pay me my compensation."

"You really think that's likely?" rejoined Thrandur.

"Pay the money," growled Sigmundur, "The alternative is worse!"

Thrandur then paid out half of the second third, saying that he had not come prepared to pay more. Sigmundur stormed up to Thrandur, holding in his hand the same silver-ornamented axe that had slain Össur. He lay the sharp tips of the double-axe on Thrandur's chest, and said he would dig them in so that Thrandur could know real pain, unless Thrandur paid him the full second share then and there.

26. Sigmundur and Thurid

Thrandur sneered, "You're a meddlesome brat." Then he ordered a servant to go into his tent to fetch his money-purse and to see how much silver was still in it. The man went and handed the purse over to Sigmundur. The money in the purse was weighed, and the amount came to what was owed to Sigmundur.

They parted ways as matters stood.

In summer, Sigmundur journeyed to Norway with Earl Hakon's tribute. He was warmly welcomed, and he delayed his return to spend some time at court, before traveling back to the Faroes where he spent the winter.

His cousin Thorir accompanied him everywhere.

Sigmundur was popular among the Faroe-Islanders. Swine-Island Bjarni and his relatives held to the settlement, and Bjarni was always visiting both Thrandur's and Sigmundur's farms; otherwise things would have been much worse.

That spring, people assembled at the *thing* on Straumey. Again, Sigmundur demanded the last share of wergild from Thrandur, and Thrandur sought compensation for Össur on behalf of Leifur Össursson. There was much talk among the Islanders that the two men should come to an agreement.

Sigmundur's response was always the same:

"Thrandur should pay the compensation to me, not to Leifur. In accordance with the proclamation of a noble man, this debt is to be repaid. I won't forgive the debt and I won't yield to any other arrangement."

After this, Thrandur and Sigmundur parted ways and went home from the *thing*.

Once again Sigmundur made preparations to sail to Norway to deliver the Earl's tribute; it was late in the season when he was ready.[1] He set sail from the harbor; Thorir was with him, but his wife Thurid remained behind. The crossing went well, and they came north to Trondheim late in the fall. Sigmundur visited the Earl and received a hearty welcome.

By this time, Sigmundur was twenty-seven years old and served Earl Hakon for the rest of the Earl's life.

---

1. Sigmundur's repeated trips to Norway to deliver tribute to the Earl in this chapter increasingly resemble the political situation in the Faroes after 1200, where an official appointed by the king, his bailiff (*fúti*), would collect taxes and enforce the law of the realm; the typical system in the days of King Magnús Hákonarson (c. 1273ff) was that the bailiff would come to the Faroes in the spring on a merchant ship, and return to Norway on one of the last boats of the fall. See Wylie (1987, 9–13).

27. The Jomsvikings

That winter the Jomsvikings invaded Norway and attacked Earl Hakon and his sons.[1] Sigmundur and Thorir took part in the battles. Sigmundur Brestirsson commanded both a ship and a detachment of the Earl's army. [...][2]

After these setbacks, the leader of the Jomsvikings, Bui, snatched up a wickedly large halberd and incited his men to attack.[3] Now he lunged into battle himself with a vengeance, striking such savage two-handed blows that all resistance gave way before him. When Earl Hakon saw what was happening on the other ship, he ordered his entire fleet to encircle Bui and drive the Viking toward him. Many of the Earl's men were exhausted from the long battle, and they quipped that Bui was better left at a distance than close at hand. It wasn't a pleasant proposition to be put to sleep by the halberd Bui was wielding in such a deadly manner.

Earl Hakon realized that nothing was coming of this plan to cut Bui off, so he brought his own ship forward as quickly as possible and tried nobly to spur on his men. Finally, he called out to Sigmundur Brestirsson to bring his ship alongside Bui's vessel and put an end to this rabble-rouser.

Sigmundur called back, "To reward those many honors you have bestowed me, your grace, and because I want you to rely on me in your hour of the greatest danger, I will move against Bui."

Earl Hakon picked his most loyal and toughest men to board Sigmundur's ship and wished them luck. Then he took his ship alongside Bui's and boarded it with a party of men, and they took the brunt of the fighting. Bui pounded them with severe blows; he was impossibly strong, and many an opponent fell before him and lost their lives.

Sigmundur exhorted his warriors to storm Bui's ship. A group thirty men strong leapt together over the gunnels; Bui and his men rushed

---

1. According to the *Jómsvíkinga saga* in *Flateyjarbók*, the Jomsvikings were an elite band of viking warriors, adhering to a strict code of discipline, who raided from an quasi-mythical base called Jómsborg on the island of Wollin on the south shore of the Baltic Sea. They invaded Norway as part of a Danish plot in c. 986 (see introduction in Blake 1962). Further accounts of the Jomsvikings appear also in *Olafs saga Tryggvasonar*. Regrettably, much of the present chapter is missing in the text of *Faroe-Islander Saga*. Appendix A provides an excerpt of the story from *Jómsvíkinga saga* which covers much of the battle which is missing from *Faroe-Islander Saga*.
2. Part of the saga text is missing here.
3. In *Jomsviking Saga*, the primarily leaders are named as Bui, Sigvaldi, and Vagn; see Appendix A.

against them sharply, and a fierce, heated melee ensued. In the thick of the fighting, Bui and Sigmundur closed on one another in single combat. Bui was the stronger man, but Sigmundur was the quicker and the better with a sword. Sigmundur switched his weapon to his other hand, as he could fight equally well with either hand—something which few or no men can do—and in a blinding slash, he cut off one of Bui's hands at the wrist; then, just as quickly, the other. Standing with two missing hands, Bui thrust the stumps into handles of his gold-chest which was full of money. He then spoke in a completely normal way: "All Bui's crew, abandon ship!"

At that, Bui leapt overboard but he never came back up to the surface. Thus Sigmundur won this victory on behalf of Earl Hakon.[1]

This is the story we have from Hallbjarn Cow-Tail and Steingrimur Thorarsson as well as the account of Ari Thorgilsson the Learned.[2]

The fighting broke up after Bui's death. Sigmundur's companions congratulated him for the great victory which he had won. [...][3]

The year when the Jomsvikings made their raid, Sigmundur Brestirsson remained alongside Earl Hakon for the winter. The following summer Sigmundur traveled to the Faroe Islands, having received splendid gifts from the Earl and his son, and he spent the winter in peace on the Islands. [...]

28. KING OLAF TRYGGVASON

At this point in the saga, Olaf Tryggvason had been king of Norway for two years and all of Trondheim had been baptized as Christians.[4] That

---

1. A very different and fantastic account as to how the battle was won is given in *Jómsvíkinga saga*, where Earl Hakon himself is reported to turn the tide of battle; see Appendix A. The present account gives prominence to a Faroe-Islander's role in this epic (and quite possibly fictional) battle, which is perhaps not unexpected in a saga about Faroe-Islanders.

2. Very little is known about the first two sources, Hallbjarn Cow-Tail and Steingrimur Thorarsson. However, Ari Thorgilsson the Learned (1068–1148) is renowned as the first Icelandic historian to record events in the Icelandic language (with Latin being used by earlier writers); he is rightly famed for writing *Islendingabók* (The Book of the Icelanders), which sketches the detail of the earliest history of the people of Iceland, and he probably wrote the original version of the important *Landnámabók* ('Book of Settlements'), which relates biographical details of the earliest settlers of Iceland and their original land claims. See the introduction to Pálsson and Edwards (2012, 3ff).

3. Part of the saga is missing here and in the next paragraph; the missing passages likely would have detailed the death of Earl Hakon and the rise of Olaf Tryggvason to power.

4. Olaf Tryggvasson was King of Norway from 995 to 1000. King Olaf founded the city of Trondheim in 997 and during his brief reign, he attempted to spread   *continued on page 78*

winter, the king sent a message to the Faroe Islands to Sigmundur Brestirsson summoning him to meet with him. In the message, the king added that Sigmundur would receive the honor that the king would make him the foremost man in the Faroe Islands if Sigmundur would swear allegiance to him.

29. Sigmundur Converts to Christianity

Toward the end of summer, King Olaf set off south from Trondheim to Sunnmøre where he held a banquet for one of his rich landholders. It was there that Sigmundur Brestirsson and his cousin Thorir traveled, having sailed from the Faroe Islands at the king's request.

When Sigmundur was brought before Olaf, the king welcomed him warmly; they quickly fell into easy conversation. The king spoke as follows[1]:

"Well done, Sigmundur, in not putting off this trip. I bade you to meet me as I have heard a great deal about your bravery and accomplishments. I would like to extend you my full friendship if you will obey and support me in those matters I consider most important. People have told me that our mutual friendship would not be unlikely: no one would deny that we are both ranked as the bravest of men, and people would find it a source of deep despair if we did not accord each other the proper respect, since we have many things in common that happened to us in our exile and oppression.

You were a child who looked after himself when your father was unjustly slain; I was in my mother's womb when my father was treacherously murdered for no reason except for the cruelty and avarice of his friends. It was also reported to me that, after this, you were seen as someday-petitioners for the wergild for your father, so your kinsmen pushed for you to be put to death along with your father. Later you were

---

Christianity by force throughout Norway, Iceland, and the North Sea Islands. Wylie remarks shrewdly of Olaf's reign: "He stands before posterity as one who in his day and place was Christ's best hatchet-man, and the Icelandic retailers of his life [i.e. the saga-writers] approved of the role" (Wylie 1987, 10). The chronology of events must be confused or greatly compressed here as the attack of the Jomsvikings in Norway purportedly took place no later than 986 (Blake 1962 sets the range of dates from 974 and 983), and King Olaf would not ascend to the throne for at least another ten years.

1. The autobiographical speech which follows is a sketch of an elaborate series of events described in King Olaf's Saga (*Olafs saga Tryggvason*).

sold as slaves, or at least money exchanged hands so that you were bound and enthralled, and by this cowardly scheme, you were driven off and taken from your farm and homelands, and for a long time, you wandered helplessly in an unknown land, until some strangers showed you mercy with their help and fosterage when all hope was lost.

In this, too, we are not unalike. As soon as I was born, things went badly for me, and I was cast aside and left for dead by my countrymen. My mother was cast into such poverty that she fled with me from her father and kinsmen and her landed estates. That's how it was for the first three years of my life. Then we were both captured by marauders, and soon afterwards I was separated from my mother, whom I never saw again. At three years old, I was sold into slavery and taken to Estland[1] and lived among foreigners until I was nine. One day, there arrived from abroad a kinsman of mine who recognized the noble paternity in my looks. He bought my freedom and took me with him east to Garda.[2] For nine years, I remained there with him in exile; though, at least I could be called a free man by then. At Garda I reached maturity and soon thereafter gained honor and redress for past wrongs from King Valdimir,[3] more than might ever have been expected for a foreigner, much in the way you have been honored by Earl Hakon.

Finally, it so happened that both of us had to win back our lands and inheritance for the sake of long-lost happiness and honor.

Most important of all, I have learned that you have never worshipped false gods like so many other heathen men. From this I have every hope that the King of Heaven on high, Maker of all things, will lead you into communion with His hallowed name and holy faith with the help of my guidance, and that He will deliver you as my companion in faith just as we are equals in physical strength, accomplishments and our other gracious gifts He granted to you and to me long before the time when I knew anything of His Glory. That same Almighty God wills it that I teach you to follow the one true faith and make you subject to His divine service, so

---

1. *Estland* or *Eistland* is modern Estonia. In historical perspective, the Scandinavians, particularly the Swedes, had extensive operations and spheres of influence on the Baltic Sea, trading in furs, spices, jewels, and other precious items with traders having connections to far-off Constantinople and the Arabian peninsula.

2. The Garda (*Garða*) was an area controlled by east Slavic tribes, the so-called Kievan Rus', which extended north to south from the Baltic Sea to the Black Sea and as far west as the Vistula river. The region was ruled by Valdimir Sviatoslavich (Vladimir the Great) from 980 to 1015.

3. Vladimir the Great (958–1015) was prince of Novgorod, grand prince of Kiev, and lord over the Kievan Rus', which he converted to Christianity in 988. His Christian teachings led to the conversion of Olaf Tryggvason.

that you, and your sons after you, with His Grace and from my example and urging, will bring all your countrymen into His Glory. It is my great wish that this shall come to pass. It shall be yours, too, if you will only be swayed by these encouragements of mine. If you serve the Lord God faithfully and steadfastly, you shall gain from me full friendship and honor, even though these things are worth nothing next to the glory and happiness which our Father, Almighty God, will bestow upon you and all those who observe His commandments and love His Holy Spirit and dwell together under the blissful protection of the King of Kings, whose eternal Glory resides in the vaults of the heavenly kingdom."

When the King finished his speech, Sigmundur replied, "As you know, my lord, I served Earl Hakon. He bestowed me with great honors, and I was very content with my position in life, as he was a gracious man, a good counselor, free-handed with his rewards, and beloved by his friends, though, to be fair, he could be harsh and treacherous to his enemies. The old faith was with us for a long time. Nevertheless, I understand from your compassionate teaching that this new faith which you have been proclaiming in every place is far more glorious and beneficent than that religion of heathen men. Thus I am willing to follow your urgings and give myself to your friendship. For this reason, I will not worship the false gods that I learned about long ago and which I later realized were useless, though I knew none better."

30. Christianity Comes to the Faroe Islands

King Olaf was pleased that Sigmundur accepted his words so sensibly. Then Sigmundur was baptized along with all his companions, and the king arranged for them to be instructed in the Holy Gospel. For some time, Sigmundur stayed with the king as an honored guest.

When autumn came, the king told Sigmundur that it was his wish to send him to the Faroe Islands to bring Christianity to the people living there.[1] Sigmundur replied it would be difficult, but nonetheless agreed to

---

1. In *Eiriks saga* (Chapter 5), King Olaf gives an identical mission to Leif Eirikursson to Christianize Greenland. In *Laxdaela saga* (Chapter 41), he sends his priest Thangbrand (in 999) to oversee the conversion of Iceland, but Thangbrand bungles the job with uninspired preaching and harsh methods, and few Icelandic chieftains are baptized; King *continued on page 81*

30. Christianity Comes to the Faroe Islands

carry out the king's wish. The king then appointed him ruler[2] over all the Faroe Islands and provided him with priests who would baptize the people and teach them the tenets of the faith. As soon as he was ready, Sigmundur set sail and the sea-crossing went well.

As soon as he arrived, he called a *thing* at Straumey, and a great crowd of Islanders made the journey there. When the *thing* was assembled, Sigmundur stood up and made a speech, in which he reported that he had gone east during the summer to Norway to meet with King Olaf Tryggvasson and that the king had placed all the Islands under his rule. Many people were delighted at this news.

Sigmundur continued, "I also wish to tell you that I have changed my faith. I am a Christian. I bring the message and proclamation of King Olaf that all Faroe-Islanders shall covert to the true faith."

Thrandur responded to this speech by saying that it was up to the Islanders to debate this serious matter among themselves; and people considered this well-said.[3]

Afterwards, Thrandur and his men moved to the opposite side of the assembly field, and Thrandur stood up and addressed the crowd: "The only thing to be done is to refuse this decree right from start. That will put an end to his preaching that we all must be agreed on the same thing."

When Sigmundur saw that everyone had drifted over to Thrandur and that the only ones standing beside him were his own men, who were already Christians, he groaned, "My authority has been undermined by Thrandur."

All of a sudden, some men came rushing back to where Sigmundur's group sat, carrying their weapons aloft, and they bore down on them aggressively. Sigmundur's men jumped up to oppose them.

But Thrandur said, "Sit down and get control of yourselves. The only thing to say to you, kinsman, is that we freedmen are all of the same opinion as to this proclamation you have delivered: no one here wants to change their faith. We'll fight you right here at the *thing* and kill you, unless

---

Olaf sends Gizur the White and Hjalti Skeggjason as missionaries who succeed in establishing Christianity in Iceland in 1000, though Olaf kept four influential Icelandic chieftains as hostages to see the deal through, including Kjartan Olafsson the hero of *Laxdaela Saga* and Gudmund the Powerful of Modruvellir, one of the main characters of Njal's saga. Sigmundur's mission to the Faroe Islands likely can be dated 999, as King Olaf is still in power the following year when Sigmundur visits him at Nidaros, and Olaf was deposed in 1000.

2. The Old Icelandic uses *valdsman* "ruler" or "regent"; the term is more autocratic than "bailiff" or "chieftain."

3. See *Laxdaela saga*, Chapter 41, for similar reluctance among the Icelanders to adopt Christianity at the *Althing*.

you surrender and make a solemn promise never to try to spread your message throughout the Islands again."

Sigmundur realized that no one was going to come over to his faith at that point, and he had no way of pacifying the anger of all these people. So he was forced to make the promise they demanded of him in front of witnesses and sealed with a handshake. Then Thrandur dissolved the *thing*.

Sigmundur sat at home that winter on Skuf Island. He seemed extremely displeased that the Islanders had kowtowed him, but he didn't let this discourage him.

31. Thrandur Forced to Accept Christianity

Sometime in the following spring when the currents were favorable but men still considered it unsafe to travel from island to island, Sigmundur and thirty men set out from his farm on Skuf Island in two ships. He said they had to run the risk that came with the king's mission or die in their attempt. They set course for Austurey and soon managed to make landfall on the island; they arrived undetected under the cover of night. Moving stealthily, they surrounded the farm at Göta. They battered logs against the door of the outbuilding where Thrandur slept, broke it open, rushed in and seized Thrandur, and manhandled him out.

Sigmundur addressed his kinsman, "Now, Thrandur, the tables are turned. You got the better of me last fall by cornering me with a difficult choice. Now I'm going to present *you* with two extremely unequal options. The better one is that you convert to the true faith and be baptized. If you are unwilling to do this, then the other option is that we'll kill you right here and now. This is clearly the poorer choice for you, as you'll instantly be deprived of all your riches and worldly comforts of your household, and in return gain only damnation and eternal suffering in your new stead in hell."

Thrandur replied, "I won't turn my back on my old friends."

Sigmundur told one of his companions to kill Thrandur, handing him a large axe, but when the man started forward, Thrandur simply stared at

31. Thrandur Forced to Accept Christianity

him and said, "Don't be so quick to kill me! I want to say something first, or where is my kinship with Sigmundur[1] to be found in all this fool's play?"

"I'm right here," Sigmundur said.

"Can we discuss this again between us?" asked Thrandur. "I'll switch to whatever faith you want!"

"Kill him now," Thorir Beinisson snarled to the man with the axe.

Sigmundur said, "Don't kill him just yet."

"We're talking about your death and mine if Thrandur gets away now," cried Thorir.

"It's time to abandon such things," said Sigmundur.

The episode ended with Thrandur and his household being baptized by the priests. After the baptism, Sigmundur had Thrandur accompany him throughout the Faroe Islands, and he did not stop before the entire population was Christian. When this was done, he outfitted his ship during the summer and planned to go to Norway to pay tribute to King Olaf along with Thrandur of Göta.

When Thrandur heard that Sigmundur wanted to bring him to the royal court, he tried to excuse himself from the trip, but Sigmundur wouldn't allow it, and they cast off from shore as soon as there was a fair wind.

Not long after they had put out from harbor, they were hit with strong currents and a big storm, and they were buffeted back to the Faroe Islands and their ship broke up into pieces on the rocks. All their livestock and tribute was lost, but many men were saved. Sigmundur rescued Thrandur and several others.

Thrandur warned them that the journey would not go smoothly if he was forced to travel against his will.[2]

Sigmundur retorted that they all would sail together no matter how much he thought it bode ill for them.

Afterwards, Sigmundur procured a new ship and provided his own money as tribute for the king, as he had no shortage of sellable property. They set off from harbor a second time, getting out to sea further than they had before, but again they met a stiff opposing wind which drove them back to the Faroes and damaged the ship.

---

1. Lit. *"where is my kinsman, Sigmundur?"* Thrandur's remark is difficult to understand as he and Sigmundur were just conversing. The emphasis is on the word, *kinsman*, as Thrandur is evoking his blood relationship with Sigmundur and a complex series of rules which govern social behavior. Thrandur is Sigmundur's first cousin, once-removed, as well as his one-time foster father (though Sigmundur cannot be all too pleased at the memory of that time in his life).

2. Throughout the saga, Thrandur appears to have the ability to control the weather; the weather is favorable when events are going his way and nasty when agents are moving against him.

Sigmundur quipped that there seemed to be a strict travel ban in place.

Thrandur stated that the journey would be like this as long as they insisted on bringing him along against his will.

Finally, Sigmundur released Thrandur from his obligation with the conditions that he swear solemnly, first, to keep and maintain the one true faith, to be loyal and faithful to both King Olaf and Sigmundur, to neither delay or hinder anyone on the islands from keeping their faith to God or obedience to the crown, and finally to promote and practice at all times the preachings of King Olaf and whichever priests he might send to the islands.

Thus swore Thrandur strictly to all the conditions that Sigmundur so carefully laid out. Then he went home to his farm on Göta, while Sigmundur stayed on his farm on Skufey for the winter, since it was already late in the fall after they had been driven back for the second time. Sigmundur had repairs made to the ship which had been slightly damaged. The winter passed quietly and uneventfully in the Faroe Islands.

32. King Olaf Turns on Thrandur

In the spring, when it seemed safe to make the voyage between countries, Sigmundur Brestirsson prepared his ship and set off at once. He let Thrandur stay behind under the conditions he had sworn to. The voyage went well, and he met with King Olaf in the north at Nidaros,[1] presenting to him the money he had gathered in tribute from the Faroe Islands in lieu of what had been lost the previous summer, as the country's tribute was now overdue. The king received him warmly, and Sigmundur stayed with the king for a time that spring.

Sigmundur and the king discussed at length everything that had happened with Thrandur and the other Islanders.

The king concluded: "Thrandur's refusal to present himself before me is base indeed, and it greatly spoils your colony out there on the Islands

---

1. *Nidaros* was an alternative name for Trondheim in medieval Norway and the home of the archdiocese established by Olaf Tryggvason.

if he cannot be driven away from them, though that would be my wish for the Faroes, seeing as there resides the vilest man who ever lived in the northern countries, Thrandur himself!"

33. Sigmundur and King Olaf

One day in the spring, King Olaf said to Sigmundur Brestirsson, "Let's have some fun today and put our athletic prowess to the test."

"I'm tired today, my lord," yawned Sigmundur, "but nevertheless let's see if you can keep up with me."

So they put themselves to the test at swimming, bow shooting, and other games, and it is retold by many that Sigmundur came second only to King Olaf in athleticism of all the men of Norway, just losing to his majesty in every contest they set for themselves.[1]

Another story is told about a time when King Olaf sat drinking and entertaining his men. Many men were gathered at the feast, and Sigmundur was there, carousing and laughing with the king; two men sat between the king and Sigmundur, whose hand rested on the table. The king noticed he was wearing a thick gold ring.

The king called over, "Let's have a look at that ring."

Sigmundur removed the ring from his hand and passed it to the king. The king studied it and asked, "Will you give me this ring?"

Sigmundur replied, "I had never planned on giving up that ring, my lord."

"I'll find you another ring in exchange," offered the king affably. "One no less precious or beautiful."

"I can't part with it," said Sigmundur with finality. "That was what Earl Hakon told me when he gave it to me with his affection, and I intend to keep this promise as the person who gave it was a great man—an earl—and he always did right by me during my years of service."

The king bridled, "Think as highly of these things as you want, about the ring and the man who gave it to you! But it won't bring you any more luck now because this ring is going to be the death of you. I don't care

---

1. This episode has its parallel in Chapter 40 of *Laxdaela saga*, where the Icelandic hero Kjartan Olafsson, newly arrived in Norway, swims in the river Nid and has a competition with a stranger who is revealed to be Olaf Tryggvason himself.

about either how you got it or where it came from. Give in to me on this demand! I don't want to lose my friend over a fight but I covet this ring!"

The king's face turned as red as blood, and the conversation in the room fell silent. Never again was the king on as friendly terms with Sigmundur as before, though he stayed on for a while with the king, until he set off for the Faroe Islands in the early summer. The two men parted as friends, but that was the last time Sigmundur would ever see the king. Sigmundur sailed out to the Faroe Islands and settled down on his farm on Skufey. [...][1]

34. Earl Eirikur and Earl Svein

After the death of King Olaf, Earl Eirikur and Earl Svein Hakonsson, ruled over Norway and they were extremely popular as the people were given more rights to govern themselves.[2] They resided at Lade in Trondheim as was their birthright; their native home also possessed the strength and resources of the country. Between the brothers, it was Eirikur who took the lead in all things.

From his many battles, Eirikur was the more famous of the two, as he had been to Svöldur and at Hjorungavagr, as had most distinguished men of his generation, and took part in the victory both times.[3] Eirikur was extremely handsome and the shrewdest of men; in these things, he took after his father, and yet he was unlike him in terms of disposition and morality, so that people came to say that he proved to be a better man than his father.

---

1. Part of the saga is missing here, which would have referred to the death of Olaf Tryggvasson and the rise to power of the brothers, earls Eirikur and Svein.

2. The half-brothers Eirikur and Svein Hakonsson co-ruled Norway from c. 1000–1014. The *Fagrskinna saga* corroborates that their rule was exceptionally peaceful and just.

3. The battle of Svöldur took place in 1000. Eirikur, Svein, and their allies ambushed King Olaf Tryggvason, waging an epic sea-battle off the island of Svöldur, one of the many islands in the Baltic Sea off what is today the north German coast. It was after this that Eirikur and Svein came to rule Norway. The sea-battle of Hjorungavágr in 986 was Eirikur's first military action; in an attempt to Christianize Norway, Haraldur Bluetooth led a Danish fleet against Earl Hakon Siguthursson, who was a firm believer in the old Norse gods. Eirikur played a critical role repulsing the Danish who were assisted by the Jomsvikings; accounts of the battle are found in the *Heimskringla*, the *Jomsvikinga saga*, and the *Gesta Danorum* of Saxo Grammaticus; see Appendix A.

35. The Earls Welcome Sigmundur

Earl Eirikur and Earl Svein sent word to the Faroe Islands to Sigmundur that he should come to meet with them. Sigmundur made the voyage to Norway without delay, and arrived at the Earls' court in the north at Lade near Trondheim. They welcomed him with great affection, remembering their early days of friendship. They made Sigmundur their bailiff and gave him the Faroe Islands to rule as a fief. Then they parted as close and dear friends, and Sigmundur sailed out to the Faroe Islands in autumn.

36. A Growing Feud

The saga turns to three young men who were raised by Thrandur of Göta. Sigurthur was the son of Thorlakur, Thrandur's brother.[1] He was a tall, strong, and handsome man with fair hair which fell in locks about his shoulders. He was very accomplished, and it was even whispered that he took after Sigmundur Brestirsson in terms of his accomplishments.

Sigurthur had a brother, Thorthur, who was called Thorthur the Short; he was compact and muscular.

The third was known as Gautur the Red, and he was the son of Thrandur's sister. The three young men were all big and strapping.

Leifur Össursson lived with them at Thrandur's farm as a foster son, and the four of them were always together.

Meanwhile, Sigmundur and Thurid had several children.

Their daughter Thora was the eldest; she had been born in the mountains of Norway. She was a tall and graceful maiden, not exceptionally pretty, but as she grew up, it became clear that she was quite clever.

Of their sons, Thoralfur was the next oldest, followed by Steingrimur, then Brandur, and their fourth son was named Heri. All four were promising young men.

---

1. Compare with Chapter 2.

By this time, Christianity had spread throughout the Faroe Islands as it had elsewhere in the Earls' kingdom, where a person could live however they wanted, so long as they observed the Christian faith.

Sigmundur and his entire household were devout Christians, and he had a church built on his farm.

On the other hand, Thrandur had cast aside his faith; he was followed in this by his family and friends.

When the Faroe-Islanders gathered for the *thing*, both families arrived with a large retinue.

Thrandur spoke with Sigmundur: "Once again, kinsman, I would ask you for compensation on behalf of Leifur Össursson to atone for his father."

Sigmundur said he would abide by the settlement Earl Hakon had handed down to them concerning any lawsuits between them.

Thrandur retorted, "Apparently, you won't give the same fair compensation to Leifur which better men than yourself have already repaid to you here on the Islands."

Sigmundur told Thrandur there was no need to row against the wind[1]; there would be no compensation.

Then Thrandur said, "You're proving to be stubborn as an ox! It so happens that those foster sons of mine think that you are a small-minded, unjust man if you won't share this fiefdom with them, when we own a bigger half than you do, and when it's clear that people have never been content with this state of affairs. You have greatly wronged me, worst of all when you forced me to convert; I was always miserable going along with that, and you should be prepared that the Islanders won't always be so happy to side with you."

Sigmundur replied that he would sleep soundly for all Thrandur's threats, and they parted ways as matters stood.

37. Hostilities Escalate

One day in the summer, Sigmundur, Thorir, and Einar South-Islander sailed over to Little Dimun, as Sigmundur wanted to collect some of his sheep which were grazing on the island for slaughter. As they came up

---

1. Lit: "to pull against the oars" (*arar at draga*), i.e. there is no point in Thrandur belaboring his case.

from the cliffs onto the island, they caught sight of men milling up on the island whose shields were gleaming in the sun; they made out twelve of them and Sigmundur wondered who they could be.

Thorir thought they were the Götuskeggjars, Thrandur and his lads, and asked, "What should we do now?"

"That's simple," responded Sigmundur. "We'll go up to them with our weapons drawn, and if they attack us, we'll run down ahead of them and meet again at the bottom of the beach path; it's the only one on the island."

Meanwhile, Thrandur's posse were discussing among themselves that Leifur, Gautur, and the two sons of Thorlak would take on Sigmundur. Their plan was overheard by Sigmundur's group, who now were coming up toward them, and Thrandur's men rushed at them at once. But Sigmundur, Thorir, and Einar turned on their heels and each raced down the path single-file, and came to the landing on the shore. A man was waiting for them at the foot of the path. Sigmundur was the first one down, and he made quick work of the sentry. Then, Sigmundur turned to defend the narrow footpath, while Thorir and Einar ran for Thrandur's ship. There was a man tending the mooring-lines on shore; another was on the ship. Thorir went for the man holding the line and killed him, while Einar ran to their own boat and launched it into the water. Sigmundur was watching the path up onto the island, but leapt down onto the pebbly beach to join them on the ships. Fighting his way past another of Thrandur's men on the beach, he caught up with Thorir and they both charged onto Thrandur's ship. Sigmundur quickly wrestled the remaining man overboard. They rowed both ships out to sea, as Thrandur's man swam safely to shore.

Thrandur and his men had to burn signal-fires until someone rowed out to get them, but eventually they returned home to Göta. Sigmundur was rounding up some men to move against Thrandur there on Dimun, when he learned that they had escaped.

Later that summer, Sigmundur was going among the Islands with Thorir and Einar to check up on the farms they had rented out. They were rowing through a narrow channel between two small islands, and as they emerged from the narrows, a ship came bearing down on them and it was very nearly upon them. They recognized the Götuskeggjars at once: Thrandur, accompanied by twelve men.

Thorir said, "They're almost on top of us. What should we do, Sigmundur?"

"There's little we can do," replied Sigmundur. "The only chance is to row straight at them and get them to drop their sail, and as our ship comes alongside theirs, you both draw your swords and try to cut the rope-lines on their gunnels so they can't raise the sail again, and I'll try to do what I can."

So they rowed directly toward Thrandur's ship, and as they drifted alongside, Thorir and Einir severed all the rope-lines on the opposite gunnel so the sail couldn't be raised. Sigmundur snatched up a gaffing-pole which was laying on his deck, and drove it into the hull of the other ship so hard that the keel nearly emerged from the water. He rammed the pole into the hull where the sail had come down and pushed the ship over still further. With Sigmundur rocking it with all his might, all of a sudden the ship capsized. In the aftermath, five of Thrandur's men drowned.

Thorir proposed that they should kill each man they could pull from the water. Sigmundur refused, saying he would rather let them suffer as much as possible. They rowed away, leaving the survivors with the overturned ship.

Watching him go, Sigurthur Thorlaksson swore, "This will certainly be a black trip for Sigmundur."

He managed to right the ship and saved many men.

When Thrandur clambered back onto the ship, he said, "Now we've had a turn of luck against Sigmundur. It was a grave mistake of him not to have killed us when he had us all at his mercy. We'll be even shrewder from now on and we won't stop until we see Sigmundur in hell."

They all agreed, and they went home to Göta as matters stood. The summer drew to an end with no further encounters between the two factions.

38. A Narrow Escape

All remained quiet until one day shortly before winter. Thrandur gathered together a group of sixty men and announced that they were going pay Sigmundur a visit. It had come to Thrandur in a dream that they had almost taken him before he narrowly escaped. The force of men loaded onto two ships. Among them were Leifur Össursson; Sigurthur Thorlaksson; Thorthur the Short; Gautur the Red; Steingrimur, a farmer on Austurey; and Eldjarn Comb-Hood, who had been Thrandur's servant all these years.[1] Swine-Island Bjarni did not take part as he had vowed when he made peace with Sigmundur.

Thrandur's posse sailed to Skufey and dragged their ships onto the beach from which they could ascend paths up onto the island.

Skufey is such a good natural stronghold that they say the island cannot be taken if just ten men are stationed on the ascending paths, no matter how many attackers try to storm it.

Eldjarn Comb-Hood went up first to take a look and caught sight of one of Sigmundur's men guarding the approach. They moved to attack each other at once; their quick skirmish ended with both men toppling down off the cliffs, plunging to their deaths.

Afterwards, Thrandur and his men ascended the path up to the farm and surrounded the farmhouse so furtively that no lookout raised the alarm against them. At last, they broke down the doors. Sigmundur's household grabbed for their weapons and charged the oncoming attackers. The lady of the house, Thurid, also snatched hold of a sword and fought no less ably than any of the men. Thrandur's followers set fire to the house, their plan being to set it ablaze and drive the occupants outside into the path of their swords. The fighting grew intense.

During this melee, Thurid appeared at the door of her farmhouse and called out, "And just how long do you intend to press your attack against leaderless men, Thrandur?"

Thrandur answered ruefully, "It's plain as day that Sigmundur isn't at home."

He turned away from the farm, walked back toward the sea, and whistled. From the echo, Thrandur detected an underground passage, the mouth of which emerged not far off from the farm. He got down in the opening and wafted his hands before his nose a few times, and then proclaimed, "The three of them got away here, Sigmundur, Thorir, and Einar."

After a moment, Thrandur climbed out and sniffed the air like a hound tracking a scent; he barked that no one should talk to him, and he kept this up until he made his way to a chasm which spanned the island of Skufey.

---

1. Eldjarn Comb-Hood was killed by Einar South-Islander in Chapter 5. The addition of the name here may be a mistake by the saga-writer. Alternatively, it may be that the saga-writer is inviting the reader to consider that Eldjarn was not killed in the incident which spurred Hafgrimur to ally himself with Thrandur to attack Brestir and Beinir. In such a scenario, the saga-writer may be building the suspicion that Thrandur is guilty of behind-the-scenes duplicity in the early days of the feud.

38. A Narrow Escape

At last, he said, "They escaped this way. Sigmundur and the rest of them must have leapt across. Let's split up our group. Leifur Össursson and Sigurthur Thorlaksson, go to the far end of the island with half the men; I'll start from this end, and we'll meet each other in the middle."

They put the plan into action.

Then Thrandur whispered to himself, "This time we've got you, Sigmundur, if you indeed possess any courage at all and if you think yourself as brave a man as people say you are."

Dusk soon fell, and it was a moonless night.

All of a sudden a figure leapt over the chasm toward Thrandur's party and struck Steingrimur, Thrandur's neighbor, with a slash of the sword between the shoulder blades. Straightaway, this powerful figure jumped right back across the chasm. There was no doubt it was Sigmundur.

"There goes Sigmundur!" growled Thrandur. "After them! Let's make for the far end of the chasm."

Thrandur's group made pursuit, but the only persons they encountered were Leifur and his men.

Sigmundur and his companions reached a cliff towering over the sea where they could hear voices coming from both directions.

"We'll have to defend ourselves here, as luck may have it," Thorir said.

"I won't be much of a defender," replied Sigmundur, "I lost my sword when I jumped over the chasm. So we'll have to jump off the cliff and land in the surf."

"We'll follow your lead," said Thorir.

So it was decided, and they plunged into the sea from the height of the cliff.

When he heard the splash, Thrandur roared, "They're getting away! Let's go back and get our ships and find them. Some men search the channel; some of you search the shoreline!"

Thrandur's men searched everywhere, but they didn't find them.

39. A Partnership Comes to an End

For a long while Sigmundur, Thorir, and Einar swam in the direction of South Island, the closest land, though it was still distant across a mile of open sea.[1]

When they had swum nearly halfway across the channel, Einar gasped, "We're not going to make it."

Sigmundur called back that they would make it: "Just grab onto my shoulders, Einar!"

Einar clutched his back, and Sigmundur and Thorir swam on.

Then Thorir, who was falling behind, called out to Sigmundur, "My brother, how long are you going to drag a dead man behind you?"

"I didn't know I was," said Sigmundur, letting Einar go.

They kept swimming until they were three-fourths of the way across the channel.

Then Thorir said, "All our lives, Sigmundur, we've been together. You've been my only family, and I've been yours. But now it seems likely that our dear partnership is coming to an end. I've swam as far as I can. I want you to save yourself ... save your own life, and forget about me. Because you'll die, my brother, if you try to save me too."

"That's not going to happen; we're not going to be separated like this," insisted Sigmundur. "Either we make it to shore together or not at all."

Sigmundur started floating and swimming with Thorir clutching his shoulders. Thorir was so faint that he could barely hang on.[1] Sigmundur swam onward until he reached South Island. Sigmundur was exhausted and the choppy surf at the island kept buffeting him away from shore, but after a while he drifted onto the beach, where Thorir slid off his shoulders. He was dead. Sigmundur crawled up the shore, so weak that he couldn't walk, and slithered up onto the rocks, finally collapsing in a bed of seaweed at the first light of dawn. There he lay until the sun was fully up.

---

1. The Old Icelandic *vika* "sea-mile" must mean something like "stretch" or "long distance" here. Foote (1965, 12) estimates Sigumundur's swim from Skufey to Suðurey to be ten miles; in the note to the Islenzk Fornrit text of *Faereyinga saga* (volume 25, p 84), the editor Olafur Halldorson notes [in Icelandic] that the distance is 12km between the closest points. It would seem like more to fully clothed swimmers, depending on the action of the ocean currents.

2. The language of this scene echoes Sigmundur carrying Thorir through the snowstorm in the mountains in Chapter 10.

A little farm was close by, up on the island, called Sandvik.[1] A man named Thorgrimur the Mean farmed there; he was tall and strong, and a tenant of Thrandur of Göta. He had two sons, named Ormstein and Thorstein; they were both promising young men.

That same morning, Thorgrimur the Mean was out walking the shore, carrying a wood axe. By and by, he noticed some red cloth caught among a heap of seaweed. He rooted in the seaweed and discovered a man laying there. He asked the man who he was, and Sigmundur told him.

"Come down in life, chieftain, eh?" grunted Thorgrimur. "What brings you here?"

Sigmundur told him the story of what had happened.

At that point, Thorgrimur's sons appeared, and Sigmundur asked if they would help him. Thorgrimur didn't respond readily to this, and turned to speak in hushed tones with his sons:

"Sigmundur possesses so much wealth—or so it seems to me—such that we've never had, and that gold-ring of his is huge. I think it's best we kill him and stash the body afterwards; no one will ever know."

Thorgrimur's sons argued against this course of action for several moments, but they finally agreed to their father's plan. They strode back to where Sigmundur lay, grabbed him by the hair, and Thorgrimur the Mean chopped off Sigmundur's head with the wood axe. Thus for the sake of a fat prize, Sigmundur, the bravest man of them all, lost his life.

They stripped off his clothes and ring, and then dragged his body up near a mound of earth and they buried him beneath it. Thorir's body was collected and thrown in next to Sigmundur; then they buried the corpses and covered up the death of the two men.[2]

40. THORA SIGMUNDURSDOTTIR

After the failed raid, Thrandur and his men made their way home. Sigmundur's farm on Skufey was saved from the flames as neighbors came

---

1. Geographically correct: Sandvík is a small village on the bay to the extreme northern end of South Island, a likely place to come ashore traveling south from Skufey.
2. Old Icelandic *víg* refers to a "slaying," what would be referred to today as murder, but this was not necessarily a vile act as the person responsible could pay compensation to the victim's family and make amends. Here, the Old Icelandic word is *morð*, which refers to the unlawful killing and concealment of a murder; this was considered a heinous crime.

rushing to help. The damage from the fire was slight and very few household items had been destroyed.

The mistress of the house, Thurid, thereafter came to be known as Thurid Strong-Widow. She ran the farm on Skufey just as ably as her husband had, and Sigmundur's children grew up at home under their mother's care; they were all promising young men and women.

Thrandur and Leifur Össursson now claimed and took control over the entire Faroe Islands. Thrandur sent word to Thurid Strong-Widow and her sons, offering to come to terms with them, but they scorned these overtures. Nothing came of it when Sigmundur's boys sought help from the crown in Norway, as they were still young and underage.

The winter passed quietly on the Faroe Islands.

One day Thrandur came to speak with Leifur Össursson. It was time to find him a wife.

"Who do you have in mind?" asked Leifur.

"Thora Sigmundursdottir," answered Thrandur.

"It's not likely she's going to look too favorably on me," said Leifur.

"It's not trying your luck if you don't even ask," countered Thrandur.

So, along with a few men, they made the trip to Skufey, where they were coldly received. Thrandur and Leifur offered to come to a settlement with Thurid and her sons, to be handled there on the Islands with the best men adjudging the matter between them. The offer was not met with a ready response. Then Thrandur brought up the matter of Leifur's marriage proposal and asked Thora Sigmundursdottir if she would have him for a husband, adding that he thought their marriage would make for a lasting settlement. Thrandur even offered to increase Leifur's prospects with a large dowry.

This proposal was met with indifference by the Skuf-Islanders, and Thora herself stood up to reply:

"You two seem to think that I'm so hotly eager to marry. However, in addition to what you're offering, I'll make these terms for my hand: First, if Leifur can swear that he is not my father's killer and, second, not until he brings to justice the men who killed him. I demand that he finds out how my father died, or who is responsible for his death. And if all these terms are met, you shall have your reconcilation with us, with the consent of my brothers, my mother and that of our relatives and friends."

Everyone felt these remarks were well-spoken and sensible. The Skuf-Islanders agreed amongst themselves that Thrandur and Leifur should meet these terms, and both families then parted as matters stood.

41. The Truth Comes Out

Shortly after this, Thrandur and Leifur set out from Göta with twelve men and traveled in a single ship to South Island. They headed for Sandvik, home of Thorgrimur the Mean; this trip was during the winter following the deaths of Sigmundur and Thorir. They arrived at the island late in the day, and walked up to the farmhouse; Thorgrimur welcomed Thrandur's group and invited them inside. Thrandur went into the sitting room with his farmer Thorgrimur, while Leifur and the other men sat near the outer door where the fire was lit for them.

The conversation in the backroom went on for a long time.

Thrandur asked, "Who do you think might have killed Sigmundur Brestirsson?"

"Seems nobody knows for sure," grunted Thorgrimur. "Some people think it were you what found 'em on the beach or in the channel and killed 'em."

"A slanderous and illogical thought," replied Thrandur silkily, "as everyone knew that we were after Sigmundur's head, so for what reason would we want to cover it up that we killed them? That's just mean-spirited rumor."

"Nevertheless, that's what people are sayin'," said Thorgrimur. "That they could've jumped down into the ocean and Sigmundur could've made it back to land, since he were a champion in so many ways, and someone could have killed him if he were too weak to fight. Then they covered it up."

"A rather attractive suggestion," agreed Thrandur, "and that's my thought as to what happened. So what now, you dolt! Am I wrong to suspect that it's you who are responsible for Sigmundur's death?"

Thorgrimur refuted the accusation, hemming and hawing.

"There's no need to deny it," continued Thrandur, "because I think we both know that you're guilty of this."

Thorgrimur stuck to his earlier denials.

Thrandur summoned Leifur and Sigurthur and ordered them to place Thorgrimur and his sons in chains; straightaway, the family was clasped in irons and they were securely bound.

Next Thrandur instructed a blazing fire be made in the fire-house, and he had four metal grates placed in a square, and Thrandur himself scored nine furrows in the earthen floor, making nine concentric circles

41. The Truth Comes Out

around the square, and he sat down on a stool between the fire and the grated pen. He asked his men not to speak to him, and they stood silently by.[1]

For a long while Thrandur sat there.

After some time had passed, a man entered the fire-house. He was all wet. Everyone recognized the man as Einar South-Islander. Einar went up to the fire and warmed his hands; he stood there a long while; then he turned and left. More time went by, and another man came into the fire-house. He went to the fire, warmed his hands, and then departed. Soon after Thorir had left, a third man came into the fire-house, a great man covered in blood, who carried his head in his hands. They all recognized him as Sigmundur Brestirsson. Sigmundur halted at a certain spot on the floor for a time, then he made his departure.

After this Thrandur rose from his stool and drew a deep, painful breath. Finally, he spoke, "Now it should be clear to you how these men met their deaths. Einar perished first, having frozen to death or drowned; he was always the weakest of them, anyway. Thorir must have died next. Sigmundur would have helped Thorir as much as possible, and we ought to respect him for that. At any rate, Sigmundur would have made it to shore utterly exhausted, where these men must have killed him, seeing as how his ghost was spattered with blood and headless."

Thrandur's men all agreed that that was what must have happened. Then Thrandur told them to ransack the house, and they uncovered some indications as to what had happened. Thorgrimur and his sons still denied everything, insisting they were innocent. Thrandur maintained that there was no need for their denials, and told his men to keep on searching.

A large, dusty chest stood in the fire-house, and Thrandur asked his men whether it had been searched yet. They broke open the latch and there seemed to be nothing inside except an assortment of rubbish which they spent some time rooting through.

Thrandur called over to them, "Dump everything out!"

---

1. This pagan ritual to summon ghosts shows that Thrandur is "old-guard," a follower of the ancient Norse gods, and staunchly anti–Christian at a time when most of the Faroes have nominally converted to the new faith. The nature of the ritual is obscure and the ritual itself is unique among the sagas. Based on comparative folklore, Foote outlines the following brief points: [1] a ritual fire is known to attract spirits, particularly those of men who died wet, cold, and exhausted; [2] in cases of divination, it is dangerous to talk to the man who is working the pagan spell, hence Thrandur's command for silence; [3] nine is a number with magical connotations, and the enclosed circles of earth create a perimeter which both protects the living and forms a barrier for the undead spirits; [4] the four-sided gates constitute some sort of barrier or door to and from the "other side" (for a full discussion of this ritual, see the article, *Faereyinga Saga, Chapter forty*, in Foote 1984, 209–221).

Junk piled onto the floor, and they came across a rag-bag which had been stuffed to the bottom of the chest. Thrandur snatched the bag out of the pile and opened it up. Inside some old rags were bundled together, and sifting through them, Thrandur found a large ring of gold and it was one which he recognized. It was the very ring which had once belonged to Sigmundur Brestirsson and given to him by Earl Hakon. Thrandur picked up the ring and stormed over to Sigmundur's murderer and recited to him precisely what they had done.

At last, Thorgrimur showed them where Sigmundur and Thorir lay dead and buried under the earthen mound. Thrandur's men unearthed the corpses and transported them home from Sandvik.

Thrandur made Thorgrimur and his sons come with him.

Sometime later Sigmundur and Thorir were buried on Skufey at the church which Sigmundur had built.

42. The End of the Feud

Directly upon returning from Sandvik, Thrandur called a *thing* on Straumey at Thorshaven, the assembly place of the Faroe Islanders. Before a great crowd of witnesses, Thorgrimur the Mean and his sons declared for all to hear that Sigmundur was dead and they had killed him. They confessed that they had murdered him and had then covered up this hateful act.

After this admission of guilt, these men were hanged right there at the *thing*, and so paid for the crime with their lives.[1]

Leifur and his foster father Thrandur now brought up the marriage proposal with Thora and asked the Skuf-Islanders to be reconciled since they had satisfied every condition. They resolved that Leifur would marry Thora Sigmundursdottir, and both sides came to a peaceful settlement with a happy outcome. Leifur settled down with Thora at the farm at Hof on South Island, which had been his father's.

For a time, events were quiet on the Faroe Islands.

Thoralfur Sigmundursson got married and farmed on Dimun; he was a good farmer. [...][2]

---

1. The punishment for the crime of *morð*, the unlawful killing and concealment of the corpse.
2. A long break in the saga occurs here, wherein Earl Eirikur and Svein ruled in Norway for ten years, before Eirikur went to join Canute the Great's conquest of England in 1014, leaving the country in the hands of his son, Hakon, and his brother, Svein Hakonsson.

43. King Olafur Haraldursson

That same summer, Olafur Haraldursson[1] had been king for ten years. A delegation travelled from the Faroe Islands to Norway at Olafur's request which included Gilli the Lawspeaker,[2] Leifur Össursson, Thoralfur of Dimun, and many other freemens' sons. Thrandur of Göta was asked to join them, but when his ship was ready to set off, he grew apprehensive and wouldn't budge, and so he stayed behind.

When the Faroe-Islanders arrived at King Olafur's court, he summoned them for an audience and addressed them; he began with the reason they had come, telling them that he wished to receive tribute from the Faroe Islands, and moreover that the Faroe-Islanders should live by the laws which he set for them.

During this audience, the king made it known that he would arbitrate all matters among the Faroese when they were presented to him in Norway, if they swore an oath of allegiance to the crown; moreover, he invited those men whom he thought worthy of the honor to become his retainers and receive his respect and friendship. Listening to the king, the Faroe-Islanders were suspicious of how their affairs would turn out if they didn't want to go along with everything the king was asking from them. Though many more appointments were made to hear cases than were ever arbitrated, everything turned out as the king wanted. Leifur and Gilli and Thoralfur clasped hands with the king and became his retainers, and their companions made oaths to the king to uphold his laws and maintain public order in the Faroe Islands, as well as to send back the tribute he claimed. At last, the Faroe-Islanders made preparations to return home. At their departure, the king presented gifts of friendship to his new retainers. When they were ready, the Faroe Islanders set off on their homeward voyage.

Meanwhile, the king had prepared a ship and assembled a crew, intending to send his agents to the Faroes to collect the tribute which the

---

1. After the joint reign of the Earls of Lade, Eirikur and Svein, Olafur Haraldursson, St. Olaf, was King of Norway from 1016 to 1030. At the beginning of his reign, pockets of paganism still existed in Norway and he aggressively worked to stamp these out and bring the population over to Christianity; his story is expounded in *St. Olaf's Saga*.

2. The Lawspeaker was elected for three years by the *thing*; the main duties included calling the assembly to order, reciting and interpreting the law, though specific duties varied throughout the Norse world. The Lawspeaker was commonly employed as an arbitrator between disputing parties. See Appendix C.

Islanders owed him. The crew were slow getting ready, and they sailed after preparations were complete. There was no report of their journey: they never returned to Norway nor was there any tribute from the following summer in the king's coffers; they had never reached the Faroes; and no agent came around to the Islands' farms to collect tribute.

44. A Bad Omen

The following summer, King Olafur received reports that the ship he had sent to the Faroe Islands the previous year had disappeared, as it had not made landfall elsewhere as far as anyone knew. The king then prepared a second ship and crew, and dispatched it to the Faroes to collect his tribute. The men weighed anchor and put out to sea. No more was ever heard from them than from the first ship, though there was much speculation as to what could have happened to them.

45. Trouble Brews Abroad

In spring of the next year a Norwegian ship travelled out to the Faroe Islands, conveying a message from King Olafur that one of his Faroese retainers should come to his court, namely Leifur Össursson or Gilli-Lawspeaker or Thoralfur of Dimun. When this message reached the Islands and was communicated to these men, they discussed among themselves what motive could be lurking behind this request. There was a consensus that they thought the king simply wanted to learn the news of whether Faroese men had accepted the arrangement he had presented to the Islands, and about the delayed arrival of the king's messengers on those two ships, which still hadn't been heard from. They decided that Thoralfur should make the trip to Norway. He made preparations for the voyage and outfitted his merchant-ship with a crew of some ten or twelve men.

While the ship was set to depart and they were waiting for fair winds, over at Göta on Austurey it happened that Thrandur was enjoying a day of absolutely lovely weather in his sitting room and that his nephews, Sigurthur and Thorthur Thorlaksson, were sprawled out idly in a natural spring with their kinsman, Gautur the Red; these three foster sons of Thrandur were accomplished young men, though the eldest, Sigurthur, was a cut above the rest in all respects. Thorthur was nicknamed the Short; he was a dangerous man, all the more so because he was compact and strongly built.

Thrandur observed, "Many things change in a man's lifetime. In my day it was considered a dreadful thing for men in their prime to sit at home and loaf around on good weather days, taking the world in stride. Your ancestors would have never believed that Thoralfur of Dimun could prove to be a braver man than you, Sigurthur! But that merchant-ship I own sits gathering dust in the boatshed and it's now so old that I expect there's rot under the pitch. Every one of our storerooms is bursting with wool which could be sold abroad; this wouldn't be the case if I were a few winters younger!"

Sigurthur leapt up and told Thorthur and Gautur to follow him, saying that they couldn't ignore Thrandur's reproach. They marched over to the shed where the servants worked, got out the merchant-ship and placed her into the water. They gathered some cargo and loaded the ship; there was no shortage of wares stored in the farm's outbuildings, and there was room for everything onboard. The outfitting of the ship took five days. There were ten or twelve men on the ship in addition to the three young men.

Meanwhile, Thoralfur's ship finally got a consistent wind in the harbor; after a few days, they reached Herna. Sigurthur's crew had put out to sea just behind them.

One evening after dark when Thoralfur's crew were getting ready to go to sleep, Thoralfur and another man went to find places for themselves on shore to lay down. As they were arranging themselves for bed, the other man complained that Thoralfur had just tossed clothes onto his head, and he stormed up off the ground. Just then they heard a crash in the underbrush; someone rushed at Thoralfur's companion and bowled him over. They happened to be above a cliff with the sea churning below, and the companion was plunged into the water. After the man had climbed up on dry land, he found his way back to where the crew were camped. He came across Thoralfur's body lying on the ground. Thoralfur had been stabbed between the shoulders; he was dead.[1]

---

1. Here as elsewhere, Peter Foote is highly suspicious of Thrandur's motives. Picking up on the detail *"storehouses bursting with wool,"* Foote's view (1965, 17–   *continued on page 102*

45. Trouble Brews Abroad

When the crew became aware of what had happened, they brought Thoralfur's body back to the ship and held a meeting during the night to discuss what to do.

King Olafur was at a banquet at Lygra,[2] so they sent word to him there. A return message ordering them to a meeting was delivered by arrow onto the ship. The king came to the *thing*, having summoned the Faroe-Islanders from both ships to appear before him. When each crew had arrived, the king stood to address them:

"The incident which occurred is as good as it is rare: life has been taken from a good-hearted and noble-minded man, and in my opinion, for no reason. So, is there anyone here who knows well enough to tell me who is responsible for this?"

None of the crew stepped forward.

The king continued, "There's no secret about what I believe to have happened among you Faroe-Islanders. In particular, it seems obvious that Sigurthur Thorlaksson must have killed Thoralfur, after Thorthur the Short chucked his friend off the cliff. Moreover, I might suggest the motive that these two men didn't want Thoralfur to reveal some acts of cowardice of theirs which he had witnessed as being true. I have no doubt that it is a case of murder and evil-doing, as one of my retainers has been killed."

After the king had ventured his thoughts, Sigurthur Thorlaksson rose to speak.

"I have never spoken at a *thing* before and I expect I won't come across as very skilled with words. Nevertheless, I think there is a vigorous need to respond to this accusation. I am adamant that this speech which the king has just made might have come from wicked tongues of men who are far less wise than he is; such rumors are our most stubborn enemy. It's falsely said that I would want to be Thoralfur's killer: he was my foster-brother and close friend.[3] Were there any other issue or source of discord

---

18) is that the saga-writer is inviting the reader to consider that Thrandur had something to do with the disappearance of the king's two lost messenger ships, which of course, would have carried a cargo for trade. This, in turn, gives Thrandur's foster sons a motive for the murder of Thoralfur; "the oblique sense of all this, suggested only by the references to Thoralf[ur], is of course that if they do not act quickly, King Olaf is going to learn something about the mysterious fate of the two ships and their crews" (1965, 18).

2. Lygra is a small island at the mouth of the Lurefjorden in the Hordaland region of Norway. The small Lyrgra Church has been an important spiritual center since the Middle Ages.

3. Thoralfur was neither Sigurthur's foster brother (*fóstbróðir*) nor good friend (*góðr vinr*), and Sigurthur's glib posturing here suggests he is guilty of what the king is accusing him of. Foote (1965, 18) is equally cynical, viewing the saga-writer engaged in a kind of "theatrical game" wherein: "The author is teasing his audience in the same way, with doubt and suspicion, only it is obvious he does not expect us to remain either as fair-minded or simple-minded as the Norwegians appear to be."

among me and Thoralfur, I am level-headed enough that I would have effected such a deed at home in the Faroe Islands rather than in your backyard, your Majesty. So I must deny your accusations on behalf of myself and my entire crew, and I offer you my solemn oath in accordance with your laws. But if you think that I'm trying to get the better of you, then I'll perform the *járnburð* so you can see for yourself I have nothing to hide."[1]

When Sigurthur had finished, many men stepped forward in his defense, pleading that the king should concede Sigurthur's innocence; they thought Sigurthur had spoken well and said that his words exonerated him of all the king's charges.

The king replied: "Concerning this young man I'm greatly divided. If he has been slandered by my words, he's a good man. On the other hand, he might be more cunning than I think he is. My intuition leads me both ways, so I guess that he's going to need to prove himself innocent."

So, contrary to the entreaties of the audience, the king accepted Sigurthur's offer to perform the *járnburð*. Sigurthur was to come back the next day to Lygra; the bishop there would put him to through the ordeal. With that decided, the assembly was concluded.

The king returned to Lygra; Sigurthur and his crewmen went back to their ship. It soon grew dark as night approached.

Sigurthur addressed his companions. "It's true we've landed in big trouble and found ourselves in a massive web of lies. The king sees cunning and deceit, and our choice is very clear, if he is going to proceed, since he first had Thoralfur killed and now he is painting us as the criminals. He's using the *járnburð* as a diversion. Now I'm getting the worse of it in trying to reason with him. Look, a light breeze off the mountains is blowing in the channel. I say that we hoist sail and leave the harbor in our wake. Let Thrandur peddle his wool abroad some other summer if he wants it sold. If I ever sail abroad again, I'll have the good sense never to come back to Norway."

His companions felt this was a good plan. They unfurled and hoisted up the sail, and that very night they put out to sea from the harbor. They didn't break their journey until they reached the Faroe-Islands and their

---

1. There were several ordeals in the pagan Norse world used to test a person's mettle or honesty. The *járnburð* "iron-carrying" was an ordeal where the accused man would carry a hot iron in his hands to prove his testimony was honest. A variant was having the accused walk across a hot-iron plate. For a discussion of the practice of ordeals, see Magnusson and Pálsson's notes to *Laxdaela saga*, Chapter 18 (1969, 81). It is curious that Sigurthur would suggest the ordeal if he was innocent, since it is an overly strong denial, something which the king seems to pick up on in the subsequent exchange.

home at Göta. Thrandur voiced his disapproval of their journey, but they muttered their excuses and remained at home with Thrandur.

46. THE KING BROODS

It did not take long for King Olafur to find out that Sigurthur's ship had left harbor. At the time, the weight of general opinion remained against the king, as many people maintained that Sigurthur and his men might have been telling him the truth when they had denied the charge and spoke against it. King Olafur was suspiciously reluctant with his words during this meeting; he felt the truth of the matter was what he had suspected originally. The king returned to Lygra and took part in the banquet which was being held in his honor.

47. KARL-MAERSKUR

The following spring, King Olafur made preparations to set out from Nidaros,[1] and gathered around him a great band of his retainers both from Trondheim and the outlying territory. When the baggage train was ready, he led his retinue first south to Møre, where he raises an army of conscripts from the region, with some coming from neighboring Romsdale. Then he moved onward to Sunnmøre, and he stayed for a time at Herøy holding court.[2] There were numerous privy-council meetings, as many people had traveled to the island to seek his advice.

It was at one of these council meetings that King Olafur spoke openly of the great loss he felt over his retainer's death, a grievance he bore on account of the Faroe Islands. He complained, "and that tribute they promised me has still not arrived! So I think it's time to send some men after it!"

These last few words were addressed to various men in attendance

---

1. Recall "Nidaros" is an alternative name for the city of "Trondheim."
2. "Møre," "South-Møre," and "Romsdale" are all regions to the southwest of Trondheim along the Norwegian coast. "Herøy" is an island to the north of Stod (noted in the maps).

with the implication that they should ready themselves for the journey. Yet the replies from the crowd were in the negative; every man refused to undertake the trip.

At last, there stood up before the assembly a tall man of noble bearing; he wore a red tunic, a helmet adorned his head, and a sword hung at his side; his hand rested on a huge halberd. The man spoke as follows:

"Here is a truly great moment for men: You have a good king and he is in bad straits. Yet you refuse the mission which he is asking of you, when he has always bestowed you with gifts of friendship and generous shares of the spoils in the past! Up until now I've been no friend of our king; in fact, he has been my enemy—he knows well enough why. But I wish to offer to your king my services for this mission, if you, his people, are so unwilling to undertake it."

The king exclaimed, "Who is this hero of men that answers my call? You do much better than all others here by offering to go when they refused, especially as I feel they could have answered better. But I cannot assign you the task without first knowing your name."

The man said, "My name is not unfamiliar, my Lord; chances are that you might have heard it before. I am called Karl Maerskur."[1]

The king replied, "You're right, Karl. I have heard your name before. It's fair to say that there were times when, if we chanced to meet, you wouldn't have lived to tell the tale. But now I would have no other champion than you, offering your assistance without seeking any thanks and gratitude in return. Karl, will you step forward and be my messenger from this day forward? Come, let us discuss this further."

Karl agreed to be the king's agent in this matter.

48. Thrandur's Foster Sons Take Action

Karl Maerskr had been on viking expeditions and was an experienced raider; time and again, the king had deputized men to track him down and kill him. But Karl was an extremely resourceful man with noble bloodlines; he kept himself in fighting-trim and his physical prowess had seen

---

1. *Maerskur* refers to an individual from the Møre district, i.e. "Karl, the man from Møre."

48. Thrandur's Foster Sons Take Action

him through several tight spots. After Karl had volunteered for this mission, the king forgave his earlier offenses and then took him into his confidence, telling him to make ready for the journey as quickly as possible. Karl took some twenty men with him on his ship.

The king composed letters to his friends in the Faroe Islands: he planned to send Karl to Leifur Össursson and Gilli Lawspeaker for help and support; and he enclosed his royal seal as proof that the messages were genuine. As soon as preparations were complete, Karl set sail. They had good weather on the voyage, and when they came to the Faroe Islands, they landed at Thorshaven on Straumey.

A *thing* was called which many people attended. Thrandur of Göta came with a large party of men, as did Leifur and Gilli.

After tents had been pitched and booths set up, they went to meet with Karl-Maerskur. Polite introductions were made, then Karl delivered the letters along with King Olafur's seal and friendly greetings to Leifur and Gilli, who received these tokens amiably. Then they invited Karl to their farms to execute his errand and they offered him any support which they could give. Karl graciously accepted their help.

Sometime later Thrandur approached and bid Karl welcome. "I am always delighted when such noble-born men come to our Islands on royal orders that we're all duty-bound to follow. I would like nothing else, Karl, than for you to accompany me to my farm to sit out the winter—you and your mates—as your trip might take longer than you thought."

Karl replied that he had already agreed to go to Leifur's farm, saying, "Otherwise I would gladly take you up on your offer."

Thrandur sighed, "Well, this time the honor falls to Leifur. Is there anything else which I can do to assist you?"

Karl thought it would be a tremendous help if Thrandur collected tribute around Austurey and the other Northern Islands.

Thrandur said it would be his duty and privilege to show such hospitality to the king's messenger. Thrandur returned to his booth; and not much else happened at the *thing*. Afterward Karl went to stay with Leifur Össursson for the winter, and Leifur gathered the tribute from Straumey and all the southern Islands.

In the spring, Thrandur of Göta's health deserted him: his eyes grew rheumy and he suffered from a range of maladies. Nevertheless, he brought himself to travel to the *thing*, though it was painful for him. When he had arrived at the *thing* and pitched his tent-booth, he had a black tent put up underneath the main tent, as if the outer tent were a layer of snow resting on the inner one.

48. Thrandur's Foster Sons Take Action

After several days of the *thing* had passed, Leifur and Karl walked over to Thrandur's booth with their companions. As they neared the booth, some men were standing in front of the entrance. Leifur asked them whether Thrandur was inside, and they confirmed he was.

Leifur told them to ask Thrandur to come out, adding, "Karl has business to discuss with him."

When the men reappeared from the tent, they said that Thrandur had sensitive eyes and would not come out; "but he asked for you to come inside, Leifur."

Leifur turned to his companions to warn them to be on guard as they went inside the booth: "Don't crowd! The first one should go out when the last one comes in."

Leifur went in first, followed by Karl. Their companions entered next, weapons at the ready as if they were about to go into battle. Leifur proceeded into the black tent; in the inner darkness, he asked Thrandur where he was.

Thrandur responded by bidding Leifur welcome.

Leifur greeted him. He then asked whether Thrandur had collected any of the tribute around the Northern Islands, or whether he had plans for raising the silver.

Thrandur replied that what he and Karl had agreed upon had not slipped his mind and that he had made arrangements for the tribute:

"Here is a purse that you should take with you, Leifur; it's full of silver."

Leifur looked around the tent and made out some men; most were lounging in the hot springs, and a few were sitting around. Leifur strode over to Thrandur, took the purse, then found his way out of the tent into the full light of day. He poured out the silver on the surface of his shield, then swept the pile into his hands, and called over to Karl to come look at it.

They both studied it for a few moments.

At last Karl asked Leifur what he thought of the silver.

He spoke, "I think that the amount is stingy for what might have come from the Northern Islands."

Overhearing this from within the tent, Thrandur responded, "But doesn't it seem like especially fine silver to you, Leifur?"

"It does," he confirmed.[1]

---

1. The detail of the silver being refined and high-quality is significant; this silver is part of Thrandur's secret cache of the fortune which he gained in Chapter 3. Audiences of the saga would have known immediately that Thrandur had made no effort to collect tribute in the Northern Islands.

48. Thrandur's Foster Sons Take Action

Thrandur continued, "Those meddling middlemen! They're not like our kinsmen who can be trusted completely. In the spring, I sent men to raise the tribute from the Northern Islands as I was in no condition to do it myself, and they have skimmed a gratuity for themselves from those poor farmers who were thus defrauded when a fraction of their tribute was taken as payment. It's likely, Leifur, that some of the missing silver has already been paid to me in my land-rents."

Leifur picked up the silver, put it in the purse along with his own collected tribute, and handed it all to Karl. They counted the money. Karl asked what Leifur thought of the sum. He said that he thought it was pitiful: "It doesn't quite come to the tribute which we talked about gathering; and I don't want to hand this paltry collection over to the king."

One of the men who had been lounging in the pools, stood, pulled on a cloak, and spoke angrily, "The old saying is true: the older one gets, the more cowardly one becomes. It's certainly true of you, Thrandur, letting Karl Maerskur nag you for money all day long."

The speaker was Gautur the Red.

At Gautur's words, Thrandur leapt up and began cursing foully, levelling strong castigations toward his kinsmen. But finally he turned to Leifur, insisting he deliver the silver to the king, "and also take this purse which my tenant farmers delivered me this spring. If I weren't so dimsighted, I would do it myself."

One of the men in the springs propped himself up on his elbows; it was Thorthur the Short. He sneered at Leifur, "we don't need meddling from this Karl Maerskur, and he might someday get his just reward for it.

Leifur retrieved the purse and brought it to Karl. They both glanced at the silver within.

Then Leifur said, "There's no need to doubt it; what's here now is better than before. We would be happier to accept this, Thrandur. Shall we get one of your men to weigh it?"

Thrandur replied that he thought it best if Leifur saw to it himself.

Leifur and Karl stepped outside the tent for a moment. They found a spot and weighed the silver. Karl removed his helmet and deposited coins into it as the money was weighed. They noticed a man come up beside them, who carried a walking staff in his hand and was wearing the hood of a green cloak over his head; he was barefoot, though linen breeches covered his legs. This fellow set his staff down on the ground, then started walking away, calling over his shoulder, "Careful there, Maerskur-Karl, that you don't get hurt by my staff."

A moment later, the man came racing back, shouting vehemently at Leifur Össursson to go as quickly as possible to Gilli Lawspeaker's booth.

"Sigurthur Thorlaksson just burst into the tent and fatally wounded one of Gilli's attendants!"

Leifur sprang up immediately and ran off to find Gilli, and his companions all went with him, but Karl stayed seated on the ground and the Norwegian men stood in a ring around him. Suddenly Gautur the Red came at a leap into the line of men, chopping down at the men's necks with a hand-axe; the axe came down on Karl's head; he was wounded, but not badly. But then Thorthur the Short snatched the staff off the ground and struck down on the axe-head, lodging it deep into his brain. More attackers rushed out of Thrandur's tent.

Karl was dead, and his corpse was carried away.

Afterwards Thrandur expressed his disapproval over these actions and offered the tribute-money to his kinsmen, Leifur, as a settlement. Leifur and Gilli brought forward a lawsuit on Karl's behalf, but no compensation came from the legal action. Nonetheless, Sigurthur was outlawed for the wound he had dealt to Gilli's attendant, and Thorthur and Gautur were outlawed for killing Karl-Maerskur.

The Norwegians prepared Karl's old ship for the voyage and sailed east to meet with King Olafur; they became embroiled in the hostilities which were then taking place in Norway.[1]

The saga now turns to those events which took place after King Olafur tried to claim tribute from the Faroe Islands.

49. A Cunning Trap

After the killing of Karl Maerskur and the wounding of Gilli Lawspeaker's attendant, Sigurthur Thorlaksson, Thorthur the Short, and Gautur the Red were driven from the Faroe Islands in exile. Thrandur provided them with a seaworthy ship and some money, and they felt somewhat free

---

1. The end of Olaf Haraldursson's reign began in 1029 when Norwegian nobles supported King Canute of Denmark in his invasion of Norway. Olaf was driven into exile in the Kievan Rus', though he returned to fight for his crown later in the same year, when Canute's regent in Norway, Earl Hakon Eirikursson, was lost at sea. In the end, Olaf was killed in 1030 at the battle of Stiklestad, a small valley north of Trondheim, against an army of peasant farmers, revolting against his reign.

of him; the Thorlakssons had rebuked Thrandur harshly for appropriating their father's inheritance to them for himself instead of sharing it with them.

Thrandur quipped they had already gotten far more of it than they deserved, arguing that he had supported them all these years, and had often given them presents of money and livestock with little thanks.

Sigurthur and his kinsmen put out to sea with twelve other men; the rumor was that they intended to make for Iceland. They had only been sailing a short while when a great storm rose up, and the foul weather prevailed for nearly a week. Observers on shore saw that Sigurthur's ship was constantly being buffeted back toward the Islands; and people talked among themselves that the prospect of the voyage seemed grim.

In the autumn, the Islanders found wreckage from the ship washing up on Austurey. As winter set in, there were terrible hauntings among the farms in Göta and widely around Austurey. There were frequent sightings of the ghosts of Thrandur's kinsmen who were known to rough up the locals during these encounters: some farmers got some broken bones and other injuries.[1] The foster sons haunted Thrandur so badly that he didn't dare to set foot outside of the house alone that winter. There was much talk about these troubles around Austurey.

During the winter, Thrandur sent word to Leifur Össurson they should meet with each other to talk, and Leifur consented. At the meeting, Thrandur said, "Foster son, last summer at the *thing*, we encountered a serious problem in that the entire assembly almost broke out into open fighting. So now I propose that it be made into law, with your consent, that men may no longer carry weapons at the *thing*, a place where men should dispute the proceedings lawfully and in a considered manner."

Leifur expressed his approval at this; he advised, "we should talk about this with my cousin, Gilli." (Gilli's and Leifur's mothers were sisters.)

Soon they met with Gilli to discuss the proposal further. Gilli agreed with Leifur, "It makes a change for me to trust Thrandur. Let's agree that those of us who are the king's retainers and some of our servants be allowed to carry weapons, but that the general assembly be weaponless."

They continued discussing the ins-and-outs of the matter.

---

1. There is nothing (overly) fantastical in Icelandic folklore about ghosts walking around and inflicting bodily harm on the living, and such troublesome ghosts make appearances in several sagas, most terrifyingly, the shepherd Glam in *Grettir's Saga* (Chapter 33) and Killer-Hrapp of Hrappstead in *Laxdaela Saga* (Chapter 17).

49. A Cunning Trap

The winter passed, and the Islanders assembled that summer at the *thing* on Straumey.

One day, Gilli and Leifur emerged from their booths,[1] positioned on a slope overlooking the island, chatting about various things. They gazed east out over the island, basked in sunlight, and noticed a not unsizeable number of men were walking their way along the headland; they counted thirty of them, their well-polished shields and metal helmets gleaming with the sunshine. The group was heavily armed with axes and spears. Gilli and Leifur made out a figure in the lead, a muscular and imposing man in a red tunic, bearing a shield painted half-blue and half-gold; a helmet adorned his head and a wicked-looking halberd was held in his right-hand. They were almost positive the man was Sigurthur Thorlaksson. Behind the leader followed a compact man in a red tunic and sporting a red shield; they knew him by sight as Thorthur the Short. The third man in line bore a red shield, a cloak billowing in the wind, and a large battle-ax in his hands; this person could only be Gautur the Red.[2]

Leifur and his men turned back quickly to their own booths. Sigurthur's force was fast approaching, weapons at the ready.

Thrandur led a large group of men out from the assembly to meet Sigurthur; his men were all armed. Leifur and Gilli had only a few men compared to Thrandur, but the more alarming difference was that still fewer of their men had weapons.

Thrandur's men and the foster sons both turned to approach Leifur's small group, and Thrandur spoke shrewdly, "It's come to this, foster son, that my wayward kinsmen have come here and will go just as quickly from the Faroe Islands with bodies in their wake. Now I can't bear the thought that we kinsmen might be cut down because of cousin Gilli, so there are two choices: either I judge what's best for all of us, or, if you don't like it, I won't try to stop them from doing what they came here for."

Leifur and his men knew they were a meager fighting force against Thrandur's numbers so they chose to follow Thrandur's judgment, and immediately he laid out his decision, saying there was hardly a wiser alternative.

---

1. Attendees of a *thing* would erect tents or booths as a temporary shelter for the two weeks the assembly was being held.

2. Following Foote's interpretation (Foote 1965, 20), this is another instance where the saga-writer seems to have deliberately mislead the reader in an effort to build the drama; Sigurthur and the others did not die in the shipwreck, and the 'hauntings' around Austurey earlier in the chapter are now revealed to be the boys sneaking around farms, scavaging for food and shaking down the locals for aid. Thrandur's plot here is shown as especially devious, as Foote explains: "The final artistic touch in this play-acting, and the cream of the joke, is the statement that the dead-walkers went most for Thrand[ur]. If this is to allay suspicion of the plot, we surely have a thoroughness in the planning which betokens a genius for fraud" (Foote 1965, 20).

Thrandur proclaimed, "It's decided, then. I want my erstwhile kinsmen to be free to remain on the Faroe Islands as they please, even though they have been outlawed, and I wish for a sum of money to be provided for each of them. The rulership over the Faroe Islands is to be divided as follows: I shall rule a third of the Islands; Leifur shall have another; and let Sigmundur's sons govern the final third. Rule over the Islands has long been a bone of contention and an endless source of ill-will. I'd ask you, Leifur, my foster son, to foster a child yourself and for my part I'll foster your son, Sigmundur. I want to make things right by you again."

Leifur replied, "I would like to foster a child, but the decision should be up to Thora whether she wants her son to go to you or stay with us."

They parted with matters thus settled.

When Thora agreed to the fostering, she groaned to Leifur, "Seems to me there might have been another way out of your jam: I wouldn't have chosen that wily foster father for my little Siggy if I had my druthers, because I've always thought that Thrandur had quite enough young men at his beck-and-call already."

Thora and Leifur's son Sigmundur was packed off to Göta to be looked after by Thrandur. He was just three years old at the time, but he was a promising little tyke, and he grew up at the farm there.[1]

50. THORHALLUR THE WEALTHY

While King Svein and his mother Alfifa ruled over Norway,[2] Thrandur resided at home in Göta with his kinsmen, Sigurthur, Thorthur, and Gautur the Red. The story goes that Thrandur never married, yet he had a daughter named Guthrun.

One day, when his kinsmen had been living with him for a while, Thrandur came to talk with them: he didn't want them to stay any longer, lazing around the farm in a stupor. Sigurthur responded in a temper. He complained that Thrandur begrudged them the slightest thing and was

---

1. Typically cynical, Foote comments here: "Thrand[ur] offers to take Leif[ur]'s young son to foster and this too is typically ambiguous, for although he is overtly making a gesture of reconciliation, he will also in effect be gaining a hostage" (Foote 1965, 20).

2. Svein Canutesson, son of Canute the Great, was regent of Norway with his mother Alfifa (*Aelfgifu* in Old English sources) from 1030 to 1035. Sent to rule Norway by Canute, who was then King of England, Svein and Alfifa were considered harsh rulers and were driven out by the Norwegians in 1035.

withholding the inheritance from Sigurthur's father. Bitter words were exchanged between them.

After this, the boys left Göta. They went to Straumey, the most thickly settled of the Faroe Islands. A man named Thorhallur the Wealthy kept a farm on the island. He had a wife named Birna, known as Straumey-Birna, who was exceptionally haughty and beautiful. At the time when this part of the saga takes place, Thorhallur was clearly showing his age; and Birna had been wed to him only on account of his wealth.

Thorhallur had nearly all his money loaned out at interest to several people, but little of it was being paid back to him.

Sigurthur, Thorthur, and Gautur arrived on Straumey and went to talk to Thorhallur at his farm. Sigurthur offered to collect half of his money from those who were the most unwilling to repay their debts. If he managed to gather any money, he would take an amount from the interest which he felt necessary to charge for his efforts, and the landowner would recoup some share of his investment. This seemed harsh to Thorhallur, but that was their bargain.

Sigurthur went far and wide around the Faroe Islands collecting Thorhallur's money and delivering him as much as he thought necessary. Soon Sigurthur had assembled such a huge sum of money that he became rich almost overnight.

Sigurthur and his two kinsmen took up residence in Thorhallur's household. More often than not Sigurthur and Birna could be stumbled upon talking together, and there was gossip among the servants that they might be having an affair.

The boys from Göta stayed the winter on Straumey.

In the spring, Sigurthur stated his wish to run the farm in partnership with Thorhallur. The farmer was rather against the idea before the lady of the house had her say; the farmer decided to let the housewife make the decision. She and Sigurthur eagerly took control of the household, while Thorhallur was essentially tossed aside and neglected, and Birna and Sigurthur managed everything on the farm the way they wanted.

51. Unwelcome Guests Arrive

The saga relates that a ship traveling to the Faroe Islands was shipwrecked off South Island that summer. Most of the cargo was lost and five

51. Unwelcome Guests Arrive

of the twelve crew members drowned, but seven made it safely to land, including the brothers who had captained the lost ship, Hafgrimur, Bjarngrimur, and Hergrimur. They were short on food and other necessities.

Sigurthur, Thorthur, and Gautur went out to meet the castaways, explained where they had come ashore, and then invited everyone to come back home with them.

When the group arrived, Thorhallur stormed off to find Birna, as he felt it had been rash to bring these men to the farm.

Sigurthur replied that everything would turn out all right.

The castaways remained at the farm as honored guests, being treated rather better than Thorhallur himself.

The farm's rightful master, Thorhallur, was intolerant of the guests; there were often nasty words between him and Bjarngrimur, in particular.

One evening when the men were gathered in the sitting room, there was a heated exchange between Thorhallur and Bjarngrimur. Thorhallur was seated on a bench, his hands playing with a stick; but as his language grew heated, he started waving it around violently. He was near-sighted and no judge of distance, and suddenly the stick hit Bjarngrimur smack on the nose. Bjarngrimur flew into a rage and groped for his axe, wanting to bury it in Thorhallur's skull. Sigurthur leapt quickly to his feet and restrained Bjarngrimur, saying that amends would be made. The anger passed, and the two men were reconciled.

The shipwrecked men stayed over the winter, and there were occasional altercations between them and Thorhallur after this episode.

When the winter was behind them, Sigurthur declared his intention to provide for the castaways in some way.

He gave them a sea-going merchant-ship which he and Thorhallur owned jointly. Thorhallur made grumblings that he was displeased about this, until the lady of the house had a word in his ear. Sigurthur arranged provisions for them, and they went down to the ship; the men slept in the ship at night, but came home to the farm during the day.

For a time they adapted to this way of living. Then, one morning, they walked up to the farmhouse; Sigurthur was away from the farm on business, taking care of errands which needed his attention; nevertheless, the men spent the day at the farm. On his way home, Sigurthur passed by the dock; the merchants were loading cargo hastily onto the ship.

When he came aboard, Sigurthur asked where Thorhallur the farmer was; the reply was given that he was sleeping.

"It's an odd time to be asleep," said Sigurthur darkly. "Is he even dressed? We should ask him if he wants dinner."

A trip was made to the sleeping loft. There lay Thorhallur asleep in his bed, just as Sigurthur had been told. Yet as Sigurthur stepped forward and approached the old man's bed, it was instantly clear that Thorhallur was dead. Sigurthur inspected the bedclothes and saw that there was blood everywhere; the wound was found beneath Thorhallur's left hand: he had been stabbed through the heart with a sharp fire-iron.

Sigurthur swore that this was the darkest of dark deeds; "Something that only that vile Bjarngrimur could have done as revenge for getting struck in the face by the old man's stick. Thorthur, Gautur, let's go back to the ship and see if we can get our own revenge for this."

The Göta-kinsmen took their weapons and they rushed down to the ship, with Sigurthur carrying a huge battle-axe in his hands. Swearing foully at Bjarngrimur, Sigurthur sprang onto the ship at once; the brothers were already on their feet at the sound of the cursing and swearing. Sigurthur charged directly at Bjarngrimur; he swung the axe in a vicious two-handed arc which plunged the axe-head deep into his chest; the blow killed him instantly. Thorthur the Short slashed at Hafgrimur with his sword, catching him on the shoulder, lopping off his arm and slicing open his entire side; he slumped down, dead. Gautur the Red made an overhead chop with his axe into Hergrimur's skull which cleaved the man in two down to his shoulders. When all three were dead, Sigurthur announced he would not harm any of the other four men, but he insisted on taking anything valuable the brothers had in their possession, though there wasn't much.

Sigurthur, Thorthur, and Gautur returned home with the valuables they claimed from the merchants. Sigurthur believed he had properly avenged Thorhallur the farmer. Not long after these events, however, a nasty gossip spread about Sigurthur and his kinsmen regarding Thorhallur's death.

Sigurthur openly courted Birna and soon moved in the house with her, raising hers and Thorhallur's many children.

52. Gautur the Red on Sandey

There was a man named Thorvaldur who farmed on Sandey with his wife Thorbera. He was a wealthy man, owning livestock and farmland, but he was getting on in years when this part of the saga takes place.

Gautur the Red went to see Thorvaldur and offered to collect the money due to him, as very few were repaying the loans they had borrowed from him. A deal was struck along the same lines as that between Thorhallur and Sigurthur.

Most days, Gautur was just as likely to be at Thorvaldur's place as at Sigurthur's, and the rumor quickly spread that Gautur was romping in the hay with Thorvaldur's wife. During this time, Gautur was raking in a tidy sum for himself.

One day a man who owed Thorvaldur money showed up at the farm; he was a fisherman. That night, the fire was burning low in the sitting room where the men were gathered, when Thorvaldur started pestering the fisherman for his money; the man responded slowly and somewhat evasively.

Gautur and some men were pacing the room in the shadows.

When nearly everyone had left the sitting-room to go to bed, Thorvaldur sneered, "Go ahead, you scoundrel! Sink your axe into the breast of an innocent old man."

His body slumped against the wall-panels, he was dead before he fell to the floor.

When Gautur heard the thump, he sprang in the direction of the fisherman and dispatched him with a single blow, saying afterward that he couldn't have let such wickedness go unavenged.

Then Gautur took up residence with the widow and took her as his wife.

53. Leifur Thorirsson

Leifur was the son of Thorir Beinirsson. His livelihood was making trading runs between Norway and the Faroe Islands, and he was well-off for money. Every now and then, when he was stopped over on the Faroe Islands, he stayed with Leifur Össursson or with Thurid Strong-Widow and her sons.

There was one time when Leifur Thorirsson's ship had just returned to the Faroe Islands that Sigurthur Thorlaksson invited Leifur to stay with him on Straumey, and the offer was accepted. But Leifur Össursson came down to the ship and didn't take it lightly when he learned that the other Leifur had agreed to stay with Sigurthur; he felt it wasn't a good idea, and stated that Leifur Thorirsson would have been more than welcome to come home with him to South Island. Leifur Thorirsson replied the matter was already settled, and he set off for Sigurthur's farm. He was seated on the high seat next to Sigurthur, who acted the gracious host toward him.[1]

Leifur Thorirsson spent the winter on Sigurthur's farm as an honored guest.

54. Death and an Omen

One day during the following spring, Sigurthur announced that he was off to collect a payment from his neighbor, Björn:

"I'd appreciate it, Leifur, if you come with me as a bit of extra muscle for our meeting. Björn is very hot-tempered, and it's been a long time since I've been repaid anything from him."

Leifur agreed to go with him, if Sigurthur wanted him to.

The two walked over to Björn's farm. Sigurthur demanded his money; Björn told him what he could do with his demands, and a brawl broke out. Björn made a swing at Sigurthur, but Leifur jumped between them, and Björn's axe caught him in the head. Sigurthur leapt at the distracted Björn and killed him with his sword, and that was the end of the fight.

News of these events spread throughout the Faroe Islands.

There was endless gossip about Sigurthur, and ill-will began to emerge toward him among the Islanders.

Thurid Strong-Widow and her daughter Thora constantly goaded Leifur Össursson about the fact that he would never lift a finger to address any of the wrongs which his Göta-kinsmen had wrought. His wife withheld sex from him, and both women regarded him with distain, but he endured this treatment civily and patiently. The women took his patience for cowardice and uselessness. The death of Leifur Thorirsson bothered his female relatives to no end; they felt it in their bones that Sigurthur had slain him.

It is said that one night Thurid, mistress of her own household, had

---

1. At meals, the family and guests were arranged at the table sitting on long benches; the high bench, or seat, was slightly elevated, reserved for the master of the household and honored guests.

a dream in which her husband Sigmundur Brestirsson appeared before her and spoke to her:

"God himself has allowed me to come here into your dreams. Don't bear resentment or ill-will toward your son-in-law Leifur, since it's destined for him to right the injustices which rankle your heart."

At Sigmundur's words, Thurid woke up, and went and told her daughter Thora about the dream. From then on, the women treated Leifur better than they had before.

55. Another Narrow Escape

The saga tells of a ship from abroad which landed on the Faroe Islands not far from Sigurthur's farm on Straumey. The eighteen-member crew was Norwegian, and their captain was a man called Arnljotur.

There was a fellow named Skopti who lived down at the wharf on Straumey; his livelihood was helping traders with their cargos and attending to their needs in harbor. Everybody liked him and treated him with respect.

Having docked the ship, the captain came over to talk with Skopti.

"I'd like a word with you in private," he began. "Those men Sigurthur Thorlaksson killed, Bjarngrimur and his brothers; they were my sons. I want you to help me find a way to take Sigurthur and his kinsmen by surprise and get revenge for my sons."

Skopti agreed Sigurthur had never received his due comeuppance, and promised Arnljotur that he would be on the lookout for the opportunity for them to attack Sigurthur.

There was a particular occasion that summer when the three kinsmen, Sigurthur, Thorthur, and Gautur, were out in a boat, heading for an outlying island to pick up some sheep for slaughter. (It is the custom of the Faroe-Islanders to eat fresh meat all year round). While they were off-island, Skopti got word to Arnljotur. The Norwegians set off after them right away, fifteen of them in the ship's dinghy, and rowed out to the island where Sigurthur and the boys were working; twelve men climbed up onto the island, while three stayed below to guard their boat.

Sigurthur noticed the men as they crested the island, and the kinsmen

55. Another Narrow Escape

contemplated who these men could be. The strangers were wearing dyed-wool clothes and carrying weapons.[1]

"Could be," mused Sigurthur, "that here are those merchants who came into harbor this summer ... and maybe, the reason they're here is to set up a trading-post and want to do business with us. Whatever the case, we should be ready to deal with them. Let's start walking toward them, but make like Sigmundur Brestirsson: if there's trouble, everybody run for themselves down to the shore and we'll all meet at the boats."

The two sides approached each other. Suddenly, Arnljotur gave the war-cry to his men to avenge his sons. Sigurthur's trio turned heel and ran down to the shore; they all made it to the boat alive, but some of Arnljotur's men were right behind them and came rushing at them. Siguthur swung low at an attacker, taking out both legs below the knees, then finished him off. Thorthur slew a second man, while Gautur dispatched a third. Then the boys leapt onto their boat and rowed parallel to shore until they found the guarded dinghy. Sigurthur jumped from one boat to the other, stabbed one of the guards, and threw two others into the sea. They stole the dinghy, rowed away in both boats, and arrived safely back home.

Sigurthur rounded up some men, headed straight back out to the island, and charged up onto the bluffs. The Norwegians sprang into formation, ready to defend themselves.

Thorthur the Short cautioned, "It would be better to make a truce with these men, Sigurthur. The advantage is clearly on our side, and we've already dealt Arnljotur heavy losses."

Sigurthur considered this. "That was well said, but they are going to have to submit themselves entirely to my authority, if they want to have a truce."

The standoff ended with the Norwegians giving Sigurthur self-judgment to arbitrate their dispute; and he fined Arnljotur three shares of wergild for the attempted murder of the three of them. Arnljotur paid the entire sum then and there (he was from the Hebrides, after all); and Sigurthur turned it back over to him in atonement for his sons; then, the Hebridean sailed abroad from the Faroes.

Sigurthur knew of Skopti's treachery, though he spared him his life. When the traders left, he sailed with them to Norway and was thereafter outlawed from the Faroe Islands.

---

1. The poorer locals would be wearing wool that was undyed; dyed fabric was outlandish and extravagant, so it is easy for Sigurthur to pick the strangers out as wealthy off-islanders.

56. An Opportunity Arises

The saga now turns to the time when Sigurthur Thorlaksson was pushing his brother, Thorthur, to get married.

Thorthur asked which woman Sigurthur had in mind.

"I won't rank the choices when it seems the best woman is right here in the Faroe Islands, namely, Thurid Strong-Widow."

"I don't think that highly of myself," replied Thorthur.

"You won't get her, if we don't ask," countered Sigurthur wryly.

"I wouldn't dare try," said Thorihur anxiously, "and I would scarcely believe that she wants to give herself away to me."

Another day, Sigurthur went over to Skufey and presented the proposal to Thurid. She didn't reply immediately, so Sigurthur talked up his kinsman's virtues. In the end, she said she would discuss the question with her sons and friends, and then she would send word to Sigurthur as to where things stood.

Sigurthur went home and reported the highlights of her reply to his brother.

"It's turned out wonderfully so far," gruffed Thorthur. "I doubt she's even taking this seriously."

Thurid met with her son-in-law and daughter, Leifur and Thora, and told them about the marriage proposal.

Thora wanted to know how her mother intended to reply.

Thurid had thought much about it, but didn't know how she felt.

"What's your advice, Thora?"

Her daughter replied, "You wouldn't be surprised if I told you there is something turning in your heart, driving you to seek a way to avenge the slights made against our family. I don't see any other bait more tempting to lure them out than this. I don't need to put words in your mouth, mother. You can draw them out several ways so that they don't suspect anything."

Leifur agreed with Thora, adding that they should take pains to ensure that they got what they deserved. They decided on the day when they would put their plan into action.

With everything arranged, Leifur offered a word of warning, "Thrandur has looked out for those boys for a long time. Ever since he raised us as our foster-father. I put it on you, Thora, that it's the death of our son Sigmundur, if he's with Thrandur when anything happens between us and Sigurthur."

Thora smiled. "I don't think little Siggy will be staying there much longer. It's time for us to be off to Austurey and for you to have a chat with your foster father, Thrandur."

And so they were all agreed.

57. Flight from Austurey

Leifur, Thurid, and Thora set out together in a ship for Austurey, with a company of seven men. Throughout the trip, they took water over the bow and nearly everyone got thoroughly soaked that day; Thora was the only one in dry clothes.[1] They marched up to the farm at Göta, where Thrandur gave them a warm welcome and ordered the servants to stoke up the fire for Leifur and his companions, while Thora was led into the sitting room where her boy Sigmundur was playing; he was already nine years old and a handful to watch.

Thora asked her son what Thrandur had been teaching him, and the boy reported that he had learned all about prosecuting lawsuits, his own legal rights and the legal rights of others; Thrandur had made everything clear to him. Then Thora pressed him about what his foster father had taught him about the Holy Scriptures. Sigmundur said he had learned the *Pater noster* and the Apostles' Creed. Thora wanted to hear him say them, which he did, and it seemed to her that he could recite the *Pater noster* fairly well, but Thrandur's version of the Creed went like this:

> *I go out not alone,*
> *following me are four,*
> *five of God's angels.*
> *I carry this prayer with me,*
> *this prayer to Christ.*
> *I sing seven psalms,*
> *May God be my rock.*[2]

---

1. This seems symbolic: A devout Christian, Thora's motherly love for Sigmundur is overcoming Thrandur's pagan magic which controls of the weather.

2. Thrandur's creed is clearly not the Apostles' Creed (*Credo in deum*), the proclamation of Christian faith which begins: "I believe in God the Father Almighty, Maker of heaven and earth" (Church of England, Book of Common Prayer). According to Foote, "The *Pater noster* and the *Credo in deum* were obligatory learning for every Christian, joined in the course of the 13th century by the *Ave*. (The absence of the last from the story in the saga may be taken as an indication of early date [of the saga's composition])" (Foote, 1984, 193). While not the Apostle's Creed, the prayer which Sigmundur recites is Christian in orgin (Foote, 1984, 193). Thrandur's prayer is of historical interest as one of the earliest *continued on page 122*

At this Thrandur burst into the sitting room, demanding to know what they were talking about.

Thora replied evenly that her son Sigmundur was reciting the lessons which Thrandur had taught to him; "but that's not the way the Creed goes."

"As you know," lectured Thrandur, "it is written that Christ had twelve disciples, maybe more, and each one understood their own creed. Now, I have my own creed, and you have the version you learned, but there are several versions, and so there is not one right way to recite it."[3]

The conversation lapsed.

The guests received every hospitality, and that evening there was very heavy drinking. Thrandur was in great spirits, and later bid them to sleep in the sitting-room and had mattresses laid out on the floor.

Leifur replied that would be perfect.

Thora said she wanted Sigmundur to tell her more about his lessons and to sleep beside her for the night.

Thrandur sighed, "Ah, maybe not. I can never sleep at night without Sigmundur in the room."

"Won't you indulge me this once, Thrandur, my dear?" wheedled Thora.

In the end, the boy slept in the sitting room with his family, while Thrandur retired for the night to one of the smaller outbuildings where

---

specimens of "a morning or going-out prayer but chiefly in use in modern Europe as a night-prayer or sleep-charm for children" (Foote 1984, 189). Linguistically and textually, these lines in the Icelandic manuscript have received much scrutiny. The "creed" text in *Flateyjarbók* was written in the 14th century, but the Old Icelandic has archaic or dialectal features, suggesting the "creed" itself far predates composition. Evidence of distortion of the original form of these lines is residual presence of the ordinal numbers: in the seven lines of verse, the numbers "one," "four," "five," and "seven" appear; "two," "three," and "six" are lacking; compare this to a modern Faroese version which runs: *"fylgja mér einn, tveir, Þrír, fjórir, fimm guðs englar"* ("one, two, three, four, five of God's angels follow me") (see Foote 1984, 203). In *A note on Þránd's kredda* (Foote 1984, 206–207), Foote argues from verb morphology that the verses may composed in an early form of the Faroese language; this would lend a vernacular and ignorant flavor to Thrandur's attempt at the Creed. For a full linguistic and textual analysis of Thrandur's "creed," see Foote 1984, 199–208.

3. The Old Icelandic text has *laerisveina* "disciples"; strictly speaking, Christ had twelve apostles, but many disciples. Thrandur's lack of specifity here, not to mention his spurious version of the Apostles' Creed, underscores that he has little true familiarity with the tenets of Christianity. Foote comments: "It seems likely for one thing that the author wanted to stress the confusion and difference between ... the familiar but still formal Latin *credo* of the catechism and hours, and *kreddan* ['prayers'], a name presumably already applied to popular, venacular morning and evening prayers of Þránd[ur]'s kind. It is also hard to avoid the thought that Þránd's defence contains an oblique reference to the well-known story concerning the composition of the creed by the apostles themselves, and that the author expects us to understand that Þránd[ur] has got hold of the wrong end of the stick" (Foote 1984, 194–195). For a revealing discussion of Thrandur and Christianity, see *Thrandur and the Apostles* (Foote 1984, 188–198).

he and Sigmundur and some of the men were in the habit of sleeping. Thrandur settled into his bunk, though he lay awake for much of the night.

Leifur got ready for bed, lay down, and rolled away from his wife. Thora tapped him on the back, warning in hushed tones that he shouldn't fall asleep.

"Get up," she whispered. "Get some men. Go round Austurey tonight and disable all the boats so that they can't put out to sea."

The men got to work. Leifur knew every inlet on the island well. Anything that could float, they sabotaged so it wasn't sea-worthy.

They didn't sleep that night. At dawn, they got up and Thora slipped down to the ship. Leifur went down to the sleeping-quarters, and said goodbye to Thrandur and thanked him for his hospitality, quickly adding, "By the way, Thora wants Sigmundur to come home with her."

Thrandur had gotten little sleep during the night, and responded groggily that it was an impossibility for Sigmundur to leave.

While Leifur raced down to the ship, the reality of what he had been saying began to dawn on Thrandur. Thrandur barked orders to his servants to take some skiffs and go after them; and a bunch of men dashed off to prepare the skiffs. The pursuers rowed from the beach, but coal-black water poured in, and they were lucky just to make it back to shore alive. There wasn't a sea-going boat on the island. In his present condition, Thrandur wasn't sure if what had happened was a good thing or a bad thing.

Leifur sailed straight home and immediately gathered a force of men at his farm. This was the day before Sigurthur and his kinsmen were to come for a visit.

58. The Vengeance of the Skuf-Islanders

The saga now returns to Sigurthur Thorlaksson and his kinsmen. The next morning while they were preparing to leave home, Sigurthur kept urging them to hurry.

Thorthur retorted that they only had a short distance to travel. "And I think you might be fated to die, as you are so eager to be on your way."

"Don't make a fool of yourself," snorted Sigurthur. "And don't be so anxious—there's no danger. We can be sure that they won't dare violate the peaceable meeting which we've agreed on."

"That's your opinion," countered Thorthur, "but it would surprise me if we all came home tonight alive."

They took twelve men with them in the ship; everyone brought their weapons. Throughout the day, the weather was stormy and the currents were threatening, but they managed to hold course, and arrived at Skufey.

At the landing, Thorthur stated that he would go no further.

Sigurthur snapped that he was going up to the farm, even if the rest of them wouldn't.

Thorthur forewarned him that he was about to die.

Sigurthur stalked up onto the island. He was wearing a red tunic under a blue cloak, the straps of which were affixed to his shoulders; a sword clanged at his hips, and he wore a helm on his head. He ascended the path up the island, and when he got closer to the farm buildings, he saw that all the doors were shut. A church stood in the home meadow across from the door of the farmhouse; it was the church which Sigmundur had built. As Sigurthur strode into the yard between the farmhouse and the church, he noticed the church door open and a woman came out of the church, dressed in a red tunic and blue cloak draped over her shoulders. Sigurthur recognized her as the lady of the house and started walking toward her. Thurid greeted him in a friendly fashion and she strolled over to a log-bench in the home meadow. As they were about to sit down on the log-bench, she wanted to sit looking at the church, but he preferred to keep an eye on the door of the house. But Thurid insisted, so they sat facing the church.

Sigurthur asked her which of her male relatives had come to meet with him.

"A few men," she replied vaguely.

"Is Leifur here?" inquired Sigurthur, uncertain.

"He's not." Thurid said simply.

"Are your sons at home?" persisted Sigurthur.

"Oh, somewhere within ear-shot," answered Thurid breezily.

"So ... what did they have to say about the proposal?" Sigurthur asked.

"We discussed it," replied Thurid, "Everyone agreed what you propose is best. Moreover, there's no need to delay the wedding on my part, if you are amenable."

"Looks like my streak of bad luck is ending!" cried Sigurthur with relief. "Could be that everything is turning out for the best! I'm a carefree man!"

58. The Vengeance of the Skuf-Islanders

"Could be," agreed Thurid stonily.

In his exuberance, Sigurthur raised his arms and tried to embrace her, but at that moment she snatched the straps of his cloak, grabbing them tightly. At this signal, the house door flew open and a man burst out, sword at the ready. It was Heri Sigmundursson. At the sight of Heri, Sigurthur fumbled down out of his own cloak, and managed to free himself of it, though Thurid tried to hold him by the cloak straps. Several more men appeared out of hiding, as Sigurthur sprinted down across the meadow. Heri snatched up a spear, and dashed across the meadow in hot pursuit. Heri caught up quickly and hurled the spear at Sigurthur. Out of the corner of his eye, Sigurthur saw the spear flying toward his back; he dove to the ground, as the spear sailed over his head, landing upright in the grasses ahead. Sigurthur sprang to his feet, grabbed the spear, and sent it hurtling back at Heri. It pierced his stomach; Heri slumped to the ground, and quickly died. Sigurthur darted down the path, as Leifur ran to where Heri lay dying, but Leifur was up again in an instant, chasing Sigurthur down the island to the landing.

People say that it was fifteen meters from the farm down to the inlet. Leifur slowed to a stop at the shore, cast around for their ship, then took off at a sprint. Sigurthur had just reached the ship and was about to jump aboard; Leifur thrust his sword at the man's side as Sigurthur turned to face him, and the sword plunged in up to the hilt, exactly as Leifur had intended. Sigurthur made a weak leap onto the ship which was moving off from shore. It was a narrow escape.

Leifur ran up onto the island to his men, instructing them to head for the boats. "We're going after them!"

They asked whether he knew Heri was dead and if he had caught up to Sigurthur.

He snapped that he didn't want to talk about it now.

Leifur took eighty men in two ships, and the difference of speed between him and his quarry was not insignificant.

Sigurthur's party landed back on Straumey. Sigurthur himself had skippered the ship, but he'd uttered few words to the crew. As they disembarked the ship, Thorthur wanted to know how bad the wound was.

Sigurthur wasn't exactly sure.

Sigurthur limped along the path to the boathouse which stood just up from the beach, his hands pressed at his side. The men began unloading the ship, and later, when they brought their gear up to the boathouse, they saw Sigurthur propped against the wall of the boathouse, rigid in death.

They carried his body to the house. No one spoke of what had happened that day.

They gathered for supper and were still eating when Leifur's men reached the farm and the assault began. Fire was set to anything that burned. Sigurthur's men mounted a noble defense; at first, there were eleven of them in the house, but thirty more came running from neighboring farms. When the farmhouse caught fire, Gautur the Red burst out, being unable to breathe inside any longer. Steingrimur Sigmundursson and two others came at him, but he fought them off. Gautur slashed at Steingrimur's knee, the blade connecting with the knee-cap. (It was a bad wound; for the rest of his days, he would walk with a limp). Gautur quickly felled both other attackers, then he rushed at Leifur Össursson. The two fought with a flash of swords, but it ended with Leifur slaying Gautur.

Then, Thorthur the Short ran from the house, only to be met by Brandur Sigmundursson, flanked by two companions. They attacked Thorthur at once; in a quick skirmish, Thorthur killed Brandur and both of his friends. But there was Leifur Össursson ready to avenge them. Leifur thrust his sword into Thorthur with the same vicious force with which he had stabbed his kinsman, Sigurthur, and Thorthur fell dead.

59. The Saga Ends

After the events at Sigurthur's farm, Leifur returned home. He earned a great reputation for what he had done.

When Thrandur found out what had happened to his foster sons, he felt such remorse that he died from grief.

Leifur now ruled alone over the entire Faroe Islands. This was in the days of King Magnus Olafsson the Good.[1]

Leifur travelled to Norway to meet with King Magnus, who granted him the right to rule the Faroe Islands as a fief. Then he returned home to the Faroes and farmed there into his old age.

His son Sigmundur lived at the farm on South Island after his father's death, and was a great chieftain among the Islanders.

---

1. Illegitimate son of Olafur Haraldursson, King Magnus Olafson the Good ruled Norway from 1035 to 1042, and over both Denmark and Norway from 1042 to 1047. There is an extant saga which details his life, *Magnus the Good's saga*.

59. The Saga Ends

Thurid and Leifur both died sometime during the reign of King Magnus, and Thora lived for the rest of her life with her son Sigmundur. She was always regarded as the most noble of women.

Sigmundur had a son named Hafgrimur, who himself had two sons Einar and Skeggi, who were both very recently king's bailiffs on the Faroe Islands.[1]

Sigmundur's son, Steingrimur the Lame farmed on Skuf Island and was considered a good man. Here the saga ends about the lives of Sigmundur Brestirsson and his offspring.

---

1. This remark is a tantalizing internal clue as to the date of composition of the *Faroe-Islander Saga*. There is conjecture that the Einar who is mentioned as bailiff (*sýslumaðr*) is the same Einar who is mentioned in the lesser known *Boglunga saga*, which is dated fairly tightly to c. 1220 (see Foote 1965, 11). The *Faroe-Islander Saga* seems to be written between 1220 and 1230, based on this and other evidence.

Appendix A: Excerpt of Jómsvíkinga saga, Chapters 31–33

The account of the invasion of Norway by the Jomsvikings and their defeat at Hjorungavágr by Earl Hakon and his sons in Chapter 27 of *Faroe-Islander Saga* is incomplete. However, a rival version of the battle is given in the following excerpt from *Jomsviking Saga* (*Jómsvíkinga saga*), Chapters 31–33. This saga survives in four Icelandic versions and in a Latin translation dating originally to the mid-13th century, and provides rich backstory on the cult of the Jomsvikings and their leaders. There is a highly readable English translation with facing Old Icelandic text, a historical introduction, notes, and appendices by N.F. Blake, *The Saga of the Jomsvikings* (London: Thomas Nelson and Sons, 1962).

Whereas *Faroe-Islander Saga* presents the Jomsvikings as vile marauders—a trial for Earl Hakon to deal with and another worthy foe to Sigmundur Brestirsson to dispatch heroically—their saga presents the Jomsvikings as a kind of viking-era Marine Corps, elite warriors who are honor-bound by a solemn vow to wage war against Earl Hakon of Norway on behalf of King Svein of Denmark. Among the Jomsvikings, there was strict discipline: only men between eighteen and fifty were admitted into their ranks; no women were allowed inside their fortress; all spoils were divided equally; and no warrior could remain a Jomsviking who had shown fear in battle (see Gordon 1956, 23; the tenth selection in that volume provides the account of the Jomsvikings from *Ólafs saga Trygvassonar*). Their legendary stronghold, Jómsborg, was established in the 10th century on the small island of Wollin, at the mouth of the Oder River on the Baltic coast, not far from modern Szczecin in Poland. While many characters in *Jomsviking Saga* are historical and the battle of Hjorungavágr is considered a genuine event, the saga itself "is of no historical worth" (Blake 1962, 7).

The Jomsvikings were clearly disciplined fighters, who probably served as a mercenary contingent of a larger Danish army in the historical battle against the Norwegians (Blake 1962, 14). According to Blake, the battle of Hjorungavágr took place some time between 974 and 983, and was likely a Danish operation against Earl Hakon's seat of power at Lade near Trondheim. Earl Hakon had refused to acknowledge the overlordship of or pay tribute to the crown in Denmark, and in the aftermath of Hjorungavágr, Earl Hakon solidified his control of much of Norway from the imperium of the Danes.

The excerpts below join the action at the climax of *Jomsviking Saga*. The Jomsviking fleet, led by Sigvaldi and his lieutenants Vagn and Bui, has been tricked into a decisive battle against the Earls' forces at Hjorungavágr, a fjord near Møre in western Norway. The chapters do more than supplement the missing scenes from *Faroe-Islander Saga*. The defeat of the Jomsvikings is rightly famous in the literary pantheon of saga battles due to Earl Hakon's pagan worship of the cult goddess Thorgerd Holgi's-Bride and her sister Irpa, who join the battle on the Norwegian side under the cover of a torrential hailstorm. It is significant that the detail of Earl Hakon's blood sacrifice of his own seven-year old boy is not mentioned in the *Faroe-Islander Saga* account of the battle; perhaps the saga-writer considered this pagan act too overpowering to the stylistic portrayal of the balanced contest between Christianity and paganism which prevails throughout the saga.

31. The Battle of Hjorungavágr

Then the two fleets drifted close enough to attack one another, and it wasn't before long that a fierce melee was underway with both sides fighting heroically. The stories relate that Sigvaldi's vikings matched Earl Hakon's and Earl Svein's crews blow-for-blow with neither side yielding an inch of their decks. Elsewhere, Earl Eirikur's men were caught up in a similar battle with Vagn's forces. But on the flank that Bui and his brother were attacking from, Bui was dropping opponents with such savage death-blows that his foes were starting to fall back from him. In their disorderly retreat to their own ships, Bui was able to punch a hole in the Earls' battle-line. Seeing this, the Jomsvikings roared their war-cry and sounded their battle-horns vigorously. When Earl Eirikur realized what was happening, he brought his ship over to the weak flank and directed the attack against Bui. The ship-to-ship fighting was the fiercest anyone had ever witnessed, and yet the Earl only managed to reestablish the battle-line; he could not press any advantage.

Just then, Eirikur's men heard a triumphant war-cry come from the direction of Vagn's ships. They rowed toward the scene of action: having burst through the front door, Vagn was ravaging the house, breaking up the entire battle-line of the Earls' forces from behind. Earl Eirikur surveyed the scene, then ordered his ship, Ironsides, to be brought alongside Vagn's war-ship; the opposing crews began fighting afresh.[1] Saga-tellers all agree that there has never been a more hard-fought battle than this one. As Eirikur's ship pulled alongside Vagn's, Vagn and Aslakur Rock-Skull leapt across onto the bow and, one going port, one going starboard, they created such havoc in clearing the decks that everyone gave ground before them. Aslakur's head was uncovered, but whenever his opponents' swords struck his skull, they bit no deeper than if they were swatting him with pieces of whalebone.

During the battle, the weather was so beautiful and the sunshine so warm that many men took off their clothes. By now Vagn and Aslakur had slain many crewmen, and Earl Eirikur was trying to rally his men with encouragements. Finally, Vigfuss Viga-Glumsson hefted up a humongous sharp-pointed anvil and brought it crashing down on Aslakur with the point gouging into the skull right up to the anvil-block. Aslakur dropped immediately to the ground, dead.[2] In the meantime, Vagn was advancing down the other gunnel, felling challengers with a vengeance. Thorleifur the Dark ran at him and made a swing at Vagn with a solid-oak cudgel. The blow landed on Vagn's helmet so hard that the helmet broke into two pieces. But Vagn steadied himself on the gunnels, made a swipe at Thorleifur with his sword, before spryly leaping over the side onto his own war-ship and rejoining the fight there without missing a beat.

---

1. Earl Eirikur's important role at Hjorungavágr is detailed in *Óláfs saga Tryggvasonar* (*Olaf Tryggvasson's Saga*) from the *Heimskringla*, which gives credit for the Norwegian success to his ferocious fighting and which backgrounds the heathen actions of Earl Hakon and supernatural intervention of Thorgerd and Irpa.

2. Intertextuality between Icelandic sagas is remarkable. Vigfúss Víga-Glúmsson, an Icelander fighting on the Norwegian side, is son of Víga-Glúm, the legendary champion and namesake hero of *Víga-Glúms Saga*.

32. The Earl and His Goddess

After this, Earl Eirikur disengaged his ship from the battle because he had lost nearly his entire crew forward of the main mast. Earl Hakon and the rest of the Norwegian fleet had also broken contact and gone ashore. There was a brief respite to the fighting, and the Earls and their crews met together on the beach. Then Earl Hakon said, "For my part, I'm of the growing opinion that the battle is turning against us. Fighting with these demons is proving to be far worse than I imagined. We can't just keep letting ourselves be cut to pieces. We need a better plan. I'm going up onto the island; you stay here with the fleet in case they attack."

Earl Hakon trekked up onto the island of Primsigd and, leaving his followers behind, entered the forest alone. Facing north, he knelt down on his knees and prayed, and in the prayers which issued from his lips, he called upon his patronness, Thorgerd Holgi's-Bride.[1] But the goddess was angry and she would not listen to his prayers. He offered to make many animal sacrifices on her behalf, but she still refused to help him. Feeling that his plight was becoming truly bleak, he next promised her human sacrifices; and still the goddess was unrelenting. At last, Hakon offered her the life of his son Erlingur, who was just seven years old, and Thorgerd accepted him. The Earl handed the boy over to his thrall, Skopti, who led him to the sacrificial spot and killed him.

33. Thorgerd and Irpa

After that the Earl went back to his ships and rallied his men with newfound spirit, "and now I know for certain that victory will be ours! Go into battle, confident that I have summoned the two sisters, Thorgerd and Irpa, to help us carry the day!" Then the Earl climbed aboard his ship and made preparations to get underway. At sea, they attacked the enemy line and immediately the heated and vicious fighting resumed. But then the winds picked up, and dark clouds rolled in from the north, blackening the

---

1. In Norse mythology, the north was associated with the home of the pagan gods and spirits.

sky, plunging day into night. Lightning flashed and with the thunder, a violent hailstorm began. The wind whipped the hail against the faces of the attacking Jomsvikings, and the hail pummeled them with such tremendous force that their warriors could barely stand. Still worse, the men who had taken off their clothing earlier because of the hot weather were now shivering in the driving sleet. Nevertheless, with their usual resilience, the Jomsvikings fought on. But it was rough going as whenever the Jomsvikings fired stones or arrows or spears on the Norwegians, the storm blew it all flying back to their side together with their enemies' missiles.

It was Cutter-Havarthur who was the first to catch sight of Thorgerd Holgi's-Bride gliding among Earl Hakon's battle line, but many men with the ability of second sight saw her, too. Through lulls in sheets of hail, they bore witness as arrows flew from each fingertip of the she-devil, each one finding a target. The Jomsvikings rushed to tell this to Sigvaldi, who reflected grimly, "I don't think we're fighting just against humans, but we need to do what we can."

After a while the storm seemed to die down, and Earl Hakon called upon Thorgerd a second time, reminding her of the great sacrifice he had made for her. Then, the sky grew dark again and the hail stones fell, now much bigger and harder than before. As this new storm began to rage, Cutter-Havarthur looked and saw that there were two women moving among the decks of the Earl's ship fighting in unison. At this, Sigvaldi cried out to his crew, "Now I'll retreat, and you men had better follow my lead! We never swore a vow to fight against these she-monsters! It's worse than ever with two of them after us."

Sigvaldi disengaged his ship and shouted to Bui and Vagn that they should retreat. Vagn snapped back that Sigvaldi was an utter coward to run.

During this confusion, Thorkell Long-Waist jumped from his ship onto Bui's and slashed at him; it all happened in a second. The sword sliced a line clear down Bui's lips and chin; teeth pelleted to the deck. Bloodily, Bui mouthed, "It'll be trickier for the Danish girls back in Bornholm to kiss me now."

In retaliation, Bui swiped at Thorkell with his sword. The deck was slick with blood and, in side-stepping the attack, Thorkell slipped and fell against the side of the ship. Bui's sword met Thorkell in the torso, slicing him in half against the gunnel. Then, Bui grabbed his gold-laden chests and called out loudly, "All Bui's crew, abandon ship!" With that, he leapt overboard with a chest under each arm.

Watching Sigvaldi's ship rowing away from the battle, Vagn composed these verses:

> *Sigvaldi helmed our ships,*
> *He himself set our scheme.*
> *Now the faint-hearted has flown,*
> *flying home to Denmark,*
> *thinking of falling into a fondle,*
> *wrapped with his ready woman,*
> *but solidly over the side*
> *went the brave Bui.*[1]

Sigvaldi was numb with cold, so he had manned an oar and was rowing to warm up, while someone else steered the ship. Just then Vagn tossed a spear at the person who he thought was Sigvaldi, and the spear pierced the helmsman, pinning him to the mast.

Thorkell the Tall broke off the attack as soon as Sigvaldi had left the battle, and Sigurthur Cowl-Hood followed him after Bui had gone overboard. They both felt they had fulfilled their solemn vow as Jomsvikings. Between them, they had twenty-four ships, which they led home to Denmark.

In a different tale, Sigmundur Brestirsson, that great hero, charged forward to attack Bui. Their duel ended with Sigmundur lopping off both Bui's hands above the wrists. Then Bui plunged the bloody stumps of his wrists into the handles of his gold-chests and called loudly, "All Bui's crew, abandon ship!"[2]

---

1. Many Icelandic sagas are studded with short verses, known as skalds, a very ancient form of poetry. Robinson comments: "Skaldic poetry was episodic and descriptive, and supposedly, under the best circumstances, extemporaneous. Given its form, however, that last adjective is hard to believe. For skaldic poetry is easily among the most artificial forms of literature ever devised by human beings. It was subject to very rigid rules of meter, alliteration, and rhyme; it deviated considerably from everyday syntax; and it used an extensive set of conventional words and expressions (kennings) that make it almost incomprehensible to the non-initiate" (Robinson 1992, 74–75). Skaldic poems are notoriously hard to translate. For the verses here, the translation is fairly loose, but the alliteration tries to give some sense of the terse poetic character of the original.

2. This spurious passage is clearly an interpolation by the author of the *H* manuscript of *Jómsvíkinga saga* which is lifted from the manuscript *Óláfs saga Tryggvasonar* or added in reference to *Faereyinga saga* (see Blake 1962, 38). Earlier Blake writes: "The Sigmundur Brestirsson episode ... is an even greater blemish [to the structure of the saga], as it introduces an unknown character and a second differing account of an episode already dealt with (Blake 1962, 23)."

Appendix B: Earl Hakon and Þorgerðr Hórðabrúðr

In Chapter 23 of *Faroe-Islander Saga*, Earl Hakon leads Sigmundur Brestirsson to a house in the woods near Lade, the home or temple of the mysterious pagan goddess, Thorgerd Horda's-Bride, where he pleads with her to surrender her golden luck-ring to Sigmundur in order to protect him on his return to the Faroe Islands. The scene alludes to and corroborates the close connection between the heathen Earl Hakon and his patroness Thorgerd which is more familiar from other sources, particularly the climactic passages from *Jómsvíkinga saga* in Appendix A, wherein Hakon mounts the island of Primsigd and sacrifices his son Erlingur to her to gain her cooperation.

Linguistically, the deity's second name varies across sources. In *Faroe-Islander Saga*, Thorgerd is referred to as *Hórða-brúðr*, where in *Jomsviking Saga*, she is *Holga-brúðr*. Variant morphological forms in other sources include *Holga-*, *Holda-*, *Hortha-* in connection with *-brúðr* "friend or bride" and *-troll* "troll or monster" (see Blake 1962, 51ff). The name's etymology is unclear, and Blake reviews the alternatives: [i] *Hortha-brúðr* or *Horda-brúðr* meaning "the friend or bride of the people of Holde/Hordaland," referring to the inhabitants of one of the northwestern regions of Norway, i.e., their special cult goddess. E.V. Gordon translates the name as "the Lady of the Horthar," following this etymology (Gordon 1956, 237). The second option: [ii] *Holga-brúðr*, refering to Holgi, the eponymous king of Halogaland, a region in the far north, i.e., "the bride of Holgi." Either etymology points to the suggestion that Thorgerd was worshipped originally as a pagan goddess regionally among peasants. Blake suggests that she might have been a kind of pagan spirit of the harvest (Blake 1962, 51).

Almost nothing is known about her sister-goddess Irpa, though her name is mentioned along with the deities Thorgerd and Thor in connection to a temple Earl Hakon had built for them in *Njal's Saga*, Chapter 88:

> *Meanwhile, Earl Hakon was attending a feast at Gudbrand's home. During the night, Hrapp the Killer went to their temple. Inside it, he saw the statue of Thorgerd Holgi's-Bride enthroned, massive as a fully-grown man; there was a huge gold bracelet on her arm, and a linen hood over her head. Hrapp stripped off the hood and the bracelet. Then he noticed Thor in his chariot, and took from him another gold bracelet. He took a third bracelet from Irpa. He dragged all three of the idols outside and stripped them of their vestments; then he set fire to the temple and burned it down* [translated by Magnusson and Pálsson 1960, 188].

It is worth pointing out that the description of this temple in *Njal's Saga* is very different from the more ambiguous scene at Thorgerd's "house" in *Faroe-Islander Saga*. In the latter, the Old Icelandic text makes it clear that Thorgerd herself is standing in her finery within the house of glass windows, not an idol or a statue as in *Njal's Saga*. Her anthropomorphic presence allows for the poignant scene of her devout subject, Earl Hakon, prostrating himself at her feet, begging her to part with her luck-ring. Both her corporeality and reluctance to yield her favors in the *Faroe-Islander Saga* echo her characterization in *Jomsviking Saga*.

Appendix C: Social Background and Technical Terms

The events in *Faereyinga saga* generally take place between 980 and 1030, roughly two hundred years before the anonymous Icelandic author penned the saga in the early 13th century. Almost nothing is known about the living conditions, legal system, and political structure on the Faroe Islands beyond the details taken from the saga itself (see Wylie 1987, 8–19). At times, the saga-writer seems to view the legal system in the Faroe Islands as equivalent to that in Iceland; at other times, he describes the Faroese system as essentially Norwegian; still again, sometimes he seems to blend the two for literary reasons. As Foote writes: "It seems safer on the whole to conclude that the author used his knowledge of Icelandic law to help his story on and his knowledge of Norwegian law to reinforce the impression of a strange setting" (1970, 173). My own impression is that the saga-writer presents the society of the Faroe Islands as very much like Icelandic society of the early saga times. Below are some terms which crop up repeatedly in the *Faroe-Islander Saga* which may require some detailed background for the general reader.

Assembly (Þing). The saga relates that the Faroese *thing* or assembly took place at Tórshavn on the large, central island of Streymoy. The saga-writer generally presents this Faroese *thing* as functionally equivalent to the Icelandic *Althing*, the open-air assembly which was held for two weeks every summer in June at Thingvellir in southwestern Iceland. Established in 930, the *Althing* was a parliamentary assembly presided over by a kind of chairperson, the **Lawspeaker** (see below). It was also the place where legal cases could be brought and tried; compensation might be paid to a victim's family or an individual might be sentenced to **outlawry** (see below). There was a legislative court of appeals, and the four judicial courts, one for each Quarter of the country. The assembled chieftains (*goðar*) would nominate judges for the Quarter Courts and the Fifth Court, thirty-six judges for each court. The chieftains also elected the Lawspeaker for his three-year term. Attendees at the *thing* would set up semipermanent booths or tents at the assembly place; merchants peddled food and drink (there is a short story about a man named Thorhall Ale-Hood [*Ölkofra Þáttr*] who sold ale around the *Althing*). With families traveling from all over Iceland and lasting for two weeks, the *Althing* was also a social occasion where family alliances could be forged and proposals of marriage might be made.

Throughout the saga, the Faroese *thing* has annual meetings in the late spring or early summer lasting for several days on the Icelandic model of the *Althing*; in later times, the Faroese assembly would meet on June 16 (see Foote 1970, 161–62). Besides for these official convocations, the saga-writer suggests that the Islanders may have called ad hoc assemblies at various times of the year, as the phrase *stefna Þing* ("to call or summon a thing") is often used to deal with more pressing business. It is unclear whether there were local assemblies among sub-communities in the Faroes of the type which were very common in both Iceland and Norway.

Lawspeaker (*Lógsógumaðr*). In Chapter 43 of the saga, the Faroese leader Gilli is introduced as the Lawspeaker, who is summoned to Norway to meet with King Olafur. The Icelandic Lawspeaker served a term of three-years, and his primary responsibility was to recite from memory the entire cannon of law at every *Althing*, one third each year; his other duty was to arbitrate disputes over legal matters. The saga-writer envisions the Lawspeaker of the Faroe Islands as equivalent to the Icelandic office, since the normal word for the cognate official in Norwegian is *lógmaðr* "law-man" (Foote 1970, 163–164). It is remarkable that the Faroese are viewed as having their own national *thing* and Lawspeaker in the saga, as it suggests an independence and self-government for the Faroe Islands in the saga period which would not be realized again for more than eight hundred years (on Faroese nationalism and independence, see Wylie 1987: especially chapters 6 and 7).

Outlawry (*útlegð/útlagi*). In the Icelandic system, the *Althing* had no executive power to enforce the judgments of the courts, nor was there a police force or legal prosecutor (see Fox and Pálsson 1974, 194–195). When a person committed a crime, such as a killing or theft, it was up to the aggrieved party to circulate news of the crime, name witnesses, summon the defendant before the *Althing*, and bring a legal suit before the proper Quarter court. If these actions were not followed precisely according to an established procedure, the guilty party could readily have the case dismissed. For example, the last day for serving a summons for someone to appear at the *Althing* was four weeks before the first day of the assembly. In the event of a killing, the man responsible needed to announce the crime (*víg* "a slaying") immediately; if the killer did not report the deed promptly, they could be charged with the more serious crime of concealed murder (*morð*). Presuming the suit was heard at trial, when the judges passed their sentence, it remained up to the aggrieved party—in wrongful killing cases, usually the family of the victim—to implement the penalty for the crime. In cases where an individual had been wounded or killed, often a fine could be paid, known as *wergild*, to compensate the family for the loss. The amount of money to be paid would be determined by a legally determined scale, based on the victim's rank as servant or freeman. Earl Hakon's settlement and the payment of wergild are at the heart of the bitter altercations between Sigmundur and Thrandur in Chapters 25–26, as Thrandur prefers not to recognize the authority of a foreign power to arbitrate a dispute which could be handled at the Faroese *thing*.

In some cases, more serious crimes would come with a sentence of outlawry. In Icelandic law there were two types of outlawry. For Lesser Outlawry, the convicted had to leave Iceland for a period of three years from the time the sentence was passed, though his physical person was inviolate both when in Iceland making preparations to leave and abroad (see Fox and Pálsson 1974, 195). Fuller Outlawry was the harsher penalty: the convicted person must leave Iceland forever, and he could be killed by any member of society either at home or abroad (Fox and Pálsson 1974, 195). No member of the community was permitted to help him and there was usually a fixed bounty on his head, generally eight ounces of silver, but "this could be raised to twenty-four ounces if he committed a killing at the *Althing*, burned someone alive in a house, or was a slave who killed a master" (Fox and Pálsson 1974, 195). Wrongful killing was not the only crime which brought a sentence of Fuller Outlawry; in the story of Thorhall Ale-Hood, Thorhall's enemies threaten him with outlawry for accidentally burning down some woodland belonging to six chieftains (see Pálsson 1971, 83). In *Faroe-Islander Saga*, only Fuller Outlawry is mentioned. For instance, Thorkell Hard-Frost is outlawed by the Frosta *thing* for murdering his neighbor Thoralfur and his men (Chapter 16); and Siguthur, Thorthur and Gautur are outlawed by the Tórshavn *thing* for killing Karl-Maerskur and attacking Gilli the Lawspeaker's attendant at the assembly (Chapter 48).

Bailiffs and Fiefdom (*fúti, lén*). As mentioned, the saga-writer often depicts the Faroes as a largely self-reliant country in his portrayal of the Faroese *thing* and office of the Lawspeaker. Elsewhere, the saga-writer points to a political connection with Norway. Foote's view is that, "politically, the author seems to think in terms of his own time: the Faroes represented a single or shared *lén* ['fiefdom'] under the rulers of Norway, and the individual in charge could be called *sýslumáðr* ['bailiff of the king']" (Foote 1970, 159). The Faroe Islands certainly had the status of a royal fiefdom of Norway in the late 12th-century but note that our only source for details of the political structure in the Islands before c. 1170 is the saga itself. Chapter 4 of the saga opens with the Faroes divided: Hafgrimur of South Island is named as the local chieftain ruling over half of the Islands as a fief for King Haraldur Grey-Cloak, while Brestir and Beinir are joint-chieftains over the other half, holding the fief for Earl Hakon. This situation must obtain between 961, when Earl Hakon rose to power in Trondheim and 975 when he becomes king of Norway. There is no discussion of evidence from the saga-writer's perspective that the situation was ever anything different. At the saga's close, in Chapter 59, Leifur Össursson is named bailiff of King Magnus Olafsson (c. 1035–1047) and rules over the Faroes as a fief. By the late 1200s, the kings of Norway appoint bailiffs (*fúti*) to the Islands, with six sheriffs (*sýslumenn*) serving under him, each with jurisdiction over one of the six districts (*sýslur*) (see Wylie 1987, 11). The bailiff was a foreigner whose main duties were to collect taxes among the Faroe Islands and to ensure the Norwegian rule-of-law was being followed (*ibid.*). Some species of this political system lasted well into the Middle Ages, though the Faroese *thing* seemed to be largely responsible for managing internal affairs (for a brilliant discussion of the development of Faroese political structures from the 13th century to modern times, see Wylie 1987, 11–18).

Appendix D: Chronology

Irish hermits in the Faroe Islands.	c. 700–800
Grimur Kamban is the first settler.	c. 825
Norse settlement of the Faroe Islands.	c. 860
Norse settlement of Iceland.	c. 870–930
King Haraldur Fine-Hair becomes ruler of Norway.	c. 872
Aud the Deep-Minded visits Faroe Islands before Iceland.	c. 915
King Haraldur Grey-Cloak rules Norway.	c. 961
Thrandur earns his fortune abroad in Denmark, settles at Göta.	c. 961–962
Brestir and Beinir rule half the Faroe Islands; Hafgrimur the other half.	c. 961
Sigmundur Brestirsson born (?)	c. 961
Earl Hakon becomes King of Norway, Brestir and Beinir killed;	c. 970
Thrandur rules the Faroe Islands alone; Sigmundur and Thorir go abroad.	c. 972
Sigmundur [18] and Thorir [20] leave Ulfur's farm.	c. 979
Sigmundur meets Earl Hakon and enters his service.	c. 980–983
Sigmundur in Denmark, defeats Randver.	c. 980
Sigmundur raids in Sweden, defeats Björn, Vandill and Athill.	c. 981
Sigmundur pursues Haraldur Iron-Skull in the Orkneys.	c. 982
Sigmundur and Thorir return to the Faroe Islands, defeats Össur.	c. 983

Earl Hakon decides settlement for Sigmundur against Thrandur.	c. 984
Thrandur agrees to pay a share of wergild.	
Sigmundur [27] marries Thurid at Lade; Thorkell reconciled with Earl Hakon.	c. 985
Jomsvikings invade Norway, Sigmundur defeats their leader Bui.	c. 986
Olaf Tryggvason rules Norway.	c. 995–1000
The Faroe Islands convert to Christianity.	c. 1000
The Earls of Lade reign in Norway, appoint Sigmundur as bailiff over the Faroe Islands.	c. 1000
Sigmundur Brestirsson murdered by Thorgrimur the Mean.	c. 1001
Thrandur and Leifur rule over the Faroe Islands.	
Leifur Össursson marries Thora, they settle at the farm at Hof.	c. 1002
Olafur Haraldursson becomes king of Norway.	c. 1016
Sigurthur Thorlakson travels to the royal court.	c. 1017
Karl Maerskur arrives at the Faroe Islands to collect tribute.	c. 1018
Sigurthur, Thorthur, and Gautur outlawed.	c. 1019
Thrandur shares rulership of the Islands with Leifur and Sigmundur's sons.	c. 1020
King Svein and his mother Alfifa rule in Norway.	c. 1030
Sigurthur marries Straumey-Birna, Gautur the Red marries Thorbera.	c. 1031
Leifur Thorirsson killed in a brawl, Thorthur seeks marriage with Thurid Strong-Widow	c. 1032
King Magnus the Good rules in Norway, Leifur rules the Faroe Islands.	c. 1035

Appendix E: Genealogical Tables

These tables are adapted from the genealogy presented in volume 25 of the Íslenzk Fornrit series which contains *Faereyinga saga* [p. 197]. NN stands for No Name.

1. Settlers on Skufey

```
                NN ~ NN {Götuskeggjar}
                         |
        Sigmundur, (Thorbjörn the Götuskeggjar)
            |                 |
Thora ~ Beinir,       Brestir ~ Cecilia
    |                         |
Thorir—NN            Sigmundur ~ Thurid Thorkellsdottir
    |                         |
  Leifur    Leifur Össursson ~ Thora, Thoralfur, Steingrimur, Brandur, Heri
                              |
                          Sigmundur
                              |
                          Hafgrimur
                              |
                             [...]
                              |
                         Einar ~ NN
                              |
                           Skeggi
```

2. Settlers on Austerey

```
                  NN ~ NN {Götuskeggjar}      NN ~ NN
                           |                     |
         Thorbjörn the Götuskeggjar ~ Guthrun, Sviney-Bjarni
                                    |
       NN ~ Thorlakur, Thrandur of Göta ~ NN, Thrandur's sister ~ NN
              |                    |                         |
      Sigurthur, Thorthur       Guthrun                    Gautur
```

3. Settlers on South Island

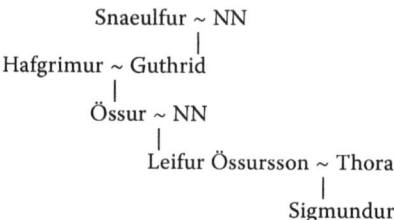

```
        Snaeulfur ~ NN
               |
    Hafgrimur ~ Guthrid
               |
          Össur ~ NN
                  |
             Leifur Össursson ~ Thora
                              |
                          Sigmundur
```

4. Settlers from Heidmark

```
    Thora ~ Steingrimur  Thoralfur ~ Idun
         |                        |
         Thorkell ~ Ragnhild
                  |
            Thurid ~ Sigmundur
                   |
                 Thora
```

References and Further Reading

The academic literature on the Icelandic sagas is vast, comparable in scope to the voluminous research and writings on, e.g., the plays of Shakespeare in English. With the majority of key works written in languages such as German, Danish, Norwegian, or modern Icelandic, much of this first-rate and extensive scholarship is also largely inaccessible or unreadable for the general reader in English. Preciously little has been written on the *Faroe-Islander Saga* in English, with the vast majority of contributions written by a single scholar, Peter G. Foote (1924–2009), formerly professor of Old Scandinavian at University College London, and a diligent student of Icelandic philology, unabashedly devoted to this particular saga. In preparing this book, I attempted to strike a balance between citing my academic sources responsibly and avoiding the exhaustive presentation of scholarly works written in less accessible languages such as Danish or Norwegian. Therefore, below I have provided some selected references of books and articles written only in English which have particularly influenced my thinking for A Note on the Translation and the Introduction. Many of these books have detailed bibliographies of literature in the wider field of the Icelandic sagas and the Viking Age, so these suggestions for further reading are given as a general point of departure for the serious student.

On the *Faroe-Islander Saga* in English

Foote, Peter. *Aurvandilstá: Norse Studies*. Viborg: Odense University Press, 1984. This is an anthology of the collected papers of Peter Foote on the occasion of his sixtieth birthday and includes in one volume some otherwise hard-to-retrieve articles, including "Thrandur and the Apostles"; "A note on Thrandur's *kredda*"; and "Faereyinga Saga, Chapter 40," all of which are important studies on aspects of the saga.

_____. "On Legal Terms in *Faereyinga saga.*" *Fróðskaparrit* 18 (1970): 159–75. A concisely written, though nonetheless somewhat technical discussion of Icelandic and Norwegian legal terms which are employed (and potentially misemployed) in the Faroe-Islander Saga.

_____. *On the Saga of the Faroe Islanders.* London: H.K. Lewis, 1965. One of the only volumes in English to explore the literary themes in the saga in any serious depth. Though extremely short, it is still useful for its insights on the question of the saga's authorship and the characterization of Thrandur.

Faroe-Islands

Wylie, Jonathan. *The Faroe Islands: Interpretations of History.* Lexington: University of Kentucky Press, 1987. Written by an anthropologist who has done extensive field work in the Faroes, this is a fascinating portrayal of the history and culture of the Faroese people, which is especially engaging on the question of Faroese national identity and the movement for independence.

_____ and David Margolin. *The Ring of Dancers: Images of Faroese Culture.* Philadelphia: University of Pennsylvania Press, 1981. A work which concentrates on the unique elements of Faroese culture, folklore, music, and art.

The Viking Age and General Background

Graham-Campbell, James., ed. *Cultural Atlas of the Viking World.* Oxford: Andromeda, 1994. There are many general introductions to greater Scandinavia in the Viking Age, but this book is especially clear and readable with lavish illustrations and detailed maps.

Richards, Julian. *The Vikings: A Very Short Introduction.* Oxford: Oxford University Press, 2005. The series, despite the title, has excellent in-depth entries into a subject by a leading expert in the field. Richards provides a thorough, highly readable survey of the notion of "Viking" and the Viking Age, with special emphasis on archaeological evidence for the Scandinavian expansion into the North Atlantic.

Translations of Other Sagas

These editions of the sagas are not intended as a replete list, rather, these are merely some editions which were referenced in the notes or Introduction. All of the introductions to these volumes are serious works of scholarship on the Icelandic sagas. Moreover, these translations are readily available and highly readable. (After *Faroe-Islander Saga*, *Eyrbyggja Saga* is a heavy favorite of mine).

Blake, N.F., trans. *Jómsvíkinga saga* [Jomsvikings' Saga]. London: Thomas Nelson, 1962.
Fox, Denton, and Hermann Pálsson, trans. *Grettir's Saga*. Toronto: University of Toronto Press, 1974
Magnusson, Magnus, and Hermann Pálsson, trans. *King Harald's Saga*. London: Penguin, 1966.
_____. *Laxdaela Saga*. London: Penguin, 1969.
_____. *Njal's Saga*. London: Penguin, 1960.
_____. *The Vinland Sagas*. London: Penguin, 1965.
Pálsson, Hermann. *Hrafnkel's Saga and Other Stories*. London: Penguin, 1971.
Pálsson, Hermann, and Paul Edwards, trans. *Eyrbyggja Saga* [Settlers of Eyr Saga]. London: Penguin, 1989
_____. *Landnámabók* [Book of Settlements]. Winnipeg: University of Manitoba Press, 1972.
_____. *Orkneyinga Saga* [Orkney-Islander Saga]. London: Penguin, 1981

Old Norse Language and Linguistics

Gordon, E.V. *An Introduction to Old Norse*, 2d ed. Oxford: Oxford University Press, 1956. Nowadays there are several Old Norse language textbooks, but Gordon's book is something of a classic with several inherently interesting and entertaining Old Norse passages for the student to translate. The introductory sections still contain tremendous insight into the history and development of saga writing.
Robinson, Orrin, W. *Old English and Its Closest Relatives*. Stamford: Stamford University Press, 1992. This book is a linguistic introduction to all the early Germanic languages such as Gothic, Old Norse, Old English, Old High German, etc. Very accessible. Chapter 4 covers Old Norse in a detailed sketch.

Index of Proper Names

Identifications and Events Referenced to Chapters

Numbers refer to chapters where events occur.

Alfifa, co-regent of Norway with King Svein 50

Alofa, grand-daughter of Aud the Deep-Minded, matriarch of the Götuskeggjar family of the Faroe Islands 1

Ari Thorgilsson the Learned, source of the Jomsvikings invasion of Norway 27

Arnljotur, a Hebridean captain, father of Bjarngrimur, Hafgrimur, and Hergrimur, conspires with Skopti, ambushes the Göta kinsmen, forced to pay wergild by Sigurthur 55

Athill and Vandill, brothers, royal-protectors of a district in Sweden 19; sea-battle against Sigmundur, Vandill fights with and slain by Sigmundur, Athill retreats 20

Aud the Deep-Minded, journeys to Faroe Islands, marries off her grand-daughter Alofa 1

Beinir Sigmundursson, Skufey farmer, brother of Brestir, nephew of Thorbjörn the Götuskeggur, chieftain over half the Faroe Islands for Earl Hakon, description, mistress Thora, father of Thorir, farm on Dimun 4; goes to Little Dimun, ambushed by Hafgrimur's posse, slain, buried in the heathen custom on Skufey 7

Birna (Straumey-Birna), wife of Thorhallur the Wealthy on Straumey, affair with Sigurthur Thorlaksson, takes control of farm with Sigurthur 50

Bjarngrimur, Hafgrimur, and Hergrimur, Norwegian captains shipwrecked off South Island, friction with Thorhallur, killed by the Göta kinsmen 51; sons of Arnljotur 55

Bjarni see Swine-Island Bjarni

Björn, sheriff of King Eirikur of Sweden, raises army against Sigmundur 19

Björn, neighbor of Sigurthur Thorlaksson on Straumey 54

Brandur Sigmundursson, third oldest son of Sigmundur and Thurid 36; takes part in final attack on Sigurthur's farm, fights with and killed by Thorthur the Short 58

Brestir Sigmundursson, farmer on Skufey, brother of Beinir, nephew of Thorbjörn the Götuskeggur, chieftain over half the Faroe Islands for Earl Hakon, description, mistress Cecilia, father of Sigmundur, farm on Dimun 4; skilled in the law, handles Einar's case, outmaneuvers Hafgrimur 5; Cecila as a wife, goes on fateful trip to Little Dimun, attacked by Hafgrimur's posse, fights pitched battle, slain by Hafgrimur, buried in the heathen custom on Skufey 7

Bui, leader of the Jomsvikings, attack on Earl Hakon, defeated by Sigmundur 27

Cecilia, Norwegian mistress of Brestir Sigmundursson, mother of Sigmundur Brestirsson 4; later wife of Brestir 7

Einar Hafgrimursson, son of Hafgrimur Sigmundursson, king's bailiff in the Faroe Islands 59

Einar South-Islander, servant of Hafgrimur on South Island 4; kills Eldjarn, sent to the Skuf-Islanders 5;

149

ambushed on Little Dimun with Sigmundur and Thorir, escapes, evades Thrandur's second attack 37; evades Thrandur by leaping into the sea with Sigmundur and Thorir 38; swims toward South Island, clings to Sigmundur, drowns 39; ghost summoned by Thrandur 41

Eirikur Bjarnsson, (*Eirikur the Victorious*), king of Sweden, son of Bjarn Eirikursson, orders killing of Norwegian merchants in his kingdom, dispatches Athill and Vandill after Sigmundur 19

Eirikur Hakonsson, earl, son of Earl Hakon, brother of Svein Hakonsson, gives men and ships to Sigmundur for raiding 17; visited by Sigmundur on the way to Sweden 19; visited by Sigmundur and Thorir on return from Sweden 20; attacked by Jomsvikings 27; rules Norway with Earl Svein, description 34; sends for Sigmundur, appoints him bailiff and ruler of Faroe Islands 35

Eldjarn Comb-Hood, servant of Hafgrimur on South Island, description 4; killed by Einar 5; reportedly takes part in raid against Sigmundur's farm (?), dies on raid 38

Gautur the Red, Thrandur's foster son and kinsman of Sigurthur Thorlaksson, Thorthur Thorlaksson, and Leifur Össursson, son of Thrandur of Göta's unnamed sister 36; takes part in ambush of Sigmundur, Thorir and Einar on Little Dimun, sea raid 37; takes part in raid against Sigmundur's farm 38; chastised by Thrandur for inactivity, outfits merchant ship 45; chastises Thrandur about Karl-Maerskr at *thing*, wounds Karl-Maerskr, outlawed 48; departs for Iceland, impoverished on Austurey, armed return to *thing* 49; kicked out of the farmhouse at Göta by Thrandur, lives at Thorhallur's farm on Straumey 50; receive castaways, kills Hergrimur 51; collects debts of Thorvaldur on Sandey, affair with Thorbera, present at Thorvaldur's death, settles on Sandey 52; ambushed by Arnljotur 55; wounds Steingrimur Sigmundursson, killed by Leifur Össursson 58

Gilli Lawspeaker, summoned to Norway by King Olafur, made king's retainer 43; attendant fatally wounded, brings lawsuit against Thorlakssons for Karl-Maerskr slaying 48; agrees to weapons-ban at *thing*, catches sight of the Göta-kinsmen at *thing* 49

Grimur Kamban, first settler in the Faroe Islands 1

Guthrid, wife of Hafgrimur of South Island, daughter of Snaeulfur 4; accompanies Hafgrimur to Sandey, mother of Össur Hafgrimursson 6

Guthrun, wife of Thorbjörn the Götuskeggur, mother of Thorlakur and Thrandur 2

Guthrun, daughter of Thrandur of Göta 50

Hafgrimur, farmer on South Island, chieftain over half the Faroe Islands, description 4; sends Einar to the Skuf-Islanders, seeks a settlement, foiled by Brestir at the *thing* 5; goes to Sandey to recruit Snaeulfur, rejected by Snaeulfur, father of Össur, visits and recruits Thrandur and Bjarni for action against the Skuf-Islanders 6; ambushes the brothers on Little Dimun, dies in duel with Brestir Sigmundursson, buried on South Island 7

Hafgrimur see Bjarngrimur, Hafgrimur, and Hergrimur 51

Hafgrimur Sigmundursson, son of Sigmundur Leifursson, father of Einar and Skeggi 59

Hakon Sigurthursson, Earl of Trondheim, grants half the Faroe Islands as a fief to Brestir and Beinir Sigmundursson 4; becomes king of Norway 10; welcomes Sigmundur and Thorir to court, father of Svein Hakonsson 16; gives men and ships to Sigmundur for raiding 17; appoints Sigmundur and Thorir as retainers 18; dispatches Sigmundur to Sweden to avenge the Norwegian merchants, provides men and ships 19; rewards Sigmundur and Thorir for service in Sweden 20; sends Sigmundur to kill Haraldur Iron-Skull, receives Sigmundur but grows angry at him, reconciled with Haraldur Iron-Skull 21; advises Sigmundur on return to the Faroe Islands, strips the luck-ring from Thorgerd for Sigmundur 23; welcomes Sigmundur back to Norway 24; makes a settlement for Sigmundur against

Thrandur *in absentia*, welcomes Sigmundur and Thorir for the winter 25; reconciles with Thorkell, grants him stewardship in Orkadale, appoints him liegeman 26; attacked by Jomsvikings, unsuccessful sea-battle against Bui, bids Sigmundur to attack 27

Hallbjarni the Tail, source of the Jomsvikings invasion of Norway 27

Haraldur Fine-Hair, King of Norway, (c. 850–c. 932) became king c. 872, tyranny contributes to men settling on the Faroe Islands 1

Haraldur Gormsson (*Haraldur Bluetooth*), King of Denmark (c. 958–985), attends market at Haleyri 2; imposes travel ban, presents Thrandur with silver 3

Haraldur Gunnhildarson (*Haraldur Grey-Cloak*), King of Norway (c. 960–975) 2; slain and deposed 10

Haraldur Iron-Skull, pirate raider in the Orkneys, allies with Sigmundur, travels to Norway, reconciled with Earl Hakon 21; accompanies Sigmundur to the Faroe Islands 23; dissuades Sigmundur from making a settlement with Össur, stays on Skufey with Sigmundur the winter, returns with Sigmundur and Thorir to Norway 24; stays in Norway after Earl Hakon's settlement 25

Harekur, retainer of Haraldur Bluetooth at Haleyri, brother of Sigurthur 2; robbed of silver 3

Hergrimur see Bjarngrimur, Hafgrimur, and Hergrimur 51

Heri Sigmundursson, fourth oldest son of Sigmundur and Thurid 36; ambushes Sigurthur Thorlaksson in ambush, slain 58

Holmgeir the Rich, ring merchant at Haleyri 2

Hrafn Holmgard-Traveler, merchant ship captain from Tønsberg in the Vik region of Norway, comes to Thorshaven, takes possession of Sigmundur and Thorir from Thrandur, takes them from the Faroe Islands to Tunsberg 8; parts ways with Sigmundur and Thorir 9

Idun, wife of Thoralfur, royal bailiff in Heidmark, mother of Ragnhild 14

Karl-Maerskr, accepts King Olafur's mission to the Faroes 47; description, leaves for Faroes, delivers letters to Leifur and Gilli, agrees to stay with them, bids Thrandur to collect tribute in the Northern Islands, stays with Leifur over the winter, visits Thrandur's black tent at *thing* with Leifur, examines tribute from Thrandur, slain by Thorthur Thorlakson 48

Leifur Össursson, son of Össur Hafgrimursson, present at his father's death at the hands of Sigmundur Brestirsson 24; becomes foster son of Thrandur 25; kinsman of Sigurthur and Thorthur Thorlaksson and Gautur the Red 36; takes part in ambush of Sigmundur, Thorir and Einar on Little Dimun, sea raid 37; takes part in raid against Sigmundur's farm, leads search for Sigmundur on Skufey 38; rules over Faroe Islands with Thrandur after Sigmundur's death, seeks marriage with Thora Sigmundursdottir 40; confronts Thorgrimur the Mean, helps Sigurthur shackle Thorgrimur and sons 41; seeks marriage with Thora a second time, settles with Thora at Hofi on South Island 42; summoned to Norway by King Olafur, made king's retainer 43; offers help and lodging to Karl-Maerskr, collects tribute among the Southern Islands, visits Thrandur's black tent at *thing*, examines tribute from Thrandur, runs to help Gilli Lawspeaker, brings lawsuit against foster sons 48; agrees to weapons-ban at *thing*, catches sight of the Göta-kinsmen, outflanked by Thrandur, receives one third rulership of Faroe Islands from Thrandur, agrees to foster 49; objects to Leifur Thorirson staying with Sigurthur Thorlaksson 53; patience after death of Leifur Thorirsson 54; conspires with Thurid and Thora against Sigurthur 56; travels to Austurey to recover Sigmundur Leifursson, disables boats, absconds with son 57; takes part in the trap against Sigurthur, fatally wounds Sigurthur, brings fight to Sigurthur's farm, kills Gautur the Red and Thorthur the Short 58; earns a good reputation, travels to meet King Magnus, rules Faroe Islands alone, dies 59

Leifur Thorirsson, trader, stays with Leifur Össursson and Thurid Strong-

Widow, winters with Sigurthur Thorlaksson 53; visits Björn with Sigurthur, slain 54

Magnus Olafsson (the Good), king of Norway, grants Leifur Össursson rule over the Faroe Islands 59

Olaf Tryggvason, King of Norway (c. 995–1000), comparison to Sigmundur 13; converts Norway to Christianity, summons Sigmundur from Faroes 28; meets Sigmundur, biographical description 29, baptizes Sigmundur, sends him on mission to Christianize the Faroe Islands 30; receives tribute from the Faroe Islands, recognizes Thrandur's opposition 32; challenges Sigmundur to sport, demands luck-ring from Sigmundur, falling out of friendship 33

Olafur Haraldursson, King of Norway, seeks tribute from Faroe Islands, appoints Gilli, Leifur, and Thoralfur Sigmundursson retainers, sends first ship to Faroes 43; sends second ship 44; accuses Sigurthur Thorlaksson of murder, insists on *járnburð* ordeal for Sigurthur 45; learns of Sigurthur's departure 46; holds a council meeting, reconciles with Karl-Maerskr, sends Karl on mission to Faroes 47; writes letters to Faroese retainers, gives Karl-Maerskr the royal seal, political unrest in Norway 48

Ormstein and Thorstein, sons of Thorgrimur the Mean on South Island, accomplices in Thorgrimur's murder of Sigmundur Brestirsson 39

Össur Hafgrimursson, son of Hafgrimur of South Island and Guthrid, description 6; taken in by Thrandur as foster son 9; marries at Thrandur's behest, rules over half the Faroe Islands formerly controlled by his father, takes possession over Brestir and Beinir's farms and livestock, builds defenses on Skufey against Sigmundur, keeps a posse in defense 22; offers terms of reconciliation, slain in fight with Sigmundur 24

Ragnhild, description 10; wife of Thorkell and mother of Thurid 11; further description 14; carried off by Thorkell, hides with him in the forest, returns home with Thoralfur after pitched fight 15; runs off to the mountains with Thorkell 16; visits Earl Hakon's court 26

Randver, Viking chieftain, fights with and slain by Sigmundur 18

Sigmundur Brestirsson, son of Brestir Sigmundursson and Cecila of Skufey 4; goes with Brestir to Little Dimun, swears vengeance on Thrandur, becomes foster son of Thrandur 7; handed over as slaves to Hrafn 8; granted freedom 9; decides with Thorir to join Earl Hakon, travels through mountains, saves Thorir, stumbles on Ulfur's farm 10; stays on Ulfur's farm, grows fond of Thurid, swears to avoid northern woods 11; trained in woodland skills and fighting by Ulfur, explores woods, encounters and slays the bear, fools Ulfur 12; description, comparison to Olaf Tryggvason, sets out from Ulfur's farm 13; confesses tryst with Thurid to Ulfur, seeks her hand in marriage, arrives at Earl Hakon's court 16; speaks with Svein and Eirikur Hakonsson, receives ships from Earl Hakon and his sons 17; raids in Denmark, storms Elfarsker, captains Svein's ship, fights and slays Randver, skill as a swordsman, gains dragon-warship, returns from Denmark, visits Earl Eirikur and Earl Hakon, made retainer of Earl Hakon 18; sent on mission to Sweden by Earl Hakon, visits Earl Eirikur, successful raids in Sweden, uses the phlanax attack, kills Björn, raids in Holmgard, prepares stone strategem against Athill and Vandill 19; sea-battle against Athill and Vandill, slays Vandill, captures five ships from Athill, visits Earl Eirikur, then Earl Hakon, earns a great fortune 20; tracks Haraldur Iron-Skull at Earl Hakon's request, captains Randver's dragon-warship, journeys to the Orkneys, allies with Haraldur and brings him to Norway, grows angry at Earl Hakon, reconciles Haraldur and Earl Hakon, stays with Earl Hakon at court 21; reputation known in the Faroe Islands 22; decides to return to the Faroe Islands to avenge Brestir, presented Thorgerd's luck-ring 23; sails to Faroe Islands, encounters a storm, separated from Thorir 23; lands on the Faroes at Sviney, accosts Swine-Island Bjarni but reconciles with him, goes to Skufey to challenge Össur, refuses terms of reconciliation, attacks fortification, description, slays Össur, reunites with Thorir on South Island, attempt at settlement with Thrandur at Thorshaven, insists on Earl Hakon's intervention, stays on Skufey, repairs his father's farm, departs for Norway in spring 24; demands Earl Hakon adjudicate against Thrandur *in absentia*, awarded four counts of wergild and complete control over the Faroe Islands, meets Thrandur at the Thorshaven *thing*, informs him of the settlement, receives one-third of the wergild, collects the Earl's tribute, returns to Norway 25; intercedes for Thorkell, propose marriage to Thurid, wedding feast at Lade, brings wife and daughter to Faroe Islands, demands and receives second count of wergild from Thrandur, trips to Norway to visit Earl Hakon to deliver tribute, his age 26; active against the Jomsvikings, engages in battle against Bui, defeats Bui in combat, stays with Earl Hakon for the winter 27; summoned to meet King Olaf 28, meets Olaf 29; baptizes, sent on mission to bring Christianity to Faroe Islands, appointed overlordship, arrives at *thing*, proclaims Christianity at Thorshavn, foiled by Thrandur, promises not to proselytize 30; makes raid against Thrandur, spreads Christianity throughout Faroes, attempts to bring Thrandur to Norway, repulsed by storms, rescues Thrandur at sea 31; brings tribute to King Olaf 32; sporting competition against King Olaf, refuses to give luck-ring to Olaf 33; children with Thurid (Thora, Thoralfur, Steingrimur, Brandur, Heri), builds church on farm, refuses to compensate Thrandur on behalf of Leifur 36; ambushed on Little Dimun, escapes, evades Thrandur's second attack, refuses to kill ship-wrecked Thrandur and foster sons 37; evades Thrandur at farmhouse, slays Steingrimur, leaps from cliff into sea 38; swims toward South Island, tries to save Einar then Thorir, hides on shore, murdered by Thorgrimur, buried with Thorir 39; ghost summoned by Thrandur, body reburied on Skufey at church 41; appears to Thurid in dream 54

Sigmundur Leifursson, sent as Thrandur's foster son, description 49; taught law and Apostles' Creed by Thrandur, rescued from Göta by Thora Sigmundursson 57; farms on South Island, becomes great chieftain, father of Hafgrimur 59

Sigurthur, retainer of Haraldur Bluetooth at Haleyri, brother of Harekur 2; robbed of silver 3

Sigurthur Thorlaksson, son of Thorlakur, nephew and foster son of Thrandur of Göta, comparison to Sigmundur 36; takes part in ambush of Sigmundur, Thorir and Einar on Little Dimun, casts curse on Sigmundur 37; takes part in raid against Sigmundur's farm, leads search for Sigmundur with Leifur 38; helps Leifur shackle Thorgrimur the Mean 41; chastised by Thrandur for inactivity, description, outfits merchant-ship, accused of Thoralfur Sigmundursson's murder, defense speech to King Olafur, proposes *járnburð*, flees Norway ahead of ordeal 45; attacks attendant of Gilli Lawspeaker, outlawed 48; departs for Iceland, impoverished on Austurey, armed return to *thing* 49; kicked out of the farmhouse at Göta by Thrandur, collects Thorhallur's assets on Straumey, seduces Birna, takes over Thorhallur's farm 50; receives castaways, provides them a merchant-ship, finds Thorhallur dead, kills Bjarngrimur, courts Birna, settles on Straumey, earns bad reputation 51; invites Leifur Thorirsson to stay 53; visits Björn with Leifur, slays Björn, reputation worsens 54; ambushed by Arnljotur, uses Sigmundur's tactics, arbitrates terms against Arnljotur 55; urges Thorthur to marry Thurid Strong-Widow, brings proposal to Thurid 56; returns to Skufey farm, ambushed by Thurid in church, attacked by Heri Sigmundursson, slays Heri, fatally wounded by Leifur, dies 58

Skeggi Hafgrimursson, son of Hafgrimur Sigmundursson, king's bailiff in the Faroe Islands 59

Skopti, dock master on Straumey, conspires with Arnljotur, outlawed from Faroe Islands 55

Snaeulfur, father-in-law of Hafgrimur of South Island, father of Guthrid, farmer on Sandey, exiled from the Hebrides 4; refuses to help and fights with Hafgrimur 6

Steingrimur, farmer in Heidmark, father of Thorkell, attempts to arrange Thorkell and Ragnhild's betrothal 14; anger at Thorkell's abduction of Ragnhild 15; suggests the cave as a hiding place to Thorkell 16

Steingrimur, tenant farmer on Austurey; takes part in Thrandur's third raid against Sigmundur's farm, slain in the night by Sigmundur 38

Steingrimur Sigmundursson (the Lame), second oldest son of Sigmundur and Thurid 36; takes part in attack against Sigurthur's farm, fights with and wounded by Gautur the Red 58; known as the Lame, farms on Skufey 59

Steingrimur Thorsson, source of the Jomsvikings invasion of Norway 27

Straumey-Birna see Birna

Svein, King of Norway with his mother, Alfifa, as co-regent 50

Svein Hakonsson, son of Earl Hakon 16; befriended by Sigmundur, gives a manned ship to Sigmundur for raiding 17; rules Norway with Earl Eirikur 34; sends for Sigmundur, appoint him bailiff and ruler of Faroe Islands 35

Swine-Island Bjarni, rich farmer on Sviney, uncle of Thrandur of Göta 5; agrees to action with Hafgrimur against Brestir and Beinir 6; takes part in the ambush on Little Dimun, refuses to murder Sigmundur and Thorir at Thrandur's suggestion 7; accosted by Sigmundur for the murder of his father, spared by Sigmundur and reconciled, accompanies Sigmundur against Össur 24; upholds settlement 26

Thora, mistress of Beinir Sigmundursson, mother of Thorir Beinirsson 4

Thora, wife of Steingrimur, a farmer in Heidmark, mother of Thorkell 14

Thora Sigmundursdottir, daughter of Sigmundur and Thurid, travels to Faroe Islands 26; description 36; rebuffs then sets conditions for marriage with Leifur 40; consents to marry Leifur, settles at Hof on South Island 42; ire at Thrandur's fostering of Sigmundur Leifursson 49; ire at Leifur Össursson after death of Leifur Thorirsson, withholds sex 54; devises revenge against the Göta kinsmen at Thurid's wedding 56; travels to Austurey, speaks to Sigmundur Leifursson about *pater noster*, schemes to disable boats, rescues son from Thrandur 57; lives with Sigmundur Leifursson, description 59

Thoralfur, prominent farmer and royal bailiff in Heidmark region of Norway, father of Ragnhild, refuses Thorkell's proposal to Ragnhild 14; pursues Thorkell and Ragnhild, spots them in the forest, fights against and slain by Thorkell 15

Thoralfur Sigmundursson, eldest son of Sigmundur and Thurid 36; married, farm on Dimun 42; summoned to Norway by King Olafur, made king's retainer 43; second trip to Norway, killed by unknown assailant 45

Thorbera, wife of Thorvaldur of Sandey, affair with Gautur the Red, re-marries 52

Thorbjörn the Götuskeggur, prominent farmer on Austurey, father of Thrandur and Thorlakur 2

Thorgerd Hörthabruthur, a pagan goddess worshiped by Earl Hakon, her priest was powerful woman in Norway in possession of a luck-ring 23

Thorgrimur the Mean, farmer at Sandvik on South Island, tenant of Thrandur of Göta, father of Ormstein and Thorstein, murders and covers up the death of Sigmundur Brestirsson 39; confronted by Thrandur, forced to go to the *thing* 41; confesses to Sigmundur's murder, hanged at *thing* 42

Thorhallur the Wealthy, farmer on Straumey, husband of Straumey-Birna, description, agrees to Sigurthur's collection of assets, cuckolded 50; quarrels with Norwegian castaways, strikes Bjarngrimur, murdered in his bed 51

Thorir Beinirsson, son of Beinir Sigmundursson and Thora of Skufey 4; goes to Little Dimun with Sigmundur and Brestir, becomes foster son of Thrandur 7; handed over as slaves to Hrafn 8; granted freedom 9; decides with Sigmundur to join Earl Hakon,

Index of Proper Names   155

travels through mountains, saved by Sigmundur, stumbles on Ulfur's farm 10; trained in woodland skills and fighting by Ulfur, explores woods and encounters bear with Sigmundur 12; sets out from Ulfur's farm with Thorir 13; arrives at Earl Hakon's court with Sigmundur 16; accompanies Sigmundur to Denmark, captains Earl Eirikur's ship, joins fight against Randver, made retainer of Earl Hakon 18; raids in Sweden, leads phlanax attack against Björn 19; fights in sea-battle against Athill and Vandill, visits Earl Eirikur and Hakon, earns a great fortune 20; goes on pursuit of Haraldur Iron-Skull with Sigmundur, captains Vandill's dragon-warship, stays at Earl Hakon's court after the reconciliation between the Earl and Haraldur 21; returns with Sigmundur to Faroe Islands, separated from his kinsman by a storm 23; makes landfall on South Island, reunites with Sigmundur, accompanies him to Thorshaven to make a settlement with Thrandur, stays on Skufey with Sigmundur the winter after their return to the Faroes, goes to Norway to seek a settlement 24; returns to Faroes with Sigmundur after Earl Hakon's settlement, helps Sigmundur deliver tribute to Earl Hakon in Norway 25; accompanies Sigmundur at all times 26; takes part in repelling the Jomsvikings 27; travels with Sigmundur to meet King Olaf 29; baptized 30; urges the killing of Thrandur 31; ambushed with Sigmundur and Einar on Little Dimun, escapes, evades Thrandur's second attack, proposes killing Thrandur and foster sons 37; evades Thrandur, leaps into the sea with Sigmundur and Einar 38; swims to South Island, clings to Sigmundur, drowns 39; ghost summoned by Thrandur, body reburied on Skufey 41; father of Leifur 53

Thorkell Hard-Frost (Ulfur), description, allows Sigmundur and Thorir to stay one night on the farm 10; invites the boys to stay as foster sons, forbids Sigmundur to explore the northern forest 11; trains Sigmundur and Thorir in woodland skills and fighting, tricked by Sigmundur with propped-up bear 12; provides supplies to the boys, tells his story 13; son of Steingrimur and Thora, description, known as Hard-Frost, seeks engagement with Ragnhild 14; absconds with Ragnhild, hides in the forest, pitched fight against Thoralfur, slays Thoralfur, returns home 15; outlawed, lives in exile, absconds with Ragnhild again, comes to mountains as Ulfur, father of Thurid, asks Sigmundur to redeem him from exile 16; pardoned by Earl Hakon, becomes steward of Orkadale, settles on a farm, made liegeman of Earl Hakon 26

Thorlakur, older son of Thorbjörn the Götuskeggur, brother of Thrandur, marries, loses his inheritance to Thrandur 2

Thorstein see Ormstein and Thorstein

Thorstein the Red, father of Alofa, matriarch of the Götuskeggjar family 1

Thorthur Thorlakursson (the Short), son of Thorlakur, nephew and foster son of Thrandur of Göta, brother of Sigurthur, description 36; takes part in ambush of Sigmundur, Thorir and Einar on Little Dimun, sea raid 37; takes part in raid against Sigmundur's farm 38; chastised by Thrandur for inactivity, description, outfits merchant ship 45; chastises Leifur about Karl-Maerskr at *thing*, attacks and kills Karl-Maerskr, outlawed 48; departs for Iceland, impoverished on Austurey, armed return to *thing* 49; kicked out of farmhouse at Göta by Thrandur, lives at Thorhallur's farm on Straumey 50; receives castaways, kills Hafgrimur 51; ambushed by Arnljotur 55; urged to marry Thurid Strong-Widow 56; premonition of Sigurthur's death, fights with and kills Brandur Sigmundursson in final attack, slain by Leifur Össursson 58

Thorvaldur, a farmer on Sandey, husband of Thorbera, lets Gautur the Red collect his debts, murdered 52

Thrandur of Göta, younger son of Thorbjörn the Götuskeggur, brother of Thorlakur, description, inherits farm on Göta (Austurey), travels to Norway and Denmark 2; earns his fortune through strategem from Haraldur Bluetooth at Haleyri, sails to Norway, buys a cargo ship, returns to Faroe Islands, settles at Göta 3; agrees to take action with Hafgrimur against Brestir and Beinir 6; takes part reluctantly in the ambush of the brothers at Little Dimun, proposes to murder Sigmundur and Thorir, dissuaded by Bjarni, offers to foster Sigmundur and Thorir, takes boys to Göta 7; attempts to sell Sigmundur and Thorir into slavery to Hrafn 8; rules Faroes alone, seizes property of Brestir and Beinir, fosters Össur Hafgrimursson 9; arranges for Össur to marry, provides his foster son with the farms of Brestir and Beinir, splits rule over the Faroe Islands, rules the fief formerly governed by Brestir and Beinir, wealth is unknown by the Islanders, secretly controls all the Faroe Islands 22; comes to Thorshaven to make settlement with Sigmundur, agrees to go to Norway to meet Earl Hakon, fails to appear at court 24; attends *thing* at Thorshaven after the king's settlement, accepts the terms of Sigmundur's settlement, pays one third of the wergild, offers to foster Leifur Össursson 25; forced to pay second third of the wergild, asks Sigmundur for compensation on behalf of Leifur 26; challenges arrival of Christianity, forces Sigmundur not to proselytize 30; nearly killed by Sigmundur, compelled to help Christianize the Faroe Islands, refuses to be brought to Norway, held back by storms, swears allegiance to Sigmundur 31; fosters Sigurthur Thorlaksson, Thorthur Thorkalsson, Gautur the Red, Leifur Össursson, abandons Christian faith, seeks compensation on behalf of Leifur 36; ambushes Sigmundur, Thorir and Einar on Little Dimun, stranded on island, second attack on Sigmundur 37; leads third raid on Sigmundur's farm, surrounds and orders the burning of the farmhouse, tracks Sigmundur and allies 38; rules over the Faroe Islands with Leifur after Sigmundur's death, seeks settlement with Thurid Strong-Widow, handles Leifur's betrothal to Thora 40; confronts Thorgrimur the Mean, summons Sigmundur's ghost, discovers luck-ring, unearths Sigmundur and Thorir 41; summons *thing*, handles marriage between Leifur and Thora 42; summoned to Norway by King Olafur but refuses 43; chastises foster sons for inaction, lends them merchant-ship, disapproves of their actions in Norway 45; meets Karl-Maerskr, agrees to collect tribute among the Northern Islands, failing health and eyesight, puts up black tent at *thing*, presents "tribute" to Karl and Leifur, chastised by foster sons, offers compensation to Leifur for Karl-Maerskr 48; helps foster sons leave Faroes, proposes a weapons-ban at the *thing*, joins forces with Sigurthur, decides rulership of Faroe Islands, takes one-third of the rule, offers to foster Sigmundur Leifursson 49; father of Guthrun, tosses foster sons out of the farmhouse at Göta 50; welcomes Leifur, Thurid, and Thora to Austerey, teaches Sigmundur *pater noster*, knowledge of Apostles' Creed, robbed of foster son 57; dies of grief 59

Thurid (Strong-Widow), daughter of Thorkell and Ragnhild, description, fond of Sigmundur 11; sad at Sigmundur's departure from Ulfur's farm 13; pregnant 16; gives birth to Thora, visits Earl Hakon's court, travels to Faroe Islands with Sigmundur and Thora 26; children with Sigmundur (Thora, Thoralfur, Steingrimur, Brandur, Heri) 36; defends farmhouse against Thrandur's raid 38; known as Strong-Widow 40; rebuffs settlement with Thrandur 40; ire toward Leifur Össursson after death of Leifur Thorirsson, sees Sigmundur Brestirsson in a dream 54; presented marriage proposal to Thorthur Thorlaksson 56; travels to Austurey in plot to recover Sigmundur Leifursson 57; lures Sigurthur to ambush in Sigmundur's church 58; later life with Leifur, dies 59

Ulfur see Thorkell

Vandill see Athill and Vandill
Vladimir Sviatoslavich (the Great), ruler of the Kievan Rus, aids Olaf Tryggvason 29

General Index

This index serves as a reference to key concepts, place names, and proper nouns from the introductory sections, the notes to the translation, and the appendices; that is, the entire content of this volume except the translation itself. Characters and place names from the saga translation are not indexed here, since the Index of Proper Names covers the appearance of historical and fictional characters by chapter. Numbers in **bold italics** indicate pages with photographs.

Agnarsson, Volundur Lars 27
Apostles' Creed (*Credo in deum*) and *Pater noster* 121–122n2, 122n3
Ari Thorgilsson (the Learned) 77n2
Aud the Deep-Minded 10, 12, 19, 31n2, 141
authorship *see* saga-writer
axes 25, 70n1
baliff 15–16, 75n1, 81n2, 127n1, 139–140, 142
Blake, N.F. (translator) 27–28, 76n1, 129–130, 134–135, 159
Boglunga saga 127n1
Borgarnes Saga Museum 2

casting of lots 32n4
Celtic Church (of Ireland) 8; Irish hermits 36n6 141
characters 2–3, 24–26; of women 3
chieftains 19, 24, 26, 36n3, 62n1, 70n1, 138
compensation *see* legal issues
conversion to Christianity 5–6, 16, 18–19, 26, 77–78n4, 79n3, 80–81n1, 86n2, 99n1, 130

Danish (language) 1–2, 16
Dano-Norwegian Kingdom 16, *50*
date of composition 17, 19, 127n1
Dicuil (Irish monk) 7–8
dragon-headed warships 57n1

dress 70n1, 119n1
driftwood 13

Edwards, Paul (translator) 6, 27, 159
Egil's Saga 6, 17, 24
Eirik Bjarnsson (king of Sweden) 59n1
Eirik Bloodaxe (king of Norway) 33n1
Eirik Hakonsson (Earl of Lade) 55n1–2, 86n2–3, 98n1, 131
Eirik's Saga 5, 34n2, 80–81n1
Elfarsker (River Skerries) 56n2
Erybyggja Saga 17, 159
Estland (Estonia) 79n1

Fagrskinna saga 86n2
Faroe Islands: Austurey (East Island) 19, 29, *30*, 31n3, 32n2, 143; bilingualism in 1–2, 16; Borðoy *30*, 31n3; conversion 5–6, 69n1, 77–78n4, 80–81n1 (*see also* conversion to Christianity); Dimum (Stóra Dímun and Lítla Dímun) 18, 24–25, *30*, 37n1, 66n1; etymology 6; farms 12–13, 46n3; Foreign Powers Policy Act 16; Fugloy *30*, 31n3; geography *30*, 31n3; Göta (Norðragøta) 19, *30*, 32n2, 141, 143; Home Rule Act 16; Hov (Hof) 12, *30*, 38n3, 41n1, 142; Kalsoy *30*, 31n3; map *7*, *30*; Northern Islands (Borðoy, Fugloy, Kalsoy, Svínoy, Viðoy) *30*, 31n3, 107n1; population 14; relation to

157

Norway 14–16, 24–25, 45n2, 75n1, 138–140; Sandoy (Sand Island) **30**, 36n5, 37n2, 94n1; Sandvík **30**, 94n1; settlement 1–2, 6, 11–16, 31n2, 33n1, 141, 143–144 (*see also* Viking Age); Skuvoy 18–19, 25, 29, **30**, 36n5, 37n1, 66n1, 93n1, 94n1, 143; Streymoy (Stream Island) 12, 15, **30**, 31n3, 38n1, 38n2, 38n3, 137; Suðuroy (South Island) 19, **30**, 36n1, 36n4, 36n5, 37n1, 39n2, 93n1, 94n1, 144; Svínoy (Swine Island) 29, **30**, 31n3, 37n3; topography 12, 40n1; Tórshavn (Thorshaven) **7**, 12, 14–15, 24, 29, **30**, 38n2, 137; Viðoy **30**, 31n3; whale-driving 13n1
Faroese (language) 1–2, 9, 16
Foote, Peter 2, 13, 18, 24, 32n1, 33n4, 39n3, 93n1, 97n1, 101–102n1, 102n3, 111n2, 112n1, 121–122n2, 137, 140, 157–158
Fóstbroeðra saga 17
foster sons and foster fathers 24, 45n1, 112n1
Fox, Denton (translator) 36n3, 159

Gordon, E.V. 18, 25, 135, 159
Götuskeggjar 19, 31n2, 36n6
Greenland 5, 11, 35n2, 80–81n1
Greenlanders' Saga 10
Grettir's Saga 1, 13n1, 17, 110n1, 159
Grimur Kamban 9, 19, 141

Hakon Eirikursson (regent of Norway) 109n1
Hakon Sigurtharson (Earl of Trondheim) 26, 36n7, 45n2-2, 54n1, 55n2, 64n1, 72n1, 77n4, 86n3; worshipper of Thorgerd 67n1, 77n1, 129–131, 135–136, 140–142
Haleyri 33n2
Harald Fine-Hair (king of Norway) 10, 19, 31n1, 33n1, 51n1, 65n1, 141
Harald Gormsson "Bluetooth" (king of Denmark) 24, 33n1, 33n3, 45n3
Harald Gunnhildarson "Grey-Cloak" (king of Norway) 15, 33n1, 36n7, 45n2, 140–141
Heimskringla 10, 17, 31n1, 86n3, 131
high seat 117n1
historical accuracy 24
Hjorungavágur (battle) **50**, 86n2, 129–131
Holmgard (Novgorod) 44n1
Hrafnkel's Saga 159

Iceland **7**; conversion 80–81n1, 81n3 (*see also* conversion to Christianity);
settlement 6, 8, 10–12, 19, 31n1–2, 77n2
Icelandic calendar 47n2
Icelandic orthography 28–29
Icelandic sagas 1–2, 5, 10, 17–19, 24, 26–27, 131; *Boglunga saga* 127n1; Egil's Saga 6, 17, 24; Eirik's Saga 5, 34n2, 80–81n1; Erybyggja Saga 17, 159; *Fagrskinna saga* 86n2; *Fóstbroeðra saga* 17; Greenlanders' Saga 10; Grettir's Saga 1, 13, 17, 110n1, 159; *Heimskringla* 10, 17, 31n1, 86n3, 131; Hrafnkel's Saga 159; Jomsvikings' Saga 26–28, 67n1, 76n1, 76n3, 77n1, 86n3, 129–135, 159; King Harald's Saga 18, 159; *Landnámabók* (Book of Settlements) 8, 11–12, 31n2, 77n2, 159; Laxdaela Saga 1, 5–6, 10, 17, 24, 27, 31n1, 80–81n1, 81n3, 85n1, 103n1, 110n1, 159; literature 157; Magnus the Good's Saga 126n1; Njal's Saga 1, 5, 17, 24, 27, 28n1, 80–81n1, 135–136, 159; Olaf Tryggvason's Saga 26, 76n1, 78n1, 131, 134; Orkney-Islander Saga 5, 18, 31n1–2, 62n2, 159; Saint Olaf's Saga 99n1; Thorhall Ale-Hood's Story 138–139; Viga-Glum's Saga 131; Vinland Sagas 159
Irpa *see* Thorgerd Horda's-Bride
Íslenzk Fornrit 2, 27–28, 93n1, 143

Johnston, George (translator) 2, 27
Jómsborg **50**, 76n1, 129
Jomsvikings 25–26, 76n1, 76n3, 129–134, 142
Jomsvikings' Saga 26–28, 67n1, 76n1, 76n3, 77n1, 86n3, 129–135, 159

Ker, William 2
Ketil Flat-Nose 10, 31n2
Kievan Rus' 44n1, 79n2, 109n1
King Harald's Saga 18, 159
kinship 25, 83n1

Landnámabók (Book of Settlements) 8, 11–12, 31n2, 77n2, 159
Lawspeaker *see* legal issues, Lawspeaker
Laxdaela Saga 1, 5–6, 10, 17, 24, 27, 31n1, 80–81n1, 81n3, 85n1, 103n1, 110n1, 159
legal issues: assault (*frumhlaup*) 39n2; courts 15, 39n3, 137–139; Lawspeaker 99n2, 137–140; murder (*vig* and *morð*) 25, 94n2, 98n1, 138–139; outlawry 53n1, 72n1, 137–139; right-to-reside (*landsvist*) 72n1; self-judgment 39n1;

General Index

system in Faroe Islands 14–15, 137–140; wergild and compensation 38*n*4, 72*n*1, 139, 142
Leif Eiriksson 10, 35*n*2
"love of stories" 2–3
luck 35*n*2, 136
Magnus Hakonsson (king of Norway) 14–15, 75*n*1
Magnus Olafsson "the Good" (king of Norway) 126*n*1, 140, 142
Magnusson, Magnus (translator) 6, 11, 24, 27, 28*n*1, 159
Magnus the Good's Saga 126*n*1
mistresses 41*n*2
money system and silver 34*n*1–2, 41*n*1
Muriel, A.C. (translator) 27

Newfoundland (L'Anse aux Meadows) 11
North Sea area 7; Caithness (Scotland) 6, 7, 8–10, 12, 19, 31*n*2, 62*n*2; Hebrides 7, 8–9, 11, 13, 31*n*1; Ireland 7, 8–9, 11; Isle of Man 7, 9, 63*n*1; Orkney Islands 5, 7, 8–9, 11–12, 19, 31*n*1–2, 62*n*2, 141; Shetlands 7, 8, 11, 31*n*1, 36*n*4; Wales 7, 9, 11, 63*n*1
Norway 5–6, 7, 10, 31*n*1, **50**; Bergen 7, **50**, 64*n*1; Dofrafjall 46*n*1, **50**, 51*n*1; Frosta 73*n*1, 139; Götland 7; Halogaland 7, **50**, 65*n*1; Heidmark 46*n*1, **50**, 144; Herøy 104*n*2; Hordaland 7, **50**, 64*n*1; invasion by Jomsvikings 129–130; Lade (near Trondheim) 7, 29, **50**, 54*n*1, 130, 135, 142; Lygra 102*n*2; Møre **50**, 71*n*1, 104*n*2, 105*n*1, 130; Nidaros **50**, 80–81*n*1, 84*n*1, 104*n*1; Orkadale 51*n*1; Oslo 7; Romsdale 104*n*2; Stod 7, **50**, 104*n*2; Tonsberg 43*n*2, **50**; Trondelag 46*n*1, 51*n*1; Trondheim 7, 36*n*8, 46*n*1, **50**, 77*n*1, 104*n*2, 109*n*1, 140 (see also Nidaros); Uppland 46*n*1, **50**, 73*n*1; Viken (The Vik) 43*n*2, **50**

Olaf Haraldursson/St. Olaf (king of Norway) 16, 17, 64*n*1, 99*n*1, 109*n*1, 142
Olaf Tryggvason (king of Norway) 5–6, 17, 19, 26, 36*n*7–8, 50*n*1, 55*n*1, 77*n*3–4, 79*n*3, 80–81*n*1, 84*n*1, 85*n*1, 86*n*1, 142
Olaf Tryggvason's Saga 26, 76*n*1, 78*n*1, 131, 134
Olafur Halldorson (editor) 26, 93*n*1
ordeal (*járnburð*) 103*n*1
Orkney-Islander Saga 5, 18, 31*n*1–2, 62*n*2, 159
outlawry see legal issues, outlawry

pagan practices: cremation 32*n*3; ghosts 97*n*1, 110*n*1, 111*n*2; human sacrifice 130, 135; magic 24, 68*n*1, 83*n*2, 97*n*1, 121*n*1; Norse gods 6, 132
Pálsson, Hermann (translator) 6, 11, 24, 27, 28*n*1, 36*n*3, 159
phalanx 60*n*1
place names see Icelandic orthography

red-headness 32*n*1
Richards, Julian (scholar) 9, 57*n*1, 158
Robinson, Orrin (scholar) 14, 134, 159
rulers of Scandinavia: Eirik Bjarnsson (king of Sweden) 59*n*1; Eirik Bloodaxe (king of Norway) 33*n*1; Eirik Hakonsson (Earl of Lade) 55*n*1–2, 86*n*2–3, 98*n*1, 131; Hakon Eirikursson (regent of Norway) 109*n*1; Hakon Sigurtharson (Earl of Trondheim) 26, 36*n*7, 45*n*2–2, 54*n*1, 55*n*2, 64*n*1, 67*n*1, 72*n*1, 77*n*1, 77*n*4, 86*n*3, 129–131, 135–136, 140–142; Harald Fine-Hair (king of Norway) 10, 19, 31*n*1, 33*n*1, 51*n*1, 65*n*1, 141; Harald Gormsson "Bluetooth" (king of Denmark) 24, 33*n*1, 33*n*3, 45*n*3; Harald Gunnhildarson "Grey-Cloak" (king of Norway) 15, 33*n*1, 36*n*7, 45*n*2, 140–141; Magnus Hakonsson (king of Norway) 14–15, 75*n*1; Magnus Olafsson "the Good" (king of Norway) 126*n*1, 140, 142; Olaf Haraldursson/St Olaf (king of Norway) 16, 17, 64*n*1, 99*n*1, 109*n*1, 142; Olaf Tryggvason (king of Norway) 5–6, 17, 19, 26, 36*n*7–8, 50*n*1, 55*n*1, 77*n*3–4, 79*n*3, 80–81*n*1, 84*n*1, 85*n*1, 86*n*1, 142; role as chieftains 35*n*1 (see also chieftain); Svein Canutesson and Alfifa (regents of Norway) 112*n*2, 142; Svein Hakonsson (Earl of Lade) 55*n*1–2, 86*n*2–3, 98*n*1

saga-writer 5–6, 16–19, 24, 26, 33*n*4, 40*n*1, 44*n*1, 57*n*1, 64*n*1, 91*n*1, 101–102*n*1, 102*n*3, 111*n*2, 130, 137, 139–140
Saint Olaf's Saga 99*n*1
Saxo Grammaticus 18, 86*n*3
Scandinavia 7, **50**; see also Norway
sea-mile (*vika*) 93*n*1
shields 60*n*1
ships and ship-building 11–13, 57*n*1; dinghy 49*n*1
Skaane (Sweden) 33*n*2, **50**
skaldic poetry 134
Snorri Sturluson 10 17, 19; see also Icelandic sagas, *Heimskrigla*

Stiklestad (battle) 109n1
Svein Canutesson and Alfifa (regents of Norway) 112n2, 142
Svein Hakonsson (Earl of Lade) 55n1–2, 86n2–3, 98n1
Svöldur (battle) 86n3

thing 14–15, 24, 34n3, 99n2, 111n1, 137–139
Thorgerd Horda's-Bride 67n1, 130–131; connection with Irpa and Thor 135–136
Thorhall Ale-Hood 138–139
Thorhall Ale-Hood's Story 138–139
Thorstein the Red 19, 31n2
translation of sagas 2–3, 24, 26–29, 158–159

Varangian Guard 10
Viga-Glum's Saga 131
Vigfúss Víga-Glúmsson 131
Viking Age 1, 9–12, 141
Viking raids 56n1
Vinland Sagas 159
Vladimir the Great 79n3

Wölck, Wolfgang (linguist) 1–2
Wylie, Jonathan (anthropologist) 6, 12–16, 38n1, 77–78n4, 158

Young, G.V and Cynthia Clewer (translators) 27

www.ingramcontent.com/pod-product-compliance
Ingram Content Group UK Ltd.
Pitfield, Milton Keynes, MK11 3LW, UK
UKHW042016140426
5217IPUK00015B/1207